PRAISE FOR

REMEMBERING SHANGHAI

"Highly enjoyable . . . an engaging and entertaining saga."
—Fionnuala McHugh, writer, *South China Morning Post*

"Absolutely gorgeous—so beautifully done."
—Martin Alexander, editor in chief, the *Asia Literary Review*

"Mesmerizing stories . . . magnificent language."
—Betty Peh-T'i Wei, PhD, author, *Old Shanghai*

"The authors' writing is masterful."
—Nicholas von Sternberg, cinematographer

"Unforgettable . . . a unique point of view."
—Hugues Martin, writer, shanghailander.net

"Absorbing—an amazing family history."
—Nelly Fung, author, *Beneath the Banyan Tree*

"Engaging characters, richly detailed descriptions and exquisite illustrations."
—Debra Lee Baldwin, photojournalist and author

"The facts are so dramatic they read like fiction."
—Heather Diamond, author, *American Aloha*

ISABEL SUN CHAO AND CLAIRE CHAO

REMEMBERING SHANGHAI

A Memoir of Socialites, Scholars and Scoundrels

Enjoy The journey!

PLUM
BROOK

Published by Plum Brook, LLC, Honolulu
www.rememberingshanghai.com

 Edited and designed by Girl Friday Productions
www.girlfridayproductions.com

Editorial: Diana Rico, Lindsey Alexander, Karen Parkin and Emilie Sandoz-Voyer;
additional developmental editing by Gali Kronenberg
Cover and interior design: Paul Barrett

Image Credits: see page 271

ISBN (Hardcover): 978-0-9993938-0-2
ISBN (Paperback): 978-0-9993938-1-9
e-ISBN: 978-0-9993938-2-6

Second Edition

Printed in the United States of America

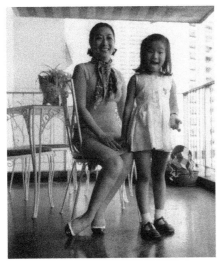

1968   *2016*

Isabel Sun Chao and Claire Chao, Hong Kong

To those who preceded us . . .   *. . . and those who will follow*
   — *Claire Chao (daughter)*   — *Isabel Sun Chao (mother)*

CONTENTS

Remembering Shanghai is being adapted
into a television drama series.

Isabel.

A magnificent illustration of Nanjing Road in the 1930s, with Wing On and Sincere department stores at the left and the right of the street.

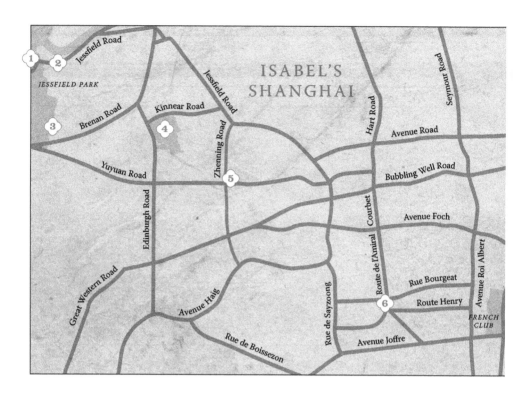

ISABEL'S
SHANGHAI

JESSFIELD PARK

Jessfield Road
Kinnear Road
Brenan Road
Zhenning Road
Yuyuan Road
Edinburgh Road
Great Western Road
Avenue Haig
Rue de Boissezon
Rue de Sayzoong
Seymour Road
Hart Road
Avenue Road
Bubbling Well Road
Avenue Foch
Route de l'Amiral Courbet
Rue Bourgeat
Route Henry
Avenue Joffre
Avenue Roi Albert
FRENCH CLUB

 1 St. John's University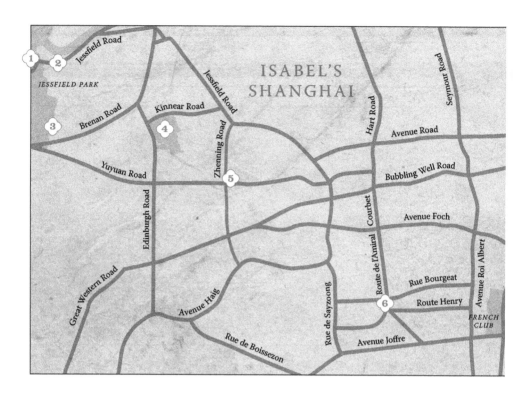

2 Xiyuan Apartments

3 St. Mary's Hall

4 McTyeire School for Girls

5 367 Zhenning Road

6 Airline Club

7 Grand Theatre

8 Huile Li

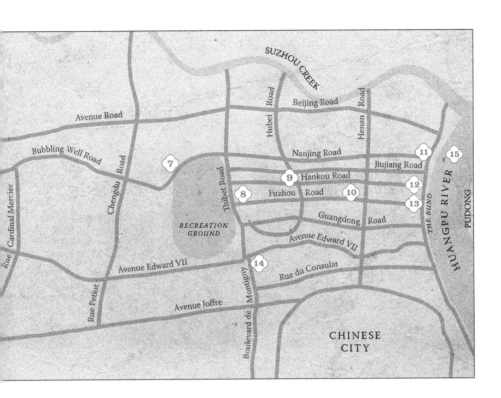

9 Huizhong Hotel

10 Commercial Press

11 Cathay Hotel

12 Customs House

13 Hongkong & Shanghai Bank

14 Great World

15 Huangpu River

JUST EIGHTEEN

SHANGHAI, 2008

THE HOUSE IS SOLID AND dignified, its high gable radiating creamy yellow under a luminous Shanghai sky. We've been standing here awhile, my daughter and I, arms linked, oblivious to the honking of impatient drivers as we gaze at the home I left behind sixty years ago. I follow the tilt of Claire's head to the second floor, where our eyes rest on a russet-framed window. Something isn't right. Despite the building's freshly painted walls, the glass is caked with grime, as if unwashed for decades.

Dust whirls, stirring memories long forgotten, now reawakened in the whoosh of Shanghai traffic.

The last image of my childhood haunts me: my grandmother rooted like a statue at that window, her unflinching stare following my every move as I prepared to leave. At eighteen, I was going to Hong Kong on my very first holiday. The sunbeams slanted through the lattice fence, bathing the garden in that mellow morning light that softened the edges of everything before it grew unbearably hot. The servants were lined up outside the front door to watch my father send me off. He clasped my shoulders with familiar affection, but his expression was solemn as he surveyed me through round spectacles. "Be careful, Third Daughter. We'll all be thinking of you."

Feeling glamorous and grown-up, I clutched my new pink valise and climbed onto the weathered seat of the pedicab that had ferried me to school every morning. We rode past the garage with the big American Buick parked inside—idle all these years since we'd had no gas to run it, yet still gleaming like an onyx sculpture in a museum.

The familiar rhythm of the driver's pedaling usually put me to sleep, but there was no chance of a nap this morning. I'd never been apart from my family or close friends before, and soon I would be boarding a train for the first time, to a destination that some claimed was even more exciting than Shanghai.

I kept peering back, inhaling the sweet traces of night-blooming jasmine. The house became smaller and smaller, my grandmother standing stock-still at her bedroom window. Somehow I knew she would not move for a long time: not when I'd turned off our little lane, not even after the pedicab picked up speed on the wide avenues of the International Settlement.

I wondered why she was so fixated on my departure, when I was going to be away only a few weeks. My mind skipped to a more amusing thought. I must find some special candies for her in Hong Kong; there'd been a shortage of nice things in Shanghai.

Claire interrupts my reverie. "Does the house look very different from what you remember?"

"Everything looks so much smaller . . . somehow sad."

"Mom, I know this is not easy for you. We don't have to go inside if you don't want to."

I pull my cardigan tightly around me. "It's okay. We've come this far."

My daughter is right. I haven't been at all keen to return to my childhood home. Claire is far more eager to look at things head on and dig into our family's colorful past. It's true, ours is a family of socialites, scholars and scoundrels. I've no doubt that despite the chaos of the Japanese occupation, a civil war and the Communist revolution, my determined daughter will somehow piece together our family story.

We turn away from the house to face the clamor of the street: motorbikes buzzing like giant mechanized honeybees, the sibilant chatter of the Shanghainese dialect, a trendy Taiwan ballad blaring from tinny speakers. I scan past the blur of traffic and dense row of shops, trying to identify where our fence had been—the bamboo lattice that had once wrapped around our entire property, enveloping my childhood in a private cocoon.

Small retail establishments occupy a space where a lifetime ago my father's study and porch overlooked our lush garden. In that once peaceful place I now see a hardware shop, a tobacconist, a ladies' boutique and a QUIK convenience store beneath a shiny red awning. "My fifth sister said the government has been expanding the road for fifty years," I tell Claire. "Each time they carve out more and more of our property. There's no sign of our fence anywhere, or the lovely garden."

My childhood home at 367 Zhenning Road, October 2008.

I gaze into my daughter's face: her upturned eyes, the wide nose with the slight hook, the rounded lips—mirror images of my own. "When the Communists came to power, I was just eighteen—carefree and hopelessly naïve," I continue. "All I cared about were films and nightclubs, the latest fashion. Even when Mao became the chairman of China, I didn't give it much thought. Some of our friends were moving away, but it didn't occur to me that we might need to leave Shanghai."

We cross the busy thoroughfare. It seems odd to enter the house directly from the street. "We always came in from the path through the garden. It must have all been paved over when they built the road."

As we stand at the entrance, long-buried memories rush into my mind. "You couldn't have found two more different personalities than my parents," I say. "Muma[1] was quite low-key about things—a gentle soul. When she was young, she lived for mahjong and nights out on the town."

"And your father? You've never talked about him much."

"I was always sorry you didn't meet him. Diedie[2] was an art collector, a Confucian scholar. It was hard for me to even think about him when you were growing up. He had a terrible time after I left Shanghai."

Claire squeezes my arm. "Your parents were divorced by then, right?"

"Yes, and Muma was living in Hong Kong. I was thrilled when Diedie said I could spend a few weeks with her. I was so innocent—I really believed it was a gift-wrapped holiday." I sigh heavily. "All I packed were a few summer dresses. I never imagined I wouldn't see my father and grandmother again. Of course, they knew I might not come back."

Claire cranes her neck upward to the bedroom window. "That's why your grandmother was standing frozen up there when you left. They'd be shocked to see what the house looks like now, don't you think?"

The brown metal gate of the house is daunting, too industrial for its surroundings; it has replaced the Spanish-style one that had graced the arched entrance to our home. We try to open it, but it is locked.

Like supplicants, we're obliged to go from shop to shop asking if anyone has a key. Each time, I explain in Shanghainese, "I lived in this house as a child, and I've come from Hong Kong with my daughter to find my memories."

Claire whispers, "I wish we'd dressed more casually. It's so obvious we're outsiders."

That is for certain. At each store, the shopkeepers appraise us warily: my daughter's suntanned, Westernized air, from years spent living in Hawaii; my own cashmere twinset and lustrous pearls. The fact is, I did dress down today! I observe a shop owner's guarded look, at first tinged with curiosity, turn to tacit empathy for what my family must have had

---

1. Muma: "mama," pronounced *moo-ma*.
2. Diedie: "daddy," pronounced *dee-eh-dee-eh*.

and what we have surely lost. One family among millions of shattered lives.

The tobacconist produces the key. "Are you ready?" Claire asks me. I adjust my shoulder bag and we step forward, leaving the tobacconist behind his counter.

The door swings open with a raspy groan. The clang as it slams shut jars me and heightens my nervousness. Inside, the frenzy of the street fades. None of the electrical switches work, and we discover there are no light fixtures anyway. The foyer takes shape as our eyes adjust to the gloom. Once elegant and inviting, it is now bare but for a rusty bicycle leaning against a wall of crumbling plaster.

A cloying odor of dank sweat and mold hangs in the air. Exposed wires dangle from corners; pipes snake haphazardly along walls. The art deco iron banister, oxidized to a cinnabar patina, ascends to a landing where watery light filters through dirty windows. Unlike the dust outside that twirls in fanciful pirouettes, inside it clings like sediment to our clothes, hair, skin; it tastes like fur on our tongues.

"Look," I call to Claire, "the banister is just as I remember—still elegant after all these years, such a beautiful red." I stroke the rail affectionately, noticing my nails are varnished the same color. Several blue-and-white porcelain pots line the wall, though the soil is bone-dry, holding the remains of plants that have long surrendered their struggle to survive.

"Here's where we had our phone." I point to the side of the stairs. "You can see the mark where it was mounted on the wall. My older sister Virginia and I were so excited when it was installed. We flew downstairs the second it rang! I still know our phone number by heart: 2-1-3-8-2."

Claire leans in for a glimpse of the vestibule, which leads to several rooms with their doors closed tight. "How many people do you think live here now—twenty-five, thirty?"

"That would be roughly the same number as when I was growing up, including the servants. Hard to figure out the layout with the rooms closed off. We always left the doors wide open, so we could see all the way through the French windows into the garden."

As much as I've been reluctant to revisit my lost and distant past, Claire's curiosity is rubbing off. I'm like a detective sleuthing for evidence of my family's life in these rooms seven decades earlier.

I walk into the small hallway. "That's the entrance to the formal dining room. The table was always set with perfectly polished European crystal and silver, but we never ate there. Ah, this is the door to Diedie's study. I loved that room and how it smelled of old books and wet ink."

The middle door is ajar. My daughter glances furtively over her shoulder and peeks through the crack; the room is empty. "Someone must have moved out recently. Let's go in, Mom."

Once inside, I picture the salon clearly, exactly as it was when I was a child. "This is where Diedie displayed his furniture and large art pieces—so many fragile things. My brother and I did break something once. I remember it was too cold to play outside, so we were in here, running around." My eyes scour the dusty hardwood for telltale marks. "There they are. See those dents in the floor?"

My daughter kneels, rubbing her finger along gouges in the weathered parquet.

"You should find four dents quite close together. It was a *gongshi*,[3] a 'scholar's rock,' one of Diedie's favorite pieces."

Claire inclines her head. "I love gongshi. I didn't know your father collected them. What happened?"

"I knocked it off its pedestal. It bounced off the floor and cracked in half. I was so traumatized by what I'd done, I didn't sleep for a week!" My daughter stands and brushes dust from the knees of her black trousers.

We carry on, up the stairs to where the bedrooms and casual living areas used to be. Each level once had three light-filled rooms, which are grim and silent behind locked metal grilles.

"It looks like a prison up here," Claire says.

In the stifling darkness at the top landing, from behind closed doors, we hear dishes clinking and a mother scolding a child. Before coming, we'd debated whether we should try to meet the residents. Now I lack the

---

3.   Please refer to the glossary for explanations of Chinese phrases.

fortitude. I may have grown up here, but I feel like an intruder; I suppose I am, in a very real sense.

Back downstairs, we tread through the dirty communal kitchen to a side door that used to open onto our garden. The lawn is concreted over and strewn with the debris of cluttered lives: plastic buckets, old shoes,

 bags of garlic, upturned pots. Lace bras and men's shorts hang from clotheslines.

In my mind's eye, I see morning glories unfurling above pots of maroon dahlias. I hear the echo of laughter as my sister and I count mulberry leaves, screeching with mock horror as insects jump out.

At one end of the courtyard, metal bars shutter the windows of a small room as if it were an animal's cage. It's unclear if it is meant to keep someone in or intruders out. Claire is taking photographs when an elderly man emerges from the cage-room, flapping his arms furiously. His close-cropped hair juts up like a lopsided bottlebrush.

"Stop that! What are you doing? Why are you taking pictures? Stop at once!" The man is yelling in Mandarin; he's not a Shanghai native.

Clad in bell-bottom trousers and a tomato-red T-shirt with the words COCKPIT SERIES emblazoned across his chest, he looks disheveled, as if we've interrupted an afternoon nap. He calms down when I give my well-rehearsed explanation of why we're here. He soon disappears into his room and returns with a jacket on over his T-shirt—eager, it seems, for a chat.

"My family name is Cheng," he offers, his suspicion having subsided. "My father moved into this house in 1966. The Cultural Revolution had just started, and there was a housing shortage. My dad was an army officer and was assigned a room here." He rubs his forehead. "The first time I visited, I couldn't believe one family lived in such a fancy place."

Claire fidgets with her camera, embarrassed by my family's former status.

My voice is hoarse as I ask, "Mr. Cheng, did you ever meet the original owner of this house? His last name was Sun."

"I remember him well. Was he your father?" He scrutinizes me with new interest. "I can still picture him . . . snow-white hair, big wire-rimmed spectacles. I remember he had the soft hands and round face of someone who'd led a pampered life."

Mr. Cheng smiles sheepishly. "We addressed him as 'Old Gentleman.' He had the bearing of someone cultured, not like my dad and me—always polite. He wasn't anything like what I'd heard about evil landlords." He shakes his head. "Ten families moved in on the same day as my father. I was living in another province and was visiting him at the time. No one was in charge—everyone argued over the rooms. I didn't understand what they were complaining about. They were lucky to be assigned to a place like this."

A gust scatters dead leaves across the courtyard.

"Your father was a puzzle to me. Everything he owned had been confiscated, including this home, yet he seemed genuinely kind. You have to understand, we had nothing in those days."

Mr. Cheng's comments about Diedie stir emotions that I've suppressed for years. Since I left Shanghai, I've rarely spoken of the past. Claire knows little of our family history, and this stranger is telling us things about Diedie's life that even I hadn't been aware of.

Claire sees I'm a bit wobbly and drags a plastic stool across the courtyard so I can perch on its cracked seat.

"My dad didn't have a teacup when he arrived," Mr. Cheng continues. "Old Gentleman gave him a celadon cup with a matching lid—much nicer than anything my father owned. He used it every day for forty years until it broke." He looks around the courtyard. "It must have been very beautiful when you lived here." Claire and I exchange a glance.

"Is it true Old Gentleman once owned entire streets of houses? People said he owned Third and Fourth Roads?"

Though he's asked, how can I, without seeming conceited, relate the glories and eccentricities of my bygone family, whose original benefactor was the empress dowager? I think of the servant boy who became an imperial minister, his playboy sons and one hundred servants; the hotels and apartment complexes; the steamships and priceless art collection; the concubines and the scandals. I am silent.

Wistfully, Mr. Cheng adds, "How strange life is that your father ended up living in the dining room." He gestures to the caged window. "It's the smallest room in the house. Even after his stroke, when he could barely walk, Old Gentleman still tried to sweep the yard, you know."

Me, September 1948.

It was painful to hear. When Diedie passed away in 1969, I had not seen him in two decades. China was closed to the outside world, and I couldn't attend his funeral. To me, it was as if he'd vanished into thin air, just like his art collection and everything he'd owned.

"The dining room stayed empty for a few years after your father died," Mr. Cheng continues, "until I moved to Shanghai and took it over." I shudder at the thought of Diedie living out his last years in that cage-room.

As if it's just occurred to him, he asks, "Are you planning to take the house back? Is that why you're here?" His narrow eyes light up. "I wouldn't mind; it could take a while, but the government might assign me a new apartment," he adds hopefully.

The conversation is almost surreal. Though not by his own design, Mr. Cheng is the face of those who seized my father's assets and stripped him of dignity.

"We don't have any plans to claim the house." I smile awkwardly. "I'm too old, and my children aren't interested in living in Shanghai."

"You still look young. What is your birth year? I was born in the Year of the Sheep," Mr. Cheng informs us.

The Chinese zodiac is a twelve-year cycle, with each year ruled by a different animal. From his astrological sign, I infer that we were born in the same year, 1931: two disparate arcs converging nearly eighty years later.

Claire asks Mr. Cheng if she can take his picture. He attempts to tamp down his uneven hair and tugs at the wrinkles in his jacket. Posing stiffly, he signals his readiness with a crooked smile.

I sound formal as I thank Mr. Cheng for his hospitality: "We hope you enjoy living in this house and wish you good health to a venerable age." Hearing Mr. Cheng talk of my father has made me revert to a long-forgotten style of speaking. The courteous words and respectful dip of my head are out of place, given the circumstances.

On the ride back to our hotel, Claire asks me about Japanese gendarmes, opium and food shortages. I prefer to tell her about Shanghai's vibrancy in the 1930s and '40s: the intimate nightclubs where jazz bands trumpeted their tunes and we waltzed and fox-trotted the night away; the grand boulevards teeming with fashion boutiques, cake shops and wonton peddlers; the entertainment palaces and opera stages and movie theaters. I remember Muma dashing off with her mink stole draped over a stylish outfit, leaving Father behind in his study, clutching an ink brush and filling a scroll with his bold calligraphy.

Before Claire and I came to Shanghai in 2008, I showed her a photograph dated in my hand, December 9, 1949. It's the last picture taken of me in Shanghai: my eyes are bright with youthful confidence as I meet friends at a popular gathering spot, the Airline Club. I am standing in front of a decorative mural, a flight of fancy by Chinese artisans depicting their version of a Pacific paradise. The scene has all the clichés of the South Pacific: an azure sea, swaying palms and lei-bedecked hula dancers. In Shanghai's quirky East-meets-West style, the figures are Caucasian beauties, dead ringers for Hollywood actresses Rita Hayworth and June Allyson—and June's ukulele bears a suspicious resemblance to a Chinese lute.

I would leave the only home I'd known a few months later. After decades of war and crisis, the city faced fresh uncertainties under the new Communist regime. Thousands of residents were getting out of Shanghai.

As our cab pulls away from Zhenning Road, I reflect on the innocent pig-tailed girl I once was, who relished Hollywood films and raising silkworms. I don't realize yet that my daughter and I have embarked on a journey into the past that will stretch over ten years and uncover a family bank heist, my grandfather's gangland kidnapping and a lifelong feud between a mob boss and my godfather, a warlord's son; or that we will discover how my glamorous mother, while trekking across war-torn China, was sold to a stranger, and how the theft of a precious art object offered redemption for my father's broken dreams.

At the Airline Club, December 9, 1949.

FAMILY TREE

This family tree focuses on Isabel's immediate relatives (it does not, for example, include her siblings' spouses and children).

Great-grandfather *Taiyeye* 太爺爺
Sun Zhutang
孫竹堂
1842–1899

Taiyeye's wife and 4 concubines
(7 sons and 5 daughters)

Grand-uncle "No. 4"
Sun Jingzhai 孫敬齋
1874–1912
(left estate to Sun Bosheng)

Grandmother *Qinpo* 親婆
Zhang Runchan
張潤禪
1879–1958

Grandfather "No. 7" *Yeye* 爺爺
Sun Zhizhai
孫直齋
1878–1950

Yeye's 5 concubines
(1st and 3rd were sisters)

Uncle Yifu 姨夫
R. C. Chen (Chen Changtong)
陳長桐
1892–1984

Auntie Ayi 阿姨
Pauline Chen (Fei Baoqi)
費寶琪
1907–2002

Mother *Muma* 姆媽
Fei Baoshu
費寶樹
1909–1988

Father *Diedie* 爹爹
Sun Bosheng
孫伯繩
1894–1969

1st daughter
Virginia Sun Shucheng
孫樹澄
1927–2015

2nd daughter
Sun Shuliang
孫樹涼
1928–1931

3rd daughter
Isabel Sun Shuying
孫樹瑩
1931–

Husband
Raymond Chao
趙梅溪
1923–2012

4th son
Sun Shufen
孫樹棻
1932–2005

5th daughter
Sun Shuquan
孫樹荃
1936–

6th daughter
Sun Shujue
孫樹珏
1937–2000

1st son
Leslie Chao
趙之浩
1956–

2nd son
Lloyd Chao
趙之仁
1959–

3rd daughter
Claire Chao
趙之蕖
1962–

THIRD DAUGHTER

I was born Third Daughter among six siblings. My father named me Sun Shuying. In Chinese, the family name comes first; siblings often share the second character to identify them as part of the same generation or nuclear family. So it's only the third character that is mine alone.

A check in the astrological almanac revealed that I lacked fire. Since a harmonious life requires a balance of all five elements (wood, fire, earth, metal and water), it was important that my name contain the missing element. Diedie selected for my third character *ying*, "luster of gems." The character is made up of the symbol for jade, with two fires atop it. I am not sure whether I fulfilled my father's aspiration for me: a precious stone that shines intensely.

My dearly loved Muma was called Third Daughter too. And Claire, my youngest child and co-author, is likewise my third daughter. *Remembering Shanghai* is our compilation of stories about four generations of my family; Claire, who represents our fifth generation, has provided notes and sidebars to help illuminate the history and culture of the times.

Claire, left, and me, 1960s.

CHAPTER 1
MOTHER'S DAY

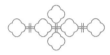

I EASED THEM OUT FROM their hiding place—a small bundle of photos tucked away in a drawer, beneath a carved inkwell next to Diedie's extra spectacles. The women in the black-and-white images were young and beautiful; I'd never seen them before.

It was the summer of 1938. Virginia and I had been playing in the garden when a sudden downpour had driven us inside. We'd dashed through the French doors directly into Diedie's study and, as he had gone out for the afternoon, decided to stay until the rain subsided. I was idly opening and closing his desk drawers when I came upon the photos.

"Eldest Sister, come look. Who are these pretty ladies?" At seven, I turned toward Virginia for guidance. She was four years older and much worldlier than I was.

"Let me see," she said, her slim fingers grabbing the photos from my chubby ones. She leafed brusquely through the images. "*Aiii*, I hate Diedie! Why does he do this?" she cried, flinging them across the room. "How can you say they're pretty? Hmmph, they're the ugliest women I've ever seen—they can't compare to Muma!"

I watched perplexed as the photos fluttered to the floor like wounded butterflies, and then I scurried over to pick them up off the maroon rug.

I couldn't understand why she was making such a fuss. "Who are they, Virginia? Why are you so mad at Diedie? Now I don't remember how to put the pictures back in the right order, and he'll figure out I've been in his desk."

"So what if he does? Throw them in the garbage, for all I care. Diedie's the one who should be ashamed, not us." She kicked a photo with the tip of her shoe. "You don't understand anything, do you? Those women are his mistresses. His girlfriends. He, he . . . *does* things with them, gives them gifts, takes them to nice meals. It's so unfair to Muma!"

Tears trickled down Virginia's face. It reminded me of lunch earlier that day, when our parents had argued about something. Virginia, who was particularly close to Muma, had started to sniffle loudly. "Eldest Daughter, stop that!" Diedie snapped. Virginia ran from the room, leaving the rest of the family to finish the meal without her. A moment later, a loud jangling from the bottom of the stairs broke the awkward silence at the table. Our majordomo, Ah Si, called up, a familiar refrain: "Shaonai,[4] telephone call for you!"

Muma headed off with uncharacteristic haste. Qinpo,[5] my father's mother, griped under her breath, "And there goes the trollop, gallivanting off again." Whatever Diedie was thinking, he kept it bottled up inside.

Downstairs, Muma accepted her friend's invitation to tea at Ciro's, mahjong at another friend's home in the French Concession, and then something about listening to jazz at a new club. We expected our mother to be gone within the hour, not to be seen again until she rose around noon the next day.

Later, in our bedroom, Virginia confided, "Muma talked to me in secret just now. She asked if I think she should divorce Diedie, and I said absolutely, yes." Her brows drew together. "I heard him talking to Qinpo, saying Muma's disgraceful. Qinpo said if he doesn't divorce her, she's going to ruin the family name. How can that be?"

I couldn't imagine Muma doing anything bad. "I want Muma to stay here with us," I said.

"She'll never be happy if she stays," said Virginia. "I wish *I* could leave. I hate being in this house. I hate being bullied by Qinpo and Diedie all the time. If Muma moves out, I'm going with her!"

It was the first time I heard the term for divorce, *lihun*. It wasn't difficult to guess the meaning, as it combined the characters for "leave" and "marriage."

---

4. Shaonai: "young mother," pronounced *shao-nigh* (*shao* rhymes with *now*).
5. Qinpo: "close (paternal) grandmother," pronounced *cheen-paw*.

Muma—Fei Baoshu in the 1930s.

"That would be awful if Muma left us," I said. "All our friends' parents live together. Why can't they both stay in the house? They already do everything separately. Muma is fine upstairs, and Diedie can stay downstairs."

I was accustomed to my parents' frequent rows: muffled yelling and slammed doors late in the night, then finding Father asleep on a cot in the salon the next morning. It had never dawned on me that they might have been interested in other people, though concubines were common and indeed expected in all but the poorest families. As a child I had met many such *yitai*, "auntie wives," living under the same roof as the first wife in our friends' families. My own grandfather had five concubines, whom I addressed as First, Second, Third, Fourth and Fifth Popo, "grandma."

Concubines may have been a normal part of our world, but divorce was unheard of. I was still a little girl, and all I desperately wanted was for Muma to remain home with us.

I couldn't take my eyes off her.

Muma was wearing the most gorgeous dress I'd ever seen. I was in her bedroom watching, enthralled, as our resident tailor gave the final fitting for her new *qipao*. Mother stood in front of the rosewood cheval mirror as Mr. Yang flitted around her, industriously pinning a tuck here, smoothing a dart there, adjusting the hemline, until every square inch draped perfectly. I bobbed and twisted to see past him, the gray silk shifting across her slim silhouette like mother-of-pearl in the midday sun.

The fitting took place in silence. Although my mother was fun and conversational in social settings, Mr. Yang was, at best, laconic. He had been living in our household and making the family's clothes since I was a toddler. Over the years, he and Muma had developed a private code of eye signals, nods, tugs, pats and small gestures that expediently conveyed all that was needed. Now, as Mr. Yang stepped back to view his creation and I finally saw the qipao in its entirety, my yelp of delight broke the silence.

Bursting from the silk were giant blooms embroidered in fluorescent hues of lavender, pink and turquoise, and outlined in silver filigree. The flowers had, on the one hand, the quality of a vivid dream, and, on the other, a startling realism as if they were living beings. Plum blossoms and peony limbs intertwined like lovers along the curves of Muma's hips, waist and chest, arching up toward her delicate features. Mr. Yang had framed the gorgeous bower with a double-piped border of cobalt and fuchsia, and finished it with a mandarin collar and satin fasteners.

I gasped. "Muma, I've never, ever seen anything so beautiful in my whole life!"

"All seven years of it? Come closer—let's look at the needlework together," she said, pulling me gently toward her. "I wanted a qipao of my favorite spring flowers, peony and plum. I sketched them in watercolors, and Mr. Yang sent the picture to the Suzhou silk makers."

"Suzhou—is that the name of a shop?"

"No, silly girl. It's a beautiful city outside Shanghai with lovely canals, gardens and pretty maidens. And also the best silk weavers and stitchers in all of China."

I recalled a scruffy stranger arriving at the servants' door a few weeks earlier, clutching a cotton *baofu* and declaring in an unfamiliar dialect that he had something from Suzhou for Tailor Yang. He had untied the topknot of the baofu to reveal several pieces of neatly folded gray silk embroidered in dazzling colors. I had marveled at how something so fabulous could emerge from so ordinary a bundle.

"Once the silk was delivered to Shanghai," Muma continued, "Mr. Yang put everything aside to make it into this qipao."

"The flowers look alive, like they're growing on your body."

"Mr. Yang gave the silk artists my measurements so he could cut the fabric exactly to my figure. We had to wait a whole year for it to be embroidered."

I pressed closer to Muma and gazed into the hollow of a teal-blue peony, stroking the lustrous stamens with my index finger. I scrutinized every meticulous detail: each flower had a dozen petals; each petal, at least five shades; each shade, dozens of stitches.

Seeing my fascination, Muma continued, "When Mr. Yang ordered the embroidery, the workshop owner guaranteed that each flower would have at least one thousand stitches."

"Did someone really count them?"

"I must say I was surprised when Mr. Yang told me that. Of course, the more stitches, the more real it looks. I'm too busy to fuss about things like that."

The tailor flinched but remained silent. He was such a perfectionist that he probably *had* counted the stitches.

"Thank you, Mr. Yang, the qipao is even lovelier than I'd hoped. Please make the final alterations right away . . . remember, I'm wearing it to my friend's wedding next Saturday." Muma adjusted a pin in her chignon. "And you needn't worry about Third Daughter's flower-girl dress. We've already been to Wing On and found a lovely five-tiered pink satin dress for her."

She stroked my cheek affectionately. "The whole theme of the wedding is pink. Nowadays, I notice more brides wearing white gowns, like the foreigners. The groom's family is superstitious about using white—the funeral color. Pink is so much happier, anyway."

With that, Muma stepped behind the lacquer screen to change. I was embarrassed to be on my own with the tailor. He had not once looked at me during the fitting; he must have still been mad about what I'd done to him the previous week.

Mr. Yang lived above our kitchen in a workshop that would have been hopelessly cluttered had he not been so fastidious. He sewed our family's clothes at a long wooden table, which he kept completely clear aside from whatever garment he was working on. From his seat at the center of his workbench, he could stretch a spindly arm up to the bamboo rods holding spools of multicolored thread; down into the cardboard boxes of brocade, sequins and lace, piping and fasteners; or back onto the tidy shelves of fabric bolts.

He kept the measurements of all our family members, and insisted that we children come see him during the first week of the lunar New Year—not in order to give us gifts, but so he could update his records. He single-handedly took care of the clothing needs of our entire family of eight—everything from Muma's couture dresses to my father's French-wool *changshan* and my grandmother's conservative gowns, as well as the children's various outfits. Even after Diedie bought him a Singer treadle sewing machine, Mr. Yang persisted in hand-stitching the family's outfits, claiming machine-made garments were suitable only for the servants' work clothes.

He took care of his responsibilities uncomplainingly, rarely leaving the house except to buy supplies. Mr. Yang chose solitude even at night, when the rest of the staff gathered in the garden to tell ghost stories and nibble watermelon seeds. He preferred a hard cot crammed into the corner of his workshop to a bed in the servants' quarters.

A week earlier, with nothing to do on my summer vacation, I had gone to Mr. Yang's room. He was in his usual position at the bench, intently weaving a bright-blue spherical knot for Muma's peony qipao. At thirteen, he had apprenticed for more than a year with an expert in handmade "frogs"—the woven, braided and spiraled knots and loops used to fasten Chinese clothes.

That morning, he glanced up but didn't greet me as I entered the workshop. I remained near the door watching him complete one knot and begin another. He did not raise his head as I sidled toward the bench. Standing directly opposite him, I removed several shiny items from my pocket and inspected his sallow face with all its angles and concavities. I reached out, gingerly at first, using Muma's Max Factor lipstick to paint plump ruby-red lips around his tightly pursed ones. Deep furrows creased his forehead, but Mr. Yang still didn't look up or utter a word. I carried on more confidently, giving him thick brows like bristly silkworms and big circular pink cheeks as he went about making his third knot.

He and I finished our handiwork at the same moment, whereupon he marched downstairs and into the study, positioning himself squarely in front of Diedie's desk. Mr. Yang croaked out two words: "Third Daughter." My father sent for me immediately and gave me a severe scolding. He then instructed my nanny to awaken Muma, and told Mr. Yang to show my mother what I'd done.

Though Diedie spared me the kneeling punishment that he periodically imposed on my siblings, I hadn't anticipated this. It was rare for Muma to arise before noon; a premature awakening would likely quash her usual equanimity. I crouched anxiously behind a curtain on the second-floor hallway. The instant Mr. Yang strode past, I scuttled toward the bedroom door to eavesdrop on their conversation.

To my relief, in stark contrast to my father's reaction, Muma let out a tinkling laugh almost immediately: "You mean, Third Daughter just painted this on your face? She's used my most expensive makeup, all the way from Hollywood, California!"

"The girl's father agrees with me." Mr. Yang sounded exasperated. "It is extremely disrespectful and unacceptable behavior."

"It seems like that, doesn't it? Have you ever noticed that she's fascinated by everything you do? She's your biggest admirer. Can you not forgive her?"

"It's no excuse for disrupting me at my work."

"Mr. Yang, have you looked at your face at all?" I heard a drawer open. "Here's a mirror. Try to put yourself in the shoes of a carefree little girl. All she knows in life is joy . . . Please, let it go."

After a pause, the tailor cleared his throat. He reemerged from my mother's room so quickly that I nearly tripped as I scrambled back to my hiding place.

At Muma's fitting the following week, I feared he hadn't forgiven me. I was alarmed when my mother passed me the qipao from behind the screen, motioning for me to take it to him. With the hanger hooked on the fingers of one hand, I folded the dress at the waist and clutched the hem in my other hand. I then crossed the room with as careful a step as I could, so nothing would drag on the floor. I held my breath as I drew near, ready to pass him the qipao with both hands respectfully extended. Our eyes met, and at last I detected the glimmer of a shy smile.

After Mr. Yang left, Muma sat down to her morning—or rather her afternoon—rituals, as it was now well past noon. I watched from my usual position, perched on the miniature replica of her white satin stool that she'd had made just for me.

She reached into the jumble of cosmetics on her rosewood dresser: Two Girls flower dew water, powder compacts, Pond's cream, crystal

atomizers. Somewhere amid the clutter, my mother found what she was looking for: a lime-green tin of The Garrick cigarettes.

I was learning English at McTyeire School for Girls. The label piqued my curiosity. I couldn't make out all the words, but I did see my oldest sister's name: *The Garrick Cigarette Virginia Blend—these cigarettes are manufactured from the choicest selected growths of ripe tobaccos, which have been blended with the utmost care.* Scroll motifs and the golden profile of a sphinx decorated the tin of fifty cigarettes. It seemed perfectly natural that this product from the American South, adorned with an ancient Egyptian icon and purveyed by English tobacconists, should now be cinched in a black holder between my mother's Chinese lips. (Muma didn't speak a word of English and used Shanghainese transliterations for foreign things: Max Factor was *Misi Fotuo*, The Garrick was *Jia-li-ke*.)

Muma lit a cigarette and inhaled luxuriantly, her large eyes dark and gleaming like oolong tea. A tendril of smoke drifted toward me. I breathed in deeply until I could discern the sweet layered scents of perfumes and powder.

Mother applied cosmetics to her oval face with languorous and practiced deliberation: a layer of powder to whiten her complexion; a touch of rouge and lipstick; matte black liner to define eyebrows and lids. She went to the hairdresser twice a week to have her hair shampooed and styled in a romantic wavy bob. She had a subtly sophisticated look—just the right amount of makeup to convey seemingly effortless femininity.

"Third Daughter, please help me find my coral brooch—you know, the one that looks like a tree?" I went to the side table, where a gilded mirror folded out from the lacquer jewelry chest. One of the drawers was slightly open to reveal a glittering mélange of jade, pearls and colored gemstones. At a time when artisans could fabricate virtually anything, my mother scoured specialty shops for confections, patiently collecting and combining them into unique pieces: Chantilly lace and beaded borders to enhance a qipao; whimsical little carvings and shiny cabochons to craft into jewelry.

The brooch I took out was a branch of actual coral polished to perfection; green jade and rose quartz butterflies flitted above the turquoise-studded bough. The individual elements were insignificant on their own, but Muma's light touch united them in an exquisite harmony of land, sea and little creatures.

I heard scrunching paper as Muma opened a package.

"Close your eyes, Third Daughter. Something arrived yesterday—it's all the rage—sold out everywhere. I had to order it from Paris."

I felt a *pfff*... something wet and cool on my neck, a heady fragrance that took over my senses. "What does that smell like to you?" Mother asked.

"Mmm, it's sweet and delicious . . . roses from our garden . . . something that reminds me of summer—peaches maybe?"

"What else?"

"Vanilla ice cream? Something sweet and nice . . ."

"Doesn't it make you think of beautiful, romantic things? Huge bouquets of roses . . . glamorous French ladies . . . It's Ye Bali perfume."

I opened my eyes and saw the cobalt bottle of Soir de Paris with its silk-webbed ball. It had come in a boxed set that included a slender flacon with a fluted lid and a tasseled vial to carry in a purse. Muma pressed the mouth of the flacon against a folded tissue. Then she tucked the tissue into her brassiere, explaining: "Most ladies like to dab their wrists and neck with perfume, but I find it too strong. This way, the scent is softer and longer lasting."

At that moment, a blur of blue-and-white fur streaked across the room, landing on a round table at the foot of the bed. Muma had placed under the glass tabletop a darling poster of two kittens looking playfully into a goldfish bowl. For a second, as the fur ball came to a halt, it appeared as if one of the painted cats had come alive and sprung out of the poster. It was my mother's fluffy kitten, Sanmi. Third Meow was the third Persian cat she'd owned. On this wintry day, he was wearing a baby-blue sweater that Muma had knitted to match his eyes. He leered at us for an instant before he launched into another frenzied flight.

The kitten leapt onto the dresser. Ever so softly, Muma said, "Sanmi, Sanmi, be careful please . . . slowly now, don't knock over my cup. There, there, you're a sweet cat." It was like trying to repel a typhoon with a paper umbrella. Yet if Sanmi had broken every cup and jar, it wouldn't have mattered to my mother; I do not recall her once raising her voice or moving with urgency.

Nothing ruffled Muma. She was nonjudgmental and unconditional in her acceptance of virtually everyone and everything, with only one exception: Diedie.

Muma and me, 1934.

CHEONGSAM OR QIPAO?

What is the correct name for that elegant Chinese dress, cheongsam or qipao? Both are correct. It depends on where you are and what dialect you're speaking.

The qipao, as it's known in Mandarin and Shanghainese, is the traditional men's "banner gown" of the Manchurians, China's Qing dynasty rulers. Women began to wear them in the 1920s as a feminist statement.

In 1930s Shanghai, the loose-fitting women's qipao evolved into a tighter, high-collared dress. Equally popular among dance-hall hostesses and the fashionable elite, the hourglass design is proper yet sensual, revealing a hint of leg under a slit skirt. The versatile qipao looks sleek and businesslike with a Western-style jacket or a flowing coat, glamorous when cut to floor length and embellished with antique embroidery or sequined designs.

Searching for fabrics, trimmings and accessories is part of the fun. Muma often went to Lao Jie Fu, a huge Bubbling Well Road emporium brimming with fabrics from all over the world. European-style boutiques such as Madame Greenhouse sold matching accessories like handbags, shoes and gloves; the Siberian Fur Store made custom fur outerwear.

With the Communists' rise to power, Shanghai tailors brought their qipao-making skills to Hong Kong. This is where it got confusing, because Hong Kong locals refer to the item as cheongsam, a loanword based on the Cantonese pronunciation of changshan, "long garment"—which outside Hong Kong describes the traditional long robe favored by men such as Diedie.

Me at eighteen in a silk floral qipao.

CHAPTER 2
THE ARTFUL SCHOLAR

DIEDIE PUSHED UP THE SLEEVE of his changshan, fingertips poised around a giant calligraphy brush. With a burst of coiled energy, he stabbed and swirled black ink onto white rice paper. The brush moved like a sinuous extension of his arm, pausing only when the character was complete.

I watched spellbound from the side of my father's desk.

"Can you read this?" he asked, gesturing at a simple character.

"Yes, Diedie, *ren*."

"What are its different parts?"

"That's a man on the left. And that's the number two."

"Good, Third Daughter. Do you know what it means?" He smiled wistfully. "Kindness between two people—one of Confucius's Five Virtues. If everyone lived by it, there would be no wars."

Diedie's study was a peaceful place. The scent that my siblings found stale—a mingling of cigar smoke, old books and wet ink—comforted me. I couldn't resist playing with the glass snuff bottles and inkstones atop his desk, though I'd been warned to be careful. His most prized objects had belonged to high officials, even emperors, long ago.

I examined his ink sticks one by one, closing my eyes to inhale the fragrance of pine needles or camellia petals. A collection of jade seals invited my caress. Even in the heat of midsummer, the jade was cool to the touch. I pressed one against my cheek and imagined a wispy-bearded mandarin extending wrinkled fingers from an embroidered robe to rub the smooth stone just as I did.

Diedie had a large assortment of brushes nestled in ceramic pots and hanging from carved wooden racks. The simplest brushes protruded from plain bamboo flutes; the most elaborate were carved in lacquer and semiprecious stone.

The French doors opposite Diedie's desk opened onto a covered porch and looked out over the prettiest corner of the garden, where indigo morning glories climbed the bamboo fence. The room did not encourage intimacy. The desk was at one end, a suite of Western-style sofas at the other. I don't recall Father ever joining anyone on the sofa for a chat—he was always seated behind his desk. On the few occasions when Muma came in, their voices suggested it was mostly to talk (or perhaps argue) about money, each of my parents speaking loudly so as to be heard from opposite ends of the room.

Unlike me, my siblings rarely ventured in unless summoned. One day my brother, Shufen,[6] got into a fight at school, and Mr. Yang had to sew yet another set of clothes to replace the torn ones. When I came home I found Shufen kneeling on the hardwood floor next to Father's sofa. He had received Diedie's maximum sentence: kneeling motionless for *yizhixiang*, the time it took to burn one stick of incense.

That afternoon, Diedie was seated at the far end of the room, head bent over his gigantic ledger. Unaware that I'd come in, he dabbed his calligraphy brush on an inkstone and wrote notes in fine, precise characters. Moving line by line down the page with a wooden ruler, his lips were pursed and he shook his head, occasionally making soft clucking noises.

"Third Sister," Shufen whispered, "I'm so bored! Open the window for me. I've been on my knees for nearly an hour."

The incense stick had burned most of the way down. My brother wanted me to open the window a crack so the breeze would make it burn faster. He nodded in silent thanks. Though a year younger, he was far taller than I. Even on his knees, his soft brown eyes were level with mine.

---

6. Shufen: pronounced *Shoo-fun*.

Diedie—Sun Bosheng in traditional scholar's robe in 1938. The calligraphy in this lifelike watercolor states, "Portrait of the scholar Po Meng, forty-three years old." Po Meng was his artistic sobriquet.

Father was fleshy in the manner of one unaccustomed to manual labor. He wore his Chineseness on his sleeve—the sleeve of his Chinese robe, that is. Fashionable men wore Western suits, but he never strayed from his black cloth shoes and floor-length changshan: dark silk in summer, European pinstripes or herringbone in the winter.

Diedie's wire-rimmed glasses were perfect moons as he looked longingly at a landscape painting that lay unfurled next to a pile of scrolls. The house didn't have enough walls to show all his artwork, so he rotated them every few weeks to reflect the seasons.

Diedie's strong baritone could be heard from just about any room in the house, but on seeing that the incense had snuffed out, he merely clapped his hands, and Shufen scurried from the room.

"Ah—Third Daughter," he said, "just in time to help hang my painting." He seemed eager to set aside his ledger. He was soon atop a wooden stool, adjusting a satin cord from which to hang the scroll. I wished the landscape and its inhabitants were real, so I could play in the rolling hills and rustic pavilion, or ride the skiff with the ducklings gliding alongside.

The sound of Diedie clearing his throat pulled me out of my daydream. He gestured toward the large square seal at the top of the painting, a red imprint nearly as big as the trees in the village grove. I couldn't make out the four old-style characters. "It's a mark of Emperor Kangxi's court," he told me. "Since it was created, this painting has been owned by nine princes."

"We don't know any princes," I said. "Where did you buy it, Diedie?"

"Well, even princes can fall onto hard times. Someone close to the imperial family sold it to me."

Father pointed to several red seals beneath a poem inked in black. "The best works of art tell you a story not only about what the artist painted, but also about the people who collected them. Even after hundreds of years, you can still trace all the owners," he explained. "Including me. See my seal here? It's this last one, 'Humble Tranquil Studio.'"

One dreary winter's day, I was keeping my father company in the salon—the *zhongjian*, or "middle room"—next to his study. I did my homework on a coffee table while he rearranged his art pieces. Normally, when no one was watching, I loved to rub my fingers over Diedie's objects, except for one type, the grotesquely pitted gongshi. Scholar's rocks struck me as boring old rocks, not pretty like porcelain vases with their bird-and-flower scenes or elaborate court vignettes.

"Diedie," I inquired, "don't be upset. These rocks are so scary looking. Why do you collect them?"

He looked up from a celadon vase and rested his gaze on a gongshi. The gray stone was balanced on a carved pedestal and towered ominously over my head. Diedie thought for a short time before replying, "The rock's beauty is not on the surface as with paintings or porcelain. Come closer, Third Daughter, and look carefully."

I moved next to the rock and peered at my father through a jagged hole.

"Unlike other artwork, gongshi are formed by nature: man has no hand in creating them. What does this stone remind you of?"

My mind was blank—all I saw was a gray rock.

Diedie stood still as I scrutinized the stone. "Take your time," he said.

"Mmm, I see a bird with wings spread wide . . . let me see, maybe a cloud?"

"Walk around it. What else do you see?"

"Oh—now it looks like a mountain, a huge mountain . . ."

He rested his hand on the pedestal. "And what is this, a path perhaps?"

"Yes, Diedie, I see the path. Look, here it splits into two—and here's a cave . . . and a bigger cave . . . I wonder if there's a fox living inside!"

"So you see, it's not just any old rock. There is mystery to it, and it's up to you to find its secrets."

I still didn't find the rocks appealing, but it felt special to be playing a grown-up game with Diedie.

"These rocks began as plain limestone boulders in Lake Tai, near where I grew up outside Suzhou." I recognized the name of the city that had produced Muma's beautiful peony embroidery. He rubbed his fingers along a crevice of the gongshi. "Time is a patient sculptor," he said. "While the rock sits at the bottom of the lake, water flows past. After hundreds of years, the rock becomes smooth. If the water is turbulent, it leaves rough edges and holes like these."

A week later, on a bitter January day, Diedie had gone out for lunch, and the ground-floor rooms were deserted. The sodden air penetrated our bones like icicles. It was too cold to play outside; I'd come home from school with chilblains the day before. And now the steam radiators on the second floor were out of order.

That's why Shufen and I were bundled up, looking like stuffed pandas in thick layers of clothing, in the relative warmth of the zhongjian. The room was all hard edges: tables with inlaid marble and glass cabinets filled with Diedie's prized Ming and Qing dynasty porcelains. I tended to avoid the room because Father's hardwood furniture was uncomfortable to sit in.

Shufen, always the restless one, started poking me, and the next thing I knew he'd chased me from the zhongjian into the study. We waddled in and out of the rooms, grabbing arms, yanking jackets, shrieking and laughing as we wove between porcelain vases and gongshi. As I made my fourth or fifth loop into the zhongjian, Shufen shouted behind me: "Careful, Third Sister, slow down, you're—"

Just inside the door to the salon, I came to a jarring halt a second too late. My padded sleeve caught the edge of a scholar's rock. Diedie had placed his prized stone at the side of the doorway. It was his favorite—the only one I quite liked—a lunar crescent pitted with deep craters and caverns.

Frozen in midstep, Shufen and I watched as the rock teetered and fell from its carved pedestal, as if in slow motion. It crashed onto the dark parquet, its top making contact first, then bouncing and flipping upside down. Finally, the bottom end hit the hardwood, snapping the gongshi into two pieces.

"*Aiya*, now you've done it!" Shufen cried. "You've broken Diedie's spooky stone! We're going to be in such big trouble. With my luck, I'm the one who'll get spanked. Father never believes that *you* could be naughty. He's going to blame it on me for sure." He scowled. "I'd better stuff padding in my pants to protect my backside."

It was true: Virginia and Shufen were punished regularly for their rebellious behavior, but Father had never struck me. I dreaded this might turn out to be my first spanking. Shufen insisted we try to glue the pieces together, and the seam was barely perceptible. The problem was, we couldn't fix the four deep gouges that the falling stone had inflicted on the hardwood floor. Diedie was bound to notice them eventually.

Shufen returned the repaired stone to its original place minutes before Father arrived at the front door.

For the next few days, I checked on the gongshi every morning and afternoon. What before had resembled gaping caverns in the rock were now accusatory eyes staring at me. After several sleepless nights, my anxiety became unbearable. I was doomed: I would have to face Father's wrath, or I would never sleep again. As the sun rose, I found him shaving in front of his bathroom mirror.

"Diedie, we've had a terrible accident," I said. My apprehension gave way to relief as I finally prepared to reveal my secret.

"What is it, Third Daughter? Shh, shh, don't be upset. What's making you cry like this? Your eyes are so red and puffy . . . Is it really that serious? Tell Diedie what's happened." I reached for his hand and pulled him toward the bedroom door. My sniffling and jerky hiccups sounded loud and ragged as we descended to the ground floor.

In the zhongjian, I blinked back tears as I pointed to the stone and the four depressions in the floor. Lather still clung to Diedie's chin and would have looked comical had his eyes not been so dark, or the purple vein in his neck so taut. My heart stopped.

Father paused, as if weighing what he'd say next. His words immediately freed me from my angst: "I see. It's all right. This isn't a valuable piece. It's just a stone after all, isn't it? But it does remind me that you're growing up, and you shouldn't be running around like a street urchin."

I hung my head in shame.

Diedie touched me under the chin and tenderly drew my face up until our eyes met. "Third Daughter, it took a lot of courage for you to tell me the truth. Try to act like a young lady from now on, all right?"

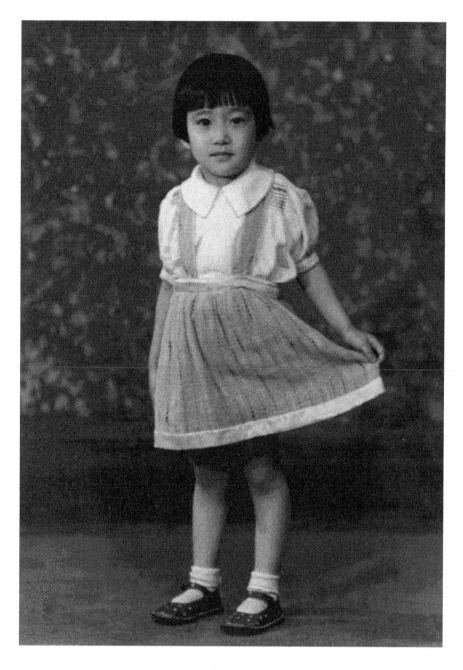

Isabel, 1936.

WRITE ON!

Chinese is a tremendously difficult language. Though speakers of, say, the Qingdao dialect in the North and Cantonese in the South are unintelligible to one another, all use the same written language.

Characters are formed in several ways and usually provide no cues as to how they are pronounced. The simplest formations use pictographs such as mu 木 *(meaning "tree" or "wood") and* senlin 森林 *("forest"). Ideographs depict more abstract concepts, such as* shang 上, *"up," and* xia 下, *"down."*

Some two hundred "radicals" or elements are combined to form characters. An 安, *the character for "peace," comprises two radicals representing a woman under a roof. Thunder,* lei 雷, *is made up of rain above a field. Radicals can be at the left, right, top, bottom or center of a character.*

Penmanship matters: every character's strokes must be written in a designated direction following a certain order. The simplest characters are one, two and three: 一, 二, 三. *The most complex contain over thirty strokes, for example the thirty-six-stroke character* nang 齉, *which connotes "stoppage of the nose." The two radicals are a nose on the left and a bag on the right.*

Suffice it to say, literacy in Chinese takes far more effort than mastering an alphabet and requires the knowledge of over three thousand characters. The amount of rote memorization needed is breathtaking—thus the ubiquitous scene of schoolchildren with heads bent over exercise books, practicing character writing in endless columns of blank squares.

In a bid to increase literacy, since the 1950s the Chinese government has simplified the written language by reducing the number of character strokes. A few examples: horse, ma 馬, *became* 马; *air,* qi 氣, *became* 气; *country,* guo 國, *became* 国.

Though my mind accepts the practicality of simplified characters, my heart laments the aesthetic loss. Consider our family names: Isabel's, Sun 孫, *has become* 孙, *the right half reduced to the character for "small." Claire's, Chao* 趙, *is now* 赵. *The "x" on the right, to us, does not look like the mark of a learned person.*

An artist's portrayal of the suppression of the Taiping Rebellion, ca. 1860.

CHAPTER 3
A PLUM POSITION

EVERY RICH FAMILY MUST START somewhere, with a progenitor who creates the wealth. In ours, it all began with Taiyeye,[7] my great-grandfather Sun Zhutang, a servant boy who became an imperial minister.

He was born in 1842 in Huiji, a hardscrabble mountain village near Shaoxing in Zhejiang Province, south of Shanghai. Taiyeye lost his father while he was an infant. The inhospitable terrain offered scant opportunity. As a child, he was always hungry, and the same was true for virtually everyone he knew.

When Taiyeye turned twelve, his mother sent him to work as a servant in the household of a renowned lawyer in Shaoxing. In addition to its scenic waterways, opera and rice wine, the city was known for its *shiye*—lawyers—and those from Shaoxing were the best in China. Before long, Taiyeye's master recognized the potential in his bright servant; he taught him to read and made him a law apprentice. Taiyeye seized every chance he was given, carefully observing and emulating his master. At twenty, with the help of his mentor, Taiyeye entered the civil service as a legal counselor.

At least, this was the story I'd heard as a girl. Claire delved further, searching historical records and interviewing relatives. Her most valuable sources proved to be the works of my brother, Shufen, a writer who penned fifty-five books, several of which were adapted into films and TV

---

7. Taiyeye: "paternal great-grandfather," pronounced *tie-yeh-yeh.*

series about life in Old Shanghai. One of his books, *Dreams of the Nobles,* includes stories about Taiyeye. Here's what Claire pieced together.

CLAIRE: Poverty wasn't Taiyeye's only challenge. In 1842, the year of his birth, the First Opium War ended with China's humiliating defeat by Britain. The earlier years of the Qing dynasty, established in 1644, had been marked by grand political and cultural achievements. However, the Chinese citizenry increasingly resented the rulers, ethnic Manchus from the North, and regarded them as ineffectual. Famine and unrest severely weakened the economy. In 1850, a charismatic leader and self-purported brother of Jesus Christ launched the Taiping Rebellion, a massive revolt against imperial rule.

It was against this tumultuous backdrop that Taiyeye charted his unconventional path to power and privilege.

Chinese society offered little social mobility. The main route to higher status was the rigorous national examination system, based on the memorization and analysis of classical texts by the philosopher Confucius. Although in theory the tests were open to all, in reality they required years of education that only the upper echelons could afford.

Students had to pass county-level exams in their late teens before progressing to ever more demanding provincial and national exams that culminated at the imperial palace in Beijing. Sequestered for three days in bare cells, the final candidates had to compose essays with distinction and precision: one incorrect character stroke meant immediate failure. The few who ultimately passed joined a bureaucracy as arcane as the system that spawned it.

Young men from affluent families coveted government positions, as they ensured lifelong financial rewards and status. Taiyeye's entry into civil service was entirely unorthodox, made possible by the patronage of the lawyer he had dutifully served. Ordinarily, a son of peasants could never have come so far; the bureaucrats would certainly have viewed him as an outsider. But it was probably this very outsider status that gave him the vision and audacity to rise above even the most seasoned officials.

The raison d'être *of Chinese officialdom was to uphold tradition. Taiyeye's colleagues resisted even the slightest departures from protocol,* seeking guidance for their decisions in the aphorisms of a philosopher who had been dead for almost twenty-four hundred years. They obsessed over the rituals and minutiae of court, such as what to embroider on their official robes—a different bird to symbolize each of the nine ranks of civil service.

Taiyeye, however, wasn't bound by the way things had always been done or by Confucian teachings: all he wanted was to do them better. When Taiyeye was nineteen, the emperor died, leaving a five-year-old son as next in line to the throne. The mother, an imperial concubine, took control of the Qing court, becoming the empress dowager Cixi. She ruled China from behind a screen of yellow silk—the color reserved for use by emperors. Cixi immediately faced the problem of recruiting conscripts to combat the Taiping rebels.

Despite being new to the court and inexperienced in battle, Taiyeye understood the local peasants and succeeded at rallying them where others had failed. Enlisting imperial troops was no easy task, as rebel ranks had swelled from a ragged band of villagers to hundreds of thousands of disciplined fighters with a reputation for brutality and fanaticism. Taiyeye's resourcefulness and ability to mobilize even the most reluctant draftee earned him the trust of two powerful military leaders, Zeng Guofan and Ronglu. At a critical juncture, he joined forces with General Zhang Yi to lead disparate militia in a unified battalion that helped destroy the Taiping regime. Historians estimate that, until then, the fourteen-year rebellion had claimed twenty million lives.

Taiyeye made history his friend. He was twenty-two, mature beyond his years at the time of the Qing victory. He continued to serve under Ronglu, the empress dowager's cousin and close confidant. Descended from Manchu royalty, Ronglu was adept at navigating the bureaucracy and intrigue of court. News spread of Taiyeye's role in defeating the Taiping uprising, soon catching the attention of Cixi herself. The shrewd, purposeful empress dowager appreciated Taiyeye's contribution to the stability of her reign, and she summoned Ronglu to court.

During the audience with his cousin, Ronglu lay prostrate in the hall, listening intently, hooded eyes gleaming. Even hidden behind her yellow curtain, Cixi wore full formal regalia—her head weighed down by a gem-encrusted coiffure, a pearl cape draped over her phoenix-embroidered robe and tasseled platform shoes. (Unlike the Chinese, Manchus did not *subject their girls to foot-binding.) With a decisive wave of her talon-like gold nail protectors, she instructed Ronglu to reward Taiyeye with a high official position.*

Like Cixi, Ronglu was well aware of the dissipation of the Manchu elites, in part due to the opium addiction that was consuming the country. He supported her break with tradition in appointing Chinese such as Zeng Guofan to senior positions that had previously been held exclusively by Manchus. Opportunities that Taiyeye couldn't have dreamed of even a few years before were now there for the taking.

First, the court appointed him head of customs of Tianjin—a plum assignment in which he received a share of fees paid by every ship entering the treaty port. More prized positions followed, including foreign minister in the capital city of Beijing and ministerial envoy in Jiangxi Province, each affording him greater wealth and influence.

When Taiyeye relinquished his official duties in his midforties, he did not retire to his barren birthplace, instead establishing a family seat about one hundred miles north, in the flourishing Yangzi Delta. Like neighboring Suzhou and Shanghai, his new base of Changshu was one of the nation's most prosperous cities.

This estate in neighboring Suzhou is in a similar style, albeit one-quarter the size of Taiyeye's Changshu compound.

He astutely used the affluence he'd gained from his government appointments to buy land—lots of it. His first purchase was a large holding at the north gate of Changshu, in the fertile Tianning Temple Lane area. The idyllic spot at the foot of Yushan Mountain offered views of verdant tea plantations, while nearby Yangcheng Lake produced the finest dazhaxie, *hairy crabs, a prized delicacy.*

Taiyeye gradually expanded his six-acre family compound of pavilions and courtyards within gracefully landscaped gardens. A serpentine bridge crossed a lotus-filled lake to a hilltop pagoda from which he enjoyed watching the moonlight shimmer on the water. Before long, more than a hundred servants and retainers looked after three generations of Suns, which included Taiyeye's wife and four concubines, their seven sons and five daughters and numerous grandchildren.

From their military triumphs, Taiyeye and his comrade-in-arms Zhang Yi forged a lifelong friendship. When Zhang's ninth daughter, Runchan, was born in 1879, she was betrothed to Taiyeye's one-year-old seventh son, Sun Zhizhai. The two wed as teenagers and became Diedie's parents.

Taiyeye still had too many ideas to fully retire, and he set about acquiring more land. At the east gate of the city's main road, he developed several dozen blocks of apartment buildings to rent to a burgeoning middle class. By the end of the century, he had purchased four thousand acres of farmland and rice paddies in the neighboring counties, becoming the richest man in the area. Much like an English lord of the manor, he took responsibility for many aspects of the townspeople's work and welfare. In addition to building a school and a town hall, he funded community enterprises such as a flour mill, an herbal medicine pharmacy and a textile factory. Once the businesses were running smoothly, he turned them over to locals to operate for their own profit.

China's interaction with the West changed dramatically in the second half of the nineteenth century. Foreign merchants had prospered by exporting opium from British-administered India and shipping it to China. Even though the Qing authorities had banned the import and use of the drug, the Chinese population and economy suffered from rampant addiction—an addiction matched only by the Westerners' dependence on its profits. During Taiyeye's youth, China's moves to halt the illicit trade erupted into two opium wars against Britain and France. The European powers' victory over China engendered a series of treaties granting them access to Shanghai and four other port cities, ending China's isolation and opening the way to international trade. This led to the creation of foreign enclaves—in Shanghai, the British and American Settlements (later merged into the International Settlement) and the French Concession, each with its own legal system, municipal council and police. Extraterritorial status allowed foreigners to live in Shanghai and the other treaty ports without a passport or visa and exempted them from Chinese law. From its prime spot at the mouth of the Yangzi River, Shanghai became Asia's largest and most prosperous city; at the start of the twentieth century she was handling two-thirds of China's foreign trade. Most of it was controlled from an area of the Huangpu riverfront known as the Bund, an Anglo-Indian word for "embankment."

Though many Chinese feared the rapid changes unsettling the established order, Taiyeye seized the very same opportunities as the foreigners. While the foreigners constructed their riverfront palaces, he quietly purchased a large swath of land on Third and Fourth Roads (also called Hankou and Fuzhou Roads), adjacent to the Bund, from which the international concessions spread westward. His Maijiaquan development on Fourth Road included twenty street-front retail buildings and more than two hundred residential apartments.

As trade flourished, Taiyeye saw the need for reliable transport to link the cities of the Yangzi Delta. His Changtong Shipping Company grew to be one of the largest passenger and cargo operations on the Yangzi River, with twelve vessels, as well as dockyards and ship repair facilities in Shanghai, Changshu, Wuxi, Suzhou and Hangzhou.

He expanded his interests beyond property development and shipping. In the 1880s, Taiyeye opened Dingtai Bank, funding it with his own capital of one hundred thousand silver taels. (The tael was a Chinese unit of currency equivalent to 1.3 ounces of gold or silver. Bank reserves during this period were held mostly in fifty-tael boat-shaped silver ingots called yuanbao, *and Spanish or Mexican dollars.)*

At fifty, Taiyeye finally withdrew from his Shanghai businesses to spend more time in Changshu. Almost all his sons had died in childhood, with only the fourth and seventh, whose mothers were No. 1 and No. 2 concubines respectively, reaching adulthood. He had named the fourth son Jingzhai, meaning "respectful." The seventh son was Zhizhai, meaning "straight"—the boy who had been promised in marriage to a general's daughter at one year old and who would become Diedie's father. Jingzhai wed the daughter of another general. (For simplicity's sake, I will refer to them as No. 4 and No. 7.)

Fourth Road (Fuzhou Road), ca. 1907.

Key to Taiyeye's success was his ability to observe and learn from anyone—be it a foreign banker or a ship mechanic. His fateful blind spot was his failure to acknowledge the shortcomings of his own sons. Like most Chinese men of his day, he maintained relationships of utmost formality with his sons. No. 4 and No. 7, in turn, behaved with great respect in his presence, kowtowing to him every morning. The brothers' names would prove eminently unsuitable: out of his sight, they did as they pleased, often to their father's detriment.

Upon his retirement, Taiyeye sent eighteen-year-old No. 4 and fourteen-year-old No. 7 to Shanghai to oversee his business concerns. Leaving No. 4's wife in the Changshu compound, the brothers arrived as immature and capricious young men—two young playboys in glittering Shanghai, free to use their father's largesse to indulge every temptation.

The rail-thin No. 4 shared his father's resourcefulness, sizing up in minutes how any situation might be molded to his advantage, except he applied it in the pursuit of hedonism rather than industry. No. 7 was the guileless and more malleable of the pair, gladly following the lead of his older brother.

The wife of No. 4 had not conceived during several years of marriage, and, as oldest son, No. 4 was under a great deal of pressure to produce an heir. At one brothel, he concocted a scheme to attract new mistresses by staging a beauty and talent show. He offered to make any contestant who became pregnant by him his official concubine. No. 4's strenuous efforts with the many willing candidates garnered him neither concubine nor child, but instead caused him to contract syphilis.

The sons' allowance from Taiyeye, though generous, wasn't enough to cover their profligate lifestyle and mounting gambling debts. They soon discovered that their father's good name could secure money and services, with the understanding that when Taiyeye passed away, the sons' inheritance would pay off creditors. Such an arrangement was glibly referred to as mayizhai, *"hemp clothes debt," referring to the plain garments worn by funeral mourners to show their humility. The brothers' extravagance was such that when No. 4 lost one thousand taels in a single mahjong game, they realized even mayizhai could not cover their debts.*

Just at that time, Taiyeye called the brothers back to Changshu for an auspicious family event.

These servants' quarters were the only surviving structure in the
Changshu family property when this photograph was taken in 2008.

Opium hulks in the Huangpu River, ca. 1901.

The Bund from the opposite side of the Huangpu River, ca. 1907.

CHAPTER 4
TAEL END

THE YEAR OF THE HORSE, 1894, *marked the birth of Taiyeye's first grandson—the firstborn of No. 7 and his wife. That infant was Diedie. It was a period of immense pride for Taiyeye, the patriarch not only of the Sun family but also of Changshu. The arrival of a male heir fulfilled his spiritual obligations and assured the family's posterity, and he wanted the whole town to celebrate. Taiyeye hosted a traditional* manyue *party when the baby, having reached one full moon of age, emerged from seclusion with his mother.*

The most important duty that morning was for the household of over one hundred residents to give thanks to the family ancestors. The men wore flowing silk changshan and ceremonial magua *jackets; the ladies, elaborate* gua *formal gowns. In hierarchical order, each family member approached the altar, knelt and paid respects: Taiyeye first, followed by his official wife, his concubines and his children. After the family came senior employees, such as accountants and foremen, and, finally, the live-in staff. Taiyeye presented red-wrapped gifts to one and all—gold and silver taels, jade carvings, imported wool for the men and handwoven silk for the women.*

Friends and townspeople streamed through the gate throughout the day, proffering gifts and congratulations. Inside the high walls, visitors' sedan chairs and horse-drawn carriages lined the courtyard alongside groves of magnificent white magnolia trees. The bearers and drivers received meals too, as well as red packets of coins for good luck.

The gardeners and house staff had decorated the great hall even more elaborately than at Chinese New Year. Taiyeye, the former servant boy, was determined to lay out the most extravagant festivities the town had ever witnessed. Red-and-gold banners, silk lanterns and hothouse orchids adorned the compound. An opera troupe from Beijing performed a tale of imperial intrigue while acrobats, magicians and jugglers displayed impossible feats.

The family's cooks had spent weeks preparing. Taiyeye's kitchen was famous for two Changshu specialties: beggar's chicken, jiaohuaji, *a whole chicken roasted in clay that according to legend was unintentionally invented by a Changshu vagrant who'd stolen a chicken and hidden it in mud; and* babaofan, *"eight precious rice" made of glutinous rice steamed with eight kinds of candied fruit, nuts and mashed red beans representing eight precious gems.*

Beyond the main pavilion, in a darkened room, male guests reclined on heated kang, *smoking pipes filled with the finest Calcutta opium.*

As the guests were enjoying the lavish event, No. 4, the heir apparent with his own outsized appetite for indulgence, begrudged what he saw as Taiyeye's vanity and wastefulness. The ne'er-do-well son of a great man, he resented living in his father's shadow. When Taiyeye began to greet visitors that afternoon, the keenly observant No. 4 immediately noticed his new festive robe—not that No. 4 was in any way concerned with his father's sartorial style. The only thing of interest was that Taiyeye's signatory jade seal—his precious mark of identification that signaled ownership in important legal documents—wasn't hanging from its usual place at the old man's waist. No. 4 hatched a plot to misappropriate his father's funds on a larger scale than ever before.

As night fell, the tables were laden with desserts and fine Shaoxing wines. Family and guests filled the courtyards and verandas; conversation paused as all eyes turned heavenward to take in a magnificent fireworks show.

With the various residential pavilions emptied of their inhabitants, No. 4 made his move. He strode purposefully through the party, No. 7 struggling to keep up on his short legs. Inside the residential wing, the brothers slowed to a stealthy pace, first stopping in their father's study, where No. 4 secreted several items from the desk. They then sneaked into the pavilion of Taiyeye's second concubine, who happened to be No. 7's mother. Pushing aside the curtains of the spacious four-poster bed, No. 4 stooped over the kang and reached past the hanging lamps to remove a small object. Until a few hours earlier, it had been suspended on a silk cord attached to Taiyeye's everyday changshan—his jade seal.

No. 7's usual genial smile disappeared, and his eyes narrowed into slits. "Fourth Brother, we can't take Father's signatory seal! We'll never get away with it—"

"Shh, shh, you dimwit. I have a foolproof plan, but I need your help. This is our only chance. He left the seal behind when he put on his formal robe. It never leaves his waist otherwise."

No. 4 laid out the items he had taken from the study. He pressed the seal onto a pad of vermilion paste, carefully making a bold red mark on a blank sheet of Taiyeye's custom-made writing paper. He wiped the seal clean and returned it to the kang, then tucked the paper into his changshan and rejoined the party with No. 7.

As a child, No. 4 had had neither the coordination nor the patience for calligraphy, but No. 7 had demonstrated talent at an early age. Taiyeye had trained his younger son to write calligraphy in the same style that he himself favored, and often had No. 7 write commemorative messages in his hand to the many people under his patronage.

No. 4 intended to put his younger brother's calligraphy to good use. Taiyeye maintained a substantial fund, set up as a renewable trust for future generations, at the Shanghai branch of the British-owned Hongkong and Shanghai Bank (the forebear of HSBC). It amounted to fifty thousand British pounds—the equivalent today of about eight million American dollars.

The brothers set to work immediately when they returned to Shanghai a few days later. Under No. 4's direction, using the stolen stationery stamped with Taiyeye's seal, No. 7 forged a letter in their father's handwriting, instructing the bank to release Taiyeye's entire deposit. The young men then headed to the bank's riverfront headquarters at 12 the Bund.

While they waited for assistance, No. 7 darted round eyes at the turbaned Sikh guards flanking the entrance, their rifles upright, belt buckles shiny and leather boots tall. No. 4 gazed upward, as if admiring the elaborate vaulted ceiling. "Don't worry, little brother," he hissed. "Very soon those guards will be grinning through their bushy beards as they help us load up the carriage with gold."

Hongkong and Shanghai Bank headquarters at 12 the Bund in the 1880s.

The head of the bank was not only Taiyeye's longtime banker but also an old friend hailing from the same hometown of Shaoxing. He personally greeted the brothers in the lobby as a courtesy to their father. As the bank's comprador—the agent between native Chinese and foreigners—Xi Zhengfu was one of Shanghai's most influential financiers. His discretion had earned him the trust of local and Western businessmen alike.

The comprador looked small in a voluminous changshan and stiff magua. The pleasant demeanor formed by his wide-set eyes and neatly trimmed beard belied an astute character. Once seated in the wood-paneled suite, he addressed the brothers across his huge desk, his words graciously formal. "Congratulations, Seventh Shaoye,[8] on the arrival of your infant son. I would have liked to come personally to Changshu for the celebration, but I have been exceptionally busy. Please accept my sincere apologies."

"We would not expect a man of your stature to travel the long distance," said No. 7, recalling the four miniature objects crafted in pure gold that the comprador had sent as gifts—a book, a sword, an official's seal

---

8. Shaoye: "young father" or "young master," pronounced *shao-yeh* (*shao* rhymes with "now").

and an abacus. "We are undeserving of your thoughtful and generous gift. It received high praise from many family members and guests. I can only hope that my son will be worthy of your good wishes."

"They are small playthings for good luck," said Xi with a dismissive wave. He leaned forward, making a steeple of his fingers. "I am pleased to receive both of you today. May I assist with a financial matter?"

No. 4 got down to business: "We've come on our father's instructions," he said, removing an envelope from his robe and holding it with two hands politely outstretched. The comprador reciprocated the courtesy, accepting the letter in both hands. Xi was expressionless as he read the letter. Having reviewed scores of Taiyeye's documents, he recognized the familiar silk stationery with the neat handwriting and distinctive seal.

After reading to the end of the page, the comprador studied the brothers in turn. He had never expected that Taiyeye might liquidate his assets in one swoop. No. 4's fidgeting may have raised suspicions, yet the letter seemed authentic, and No. 7's affable manner was reassuring. Xi bobbed his head, rising from his desk. "I understand. If there are no special instructions, I will arrange for the yuanbao to be prepared."

After the comprador had left the room, No. 4 said to his brother, "Finally, something useful from all the time you wasted practicing calligraphy."

Xi soon returned with the bank's accountant. The blue-eyed Englishman held open a dark leather ledger to which No. 4 affixed his own seal. The transaction was complete.

Once the carriage had been loaded with the trunks of gold and silver yuanbao and bank notes, Comprador Xi bid the brothers farewell. "Please give my best regards to your father," the banker said. "Ordinarily I would not dare intrude, but, as we are family friends, I wonder what you are planning for the funds? If I can help in any way, I would be most honored."

No. 4 had a pretext prepared: "Recently, a property agent told us that several acres of land have become available near our properties on Fourth Road. Our father thinks it's a good idea to buy all of it and build a few more longtang of rental apartments."

"Opportunities abound in Shanghai these days," Xi observed. "I heard that new roads and utilities are being constructed in the area. When that happens, you will enjoy excellent profits."

"We certainly hope so," No. 4 said, closing the carriage curtain. Though he had thought ahead to secure a four-horse carriage, the animals strained to pull the heavily laden vehicle along the cobblestones.

And that is how No. 4 and No. 7 peacefully hijacked their father's fortune from the largest foreign bank in Shanghai.

Months later, newspapers reported on the sale of the land that No. 4 had mentioned. Comprador Xi was perturbed to read that the Sun family was not the buyer. The financier had sensed that something had been amiss when he had met with the brothers; his banker's discretion wrestled with his personal loyalty to their father. Finally, he followed his intuition and wrote to Taiyeye.

When Xi's letter arrived in Changshu, Taiyeye had just awakened from a nap in his second concubine's pavilion, a few feet away from where his sons had pilfered his legal seal. An ominous feeling rose from deep in his gut as soon as he saw the Hongkong and Shanghai Bank insignia on the envelope. The missive began innocently enough, with the comprador dutifully inquiring after his client's health and retirement, and offering his congratulations once again on the birth of his first grandson.

Taiyeye's face contorted as he reached the end of the letter, written as if it had been a postscript: "After your sons' recent withdrawal of your funds from our bank, I trust you had no problems acquiring the land that you sought. As always, it would be my distinct honor to facilitate any financial arrangements that you might require."

His roar of fury and anguish reverberated across the six-acre estate.

When Taiyeye went to Shanghai in search of his sons the next day, they were nowhere to be found. They were already in hiding and remained one step ahead of Taiyeye's investigators for the next three months. The foreign settlements were a perfect haven for people hiding from the law. The International Settlement had Sikh constables under British command, and most of the French Concession's policemen were from Vietnam. The two international police forces operated independently from each other as well as from the Chinese authorities in the rest of the city. Eluding one's pursuers was as simple as crossing the street into another jurisdiction.

The brothers had stolen their father's entire Hongkong and Shanghai Bank deposit and also all the cash from the family businesses. After suffering a stroke, Taiyeye returned to Changshu empty-handed.

Betrayal of one's father in a Confucian culture was deemed to be one of the gravest transgressions. Taiyeye removed the names of No. 4 and No. 7 from the family ancestor hall and took out full-page newspaper ads disowning them. He even visited relatives in Shaoxing, seeking suitable teenagers whom he could formally adopt and train to run his businesses (he found none). Forced out of retirement, Taiyeye was as despondent over his sons' treachery as he was over his massive monetary loss. The theft hadn't bankrupted him, but it broke his spirit. With his sole grandson still a toddler, he faced the possibility of dying with no adult heirs and failing to perform his duty to carry on the family line.

Constantly on the move to dodge their father's detectives, the dissolute brothers managed to deplete their funds again. They stretched their imaginations to contrive another scheme, this time playing on the old man's desire to see their remorse.

While hiding out in a town outside Shanghai, No. 7 wrote Taiyeye to break the news that No. 4, ashamed and contrite over what he'd done, had committed suicide by swallowing raw opium. As No. 4 had taken his last breath, the younger brother wrote, he had pleaded to be buried in the family's Changshu cemetery. Taiyeye could not refuse his oldest son's final wish and arranged shipment of No. 4's coffin from Shanghai. When No. 4's wife found out, she made a failed suicide attempt and went to live in a nunnery.

Taiyeye now believed he had only one surviving son among twelve children. No. 7 begged his father for forgiveness, pledging to reform if given one more chance. Taiyeye acquiesced, placing him under house arrest for two years, during which No. 7 read Chinese classics and became even more accomplished in calligraphy. Over time, Taiyeye became more lenient, allowing his son to visit teahouses and meet friends. Never one to sit still for long, No. 7 quickly acquired three concubines, all of whom came to live in the same pavilion as his long-suffering wife.

Taiyeye lost faith in banks after the Hongkong and Shanghai Bank disaster. He instead stored his assets as gold and silver yuanbao inside one of his warehouses. The boat-shaped ingots were stacked neatly from floor to ceiling and protected by guards—a verifiable system, Taiyeye thought, to protect his assets from another theft. He visited the warehouse every full moon to ensure that his holdings were intact. Even in his final years, partially paralyzed and nearly blind, he took comfort in running his hands up and down the shelves as far as his arthritic fingers could reach, slowly stroking the sides of his precious yuanbao.

The day after Taiyeye's death, No. 7, his supposed sole heir, set out from the family compound to inspect the warehouse. He had arranged to meet someone at the entrance; it was none other than No. 4. He had been alive all this time, hiding out in Shanghai! The coffin that No. 7 had shipped to Changshu for burial years earlier had contained nothing but rocks—it had all been the brothers' ruse to escape Taiyeye's retribution.

Astonishingly, the brothers succeeded in double-crossing their father one more time. Years before, No. 7 had bribed the warehouse caretaker and stolen all but the front rows of yuanbao, replacing the rows behind with ingots of worthless lead. Perhaps it's just as well that Taiyeye never knew about the final grand deception. After rising from abject poverty to amass a fortune and then losing much of it to his scheming sons, he had derived profound consolation in his last years thinking he still had all that gold.

The two brothers reclaimed their late father's companies and resumed business. No. 4's wife left the nunnery to rejoin her husband.

No. 4's excessive lifestyle did catch up with him; he died childless two years shy of his fortieth birthday. For a peaceful afterlife, it was essential that a male descendant pay ancestral respects. That became the responsibility of the only boy in his generation, No. 7's son and No. 4's nephew. The sole heir was eighteen-year-old Diedie.

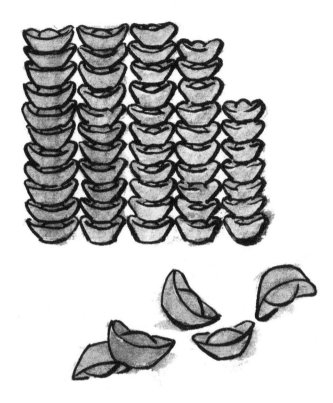

IT'S ALL RELATIVE

The many Chinese monikers for relatives are extremely effective for pinpointing an individual's position in a family. At the simplest level, we have gege, "older brother"; didi, "younger brother"; jiejie, "older sister"; and meimei, "younger sister." To these, the siblings' birth order is added: first son, second daughter and so on.

In English, "uncle" is all-encompassing. Introducing your uncle inevitably leads to the question of how, exactly, he's related. Chinese distinguish the various kinds of uncle with different words: bobo, your father's older brother; shushu, your father's younger brother; jiujiu, your mother's brother; gufu, the husband of your father's sister; and yifu, the husband of your mother's sister. (Typically, when Chinese people call someone "uncle" and "auntie" in English, they are good friends rather than blood relations.)

Specific forms of address extend to distant branches of the family tree. There are appellations for every kind of cousin—paternal or maternal, male or female, older or younger and by blood or marriage. One or two Chinese characters conveys all the information that in English would require perhaps ten words. For instance, tangsao means "the wife of the older son of one's father's brother."

Understanding these designations from childhood means that you know immediately how someone is related to you. Your designation gives you a permanent, unassailable position among your kin.

This elaborate and yet economical naming system was needed in the past because people had large, multigenerational households. Expressions like tongfuyimu, "same father, different mother," and yiniang, "auntie mother" (for your father's concubine), were useful descriptors.

Western culture tends to focus on individuality. Traditionally, Chinese have thought of themselves as being a small part of a larger group. The surname comes first in Chinese, so you grow up with an inherent awareness that the individual is subordinate to the family. And when you're addressing an envelope, the country comes first, then the city, the street address and, finally, the personal name.

Although nowadays the order of Chinese names is sometimes switched to conform with Western practice, the conventional style still used in China is

surname first, followed by given name. *In other words, identify your family, then
reveal yourself as an individual.*

gege 哥哥 older brother
didi 弟弟 younger brother
jiejie 姊姊 older sister
meimei 妹妹 younger sister
yitai 姨太 concubine

bobo 伯伯 father's older brother
shushu 叔叔 father's younger brother
jiujiu 舅舅 mother's brother
gufu 姑夫 husband of father's sister
yifu 姨夫 husband of mother's sister

Muma with Virginia, eight, and me, four, in a Shanghai photo studio. (I looked
tense because I was worried about falling backward through the open window.)

CHAPTER 5
FOOTLOOSE

"Qinpo, why do your feet look like that?"

I'm not sure what made me ask. I had seen her strange feet hundreds of times before, soaking in a tub of warm, vinegary water as we whiled away evenings together, and I had not inquired before. As a child I spent a great deal of time with my grandmother, but it's hard to recall many conversations beyond what was practical and necessary. Usually, we shared our companionship in comfortable quietude, sitting at her bedroom table listening to traditional storytelling or Beijing opera on the radio. Sometimes, Qinpo played consecutive games of solitaire *paigow* using thirty-two domino tiles, with me watching by her side.

Her silence was benevolent. It was rare for her to smile in the way others did, with lips upturned. If she was content, her close-set eyes became rounder and sparkled like black buttons. Though she wasn't one to coddle or compliment, her presence instilled peace and confidence in me. Not everyone in the family felt that way; all my siblings and even my mother were afraid of her. Qinpo didn't hide her displeasure if something annoyed her. Thankfully, I was never the target of her temper.

That is why, after I asked about her feet, the look on her face bewildered me. Her wide-eyed expression made me think of when I'd pulled my kitten's tail too hard.

Qinpo lowered her head after a long pause and rested her gaze on her feet. "It happened when I was younger than you are now. Everything was different then. It was expected for girls from good families. If a mother did not do it, her daughter might never find a suitable marriage." Qinpo's eyes moistened as she looked lovingly into mine. "I thank Buddha that it will never happen to you or your sisters."

Qinpo—Zhang Runchan, ca. 1895, wearing special shoes to give the illusion of bound feet.

She sighed deeply and returned to her paigow tiles. The discussion was over.

"It" had not entered my mind before our conversation. My grandmother's reticence to tell me what made her toes fold down like squishy chicken feet only fueled my interest.

I had noticed other older women with small feet, but no one talked about it openly. It was only after I'd grown up that I became aware Qinpo's feet had been bound when she was a girl. I shared this with Claire one day when she was visiting me in Hong Kong from her home in Hawaii. She was aghast that her own grandmother had been subjected to this horrific treatment.

"Of course, I'd known about foot-binding," my daughter said. "It never hit home, though, until I heard your stories about Qinpo."

I'll let Claire explain.

Ten centuries of Chinese women submitted to the cruel custom of foot-binding in the name of feminine beauty. Around age five, a girl's feet were bound tautly, using long strips of silk or cotton. Over time, her toes were broken and folded under the balls of her feet. The tight bindings served two purposes: to stop the feet from growing and to reshape them into an ideal form.

It's hard to understand that this had sexual connotations—in extreme cases, the heels were forced toward the toes, exaggerating the arch of the foot to create a cleft that was considered erotic. The smaller a woman's feet, the more desirable; under four inches in length was ideal. Balanced atop her "golden lotuses," she tottered along with a swaying gait that was thought to be the pinnacle of grace. It came at a high price: excruciating pain, frequent infection and dependence on others for nearly everything.

In a family of means, it was natural for women to have servants assisting them. Yet it wasn't only the well-to-do who bound their daughters' feet. Even villagers of modest means believed it would improve a girl's marriage prospects. What a double injustice if she didn't marry well and wound up laboring in a field on her mangled feet.

How could such a disfiguring practice stem from a mother's love and the desire to win a man's affection? As one author put it, "The driving force

*behind this desire was complex: it had to do with marriage; it had to do
with sex; it had to do with status; it had to do with beauty; it had to do
with duty."[9]*

*I was relieved when Mom told me Qinpo had been spared the worst of
the sadistic practice.*

Qinpo was born in Jingdezhen, a town in Jiangxi Province that was famed
for its fine porcelain. One of her helpers told me Qinpo was too small to
protest when her feet were bound at the age of five. I suppose the strong
will that characterized her adult life developed quickly after that. At ten,
she objected so vehemently that her parents agreed to have the bindings
removed.

Qinpo was Runchan, the daughter of the general who had been
Taiyeye's friend. Since she had already been promised at birth to Taiyeye's
No. 7 son, she didn't need golden lotuses to lure a man into marriage.
Her feet remained deformed and pained her all her life, but she could
walk more or less unrestrictedly.

Qinpo became the official wife of No. 7, whom we would call Yeye,[10]
in an elaborate ceremony at Taiyeye's Changshu estate when she was
fourteen and Yeye was fifteen. She had anticipated this day for as long as
she could remember and had no inkling of what he looked like. In their
bedchamber after the wedding, she saw her groom for the first time as
he lifted the red veil from her lacquered hair. She was surprised at how
short he was, with a dark complexion more befitting a farmer than a
member of the landed gentry.

It turned out Qinpo had scant opportunity to get to know her
new husband. He left her in Changshu a few days later and returned
to Shanghai, where he and No. 4 were ostensibly running their father's
enterprises. Yeye did not come back to the Changshu compound until ten
months later, to join the first-month celebration of his and Qinpo's son.

9. Beverley Jackson, *Splendid Slippers: A Thousand Years of an Erotic Tradition*
    (Berkeley: Ten Speed Press, 1998).
10. Yeye: "grandfather," pronounced *yeh-yeh.*

Not long after that, he and No. 4 pulled their Hongkong and Shanghai Bank heist and went into hiding.

When Yeye came home to Changshu several years later and was confined to house arrest by Taiyeye, it could have been the perfect opportunity to become acquainted with his wife, but Yeye was an unapologetic philanderer. To Qinpo, it didn't matter that Chinese men had been taking concubines for centuries; she would have none of it. She had put a stop to her foot-binding, and she was not about to welcome concubines into her pavilion.

Qinpo may have been the official wife but, as a woman, she was powerless. Her protests failed to have any effect on her husband. She watched in silent fury as Yeye acquired three concubines—of whom the first and third were sisters—and consorted with an untold number of mistresses in brothels and teahouses. The concubines' children, who were Diedie's half-siblings, all lived with their mothers in the increasingly complicated Changshu compound.

Divorce wasn't an option, so Qinpo simply refused to have anything further to do with her husband. She instead turned to Amitabha Buddha for spiritual solace and remained deeply devout to the end of her life.

Things did work out in the end. Just as my favorite expression says, "When the boat reaches the bridge, it will naturally straighten."[11] In Qinpo's case, salvation came because, as Yeye's official wife, she had produced the only "legitimate" son in that generation. When No. 4 died in 1912, he left everything to Diedie, his eighteen-year-old nephew. The windfall enabled Diedie to assume responsibility for Qinpo's support. Mother and son left Changshu immediately, journeying sixty miles toward the coast to start a new life in Shanghai.

My grandmother was a devout Buddhist, and for several hours each day she practiced *nianfo*, a form of meditation from the Pure Land school. As a child, I'd sit by her and calm down the moment I heard her chanting and the muffled click-click of beads while she recited her mantras. Her sandalwood rosary, rubbed smooth by thousands of small strokes, lay loosely coiled in the soft cradle of her rice-paper hands. My eyes followed, as if hypnotized, her thumb sliding the beads forward one by one: 108 repetitions of "Amitabha Buddha"—"*Namo Emituofo, Namo*

---

11. *Chuan dao qiaotou zi hui zhi.*

Emituofo, Namo Emituofo"—a graceful turn of the rosary, then back to the beginning again.

Qinpo was never alone. She had two helpers dedicated to her care, who assisted with her clothes and toilette. She wore almost no makeup, just a little rouge on her translucent cheeks. A helper brushed a black crayon along Qinpo's hairline every morning, to cover the gray hair.

Grandmother also had a Buddhist companion whose main duty was to be at her side during prayers and meditation. I called her companion Gonggong, "grandfather," and had always thought he was a man until I saw him changing and realized that Gonggong had a woman's breasts hidden by a loose-fitting robe. Since, in spoken Chinese, "he" and "she" sound the same, we were able to skirt the issue, so to speak. Years later, I learned that imperial court eunuchs were addressed as Gonggong too.

OUT OF A BIND

By the time foot-binding was finally outlawed at the end of the Qing dynasty in 1912, it is estimated that more than one billion Chinese women had had their feet bound and broken since the custom began. Although the government imposed fines on families who continued the practice, decades passed before foot-binding came to a full stop.

When the last factory making bound-feet shoes ended production in 1998, China's Xinhua News Agency reported:

"Special shoes for bound-feet women [are] now a thing of the past. Elderly Chinese women whose feet were bound since childhood to keep them small have fewer shoes to choose from in Harbin, the capital of northeast China's Heilongjiang Province, because shoe factories no longer produce them. . . . The factory added small shoes for old women to its product range in 1991 to fill a gap in the shoe market. . . . In the first two years, more than two thousand pairs of the shoes were sold annually, but now the factory has to think of what to do with the stockpile of tiny pointed shoes, which are not even suitable for babies."[12]

At last—the end of an abominable tradition.

---

12. October 26, 1998, Xinhua News Agency report, cited in the Virtual Museum of the City of San Francisco, www.sfmuseum.org/chin/foot.html.

House 15, Lane 668 (later named Zhenning Road).

CHAPTER 6
MISTER STREET

IT IS NOT EVERY DAY that you have a street named after you. That's what happened to Diedie—but unfortunately not for honorable reasons.

My father, Sun Bosheng, grew up in the lap of luxury on his grand-father's sprawling estate in Changshu, a full day and night's journey from Shanghai aboard one of Taiyeye's steamboats on the Yangzi River. Changshu had flourished for centuries, with its fertile terrain, crisscross-ing rivers and lakes yielding an abundance of fish and shrimp. The city's very name—*chang* meaning "ever," and *shu* meaning "harvest"—was a testament to its bounty.

Surrounded by tea plantations, the high whitewashed walls of the Sun family property shielded twenty gray-tile-roofed buildings. Connected by meandering paths and covered galleries, the pavilions housed a dozen wives and concubines. The estate had a staff of eighty for the residences, as well as laborers who tended the orchards and vegetable gardens.

For the women with bound feet, it was too difficult to walk the estate's entire six acres. On the rare instances when they needed to reach another pavilion, they would call for a sedan chair carried by four man-servants. The elaborate central hall with its table for thirty was used during Chinese New Year and festive celebrations. The rest of the time, the women mostly kept to their own families.

Taiyeye oversaw his assets with more vigilance than he did his house-hold. The soothing views of gardens through circular moon gates and willow trees nodding over koi ponds did little to quell the conflicts and jealousies among the female residents.

Although he grew up in affluence as the first and only son of the first wife, Diedie's childhood was a somber affair. The men in the family were at best troubled, and more often than not absent. Qinpo's only child, Diedie was barred from playing with his half-siblings, whose mothers she considered adversaries.

Diedie found solace exploring the estate's secret courtyards and rock grottos, taking a poet's delight in the subtleties of the shifting seasons. In later years he socialized in intellectual circles, but the love of solitude he developed in his youth continued into adulthood.

A student of art history, Claire possessed a special affinity for my father even though she never met him.

The more I learned about Mom's family, the more I came to understand how twentieth-century developments made Diedie an anachronism. His life spanned some of the most radical and disruptive changes in China's long history. The Qing dynasty collapsed when he was eighteen, ending two thousand years of imperial rule.

Taiyeye's rise from pauper to government minister afforded Diedie the classical upbringing of a Confucian scholar preparing for the imperial examination that had dominated education from the tenth through the nineteenth centuries. But unlike scholars from families with a long intellectual history, Diedie did not aspire to serve in court, and the national examination system was abolished when he was eleven. He was an exemplar of China's great literati tradition, yet was under no obligation to join the civil service. The teachings of Confucius, which provided a strong moral grounding and a deep reverence for the arts and letters, remained a constant in his life.

By the time Diedie was born, trade in agriculture, silk and cotton in the Changshu area had created a prosperous merchant class, who poured their wealth into culture as a way of enhancing their social standing. Patrons from Changshu, such as the Four Wangs, seventeenth-century landscape scholar-artists all surnamed Wang, assembled exceptional art collections. The rich cultural environment provided opportunities for Diedie to learn about fine art at an early age.

Claire observed that a story I'd told her about a lapse in judgment in my father's youth helped explain his character as an adult. In his early teens, Diedie was already an avid collector of Chinese paintings, porcelains and objets d'art. One steamy summer afternoon, a young art dealer pulled up to the Sun compound in a horse-drawn cart. Intrigued by the wooden crates loaded onto the back of the carriage, Diedie went out to the gate to meet him.

The dealer jumped down from the cart and squared his shoulders to face Diedie. "I have excellent things to show you that have just arrived from Beijing," he said. "They were consigned by a relative of the Qianlong emperor, rare and unusual pieces. Sun Xiansheng, Mister Sun, I'm sure you'll—"

Before he could finish, Diedie delivered a sharp slap to the vendor's cheek. It was a reflexive response to a perceived insult. Traditionally, a merchant—even one engaged in art and antiquities—was not of Diedie's social rank, and should have shown humility by using an honorific address such as Shaoye, "Young Master." Calling my father "Mister" was unacceptable.

"How dare you address me with such discourtesy?" Diedie exploded. He rubbed his thumb against his fingertips, feeling the sticky perspiration where they'd made contact with the man's face. In Father's rarified existence, his family's landed status warranted a level of respect akin to aristocracy. A swift slap, in Diedie's adolescent judgment, had been an appropriate response.

The art dealer took exception, suing Diedie in the Changshu municipal court. The shifting tide of social mores influenced the judge to rule in the vendor's favor. The court demanded that Father pay a hefty fine for his misdeed, and the proceeds were used to build a street in Changshu. The aggrieved vendor, albeit not a literary man, received his poetic justice. The municipal authorities named the new thoroughfare MISTER STREET.

As a child in Shanghai, I heard whispers about Mister Street from the servants, though Diedie never once mentioned it. The slapping incident was so at odds with my memories of Father—returning home with armloads of books for us, indulging us with tasty morsels at the dinner table, patiently teaching me Chinese characters—that for many years I couldn't believe it.

But the stories persisted for a half century, when my husband and I were raising our own children in Hong Kong and interviewing a potential cook from Changshu. When I told her my maiden name was Sun, the prospective helper asked if I was related to the infamous Mister Sun from her hometown.

I long ago reconciled the thoughtless teenager in the story with the courteous and caring, if aloof, father who raised me. Claire believes, and I agree, that Mister Street must have been his defining lesson in humility; that the comeuppance of the lawsuit and his ensuing self-reflection forged the respectful and charitable nature that became his hallmarks.

After inheriting his uncle No. 4's estate in the 1910s, Diedie left behind his scholarly roots to become a businessman in Shanghai. He worked hard, if reluctantly, for more than a decade, focusing on the family enterprises instead of his true passion, collecting art. On a return visit to Changshu, he was thirty-two—middle-aged by the day's standards—and it was high time to find a wife and raise his own children. According to family lore, Muma was walking on the main road as Diedie passed. At seventeen, she was a classic beauty, endowed with a lissome frame and flawless features. Her large, liquid eyes looked up alluringly as Diedie's sedan chair swayed along the cobblestoned roadway. The unhurried tilt of her head and her gentle countenance were irresistible—a sort of old-world grace that was lacking among Shanghai's fast city girls. Diedie was smitten, and proposed after a short courtship. Muma, who came from a well-off family but had been orphaned a few years earlier, was thrilled to move to Shanghai as the wife of a property scion.

I'm not sure if the story is entirely true; I am certain that for my mother the marriage was a godsend. Muma left Changshu and never looked back. Within a year, her transformation was complete. She had become a wife, mother and bon vivant in one of the world's most glamorous cities.

When they first married, my parents lived in No. 4's spacious house, which Diedie had inherited, on a one-acre lot on Avenue Road (not the International Settlement's most inspired street name). After four-teen years of overseeing the family investments, Diedie remained better suited to being a scholar than a capitalist. Around the time I was born, he tried to expand the company portfolio, using investors' and his own capital to establish Huadong Commercial Bank. It was a risky undertak-ing, given the uncertain times: a civil war in full swing, Communists and Nationalists struggling for power, and the Japanese steadily carving their way deeper into China.

The new venture ended in less than two years, with the bank going into receivership. To pay off creditors, Diedie was obliged to liquidate stocks and other assets, a process that included auctioning off the home where we lived. He lost more than half his holdings but managed to retain the properties on Third and Fourth Roads, which would sustain generations of our family for years to come.

With the financial disaster casting a pall over the family, our lifestyle—while still securely upper-class—became more modest by our former standards. The biggest change was our move from Uncle No. 4's Avenue Road house to a new home in Yuejiezhulu, an area known as the External Roads, on the western edge of the International Settlement. The address was House 15, Lane 668; the street was later dubbed Zhenning Road. Diedie leased the land from a friend and had our new home built on it. It was an easy bike or pedicab ride to McTyeire, where we went to school.

Our lane was north of Yuyuan Road, a wide residential street lined with lush plane trees. The houses and gardens were well kept—like ours, gracious but unpretentious. There were one or two larger mansions, albeit not on the scale of the estates in the French Concession. Our immediate neighbors were mostly Shanghainese households, as well as an English family and a Japanese family. The owner of the home directly opposite ours was descended from the infamous general Yuan Shikai. The elder Yuan, who had been instrumental in the abdication of the last Qing ruler, the child emperor Puyi, in 1912, served briefly as president and later proclaimed himself emperor of China.

Perhaps chastened by his financial humiliation, Diedie's design for our new home was solid and unpretentious. Above the front gate hung a carved wooden plaque identifying the family as Huiji Sun. Huiji, a county in Shaoxing, was Taiyeye's birthplace. Though we children were all born in Shanghai and had never been to Huiji, Father valued its significance as the earliest point from which he could trace our family history.

The house was a Chinese architect's rendition of a Spanish villa, with Mediterranean touches like stucco walls, brick accents and terra-cotta tiles. It had curves everywhere: over windows, above arches, woven into gates, intertwined in railings. Our home's most prominent exterior feature was its façade, a three-part scalloped silhouette that curved and swooped against the sky, projecting a strength that was more reassuring than showy, more earthy than sophisticated.

We entered the house through the front garden, where seasonal blooms greeted us at all times of the year. An entry arch with a carved molding led to the high-ceilinged foyer, where a blue-and-white Tianjin rug shimmered in the soft light. All three levels of our home had wide covered porches that provided shade and breezes during the humid summers.

While the exterior was Western in style, the interior floor plan followed the Chinese design principle of threes: three stories, each divided into three large rooms. Diedie's study was at street level together with the zhongjian and dining room. The kitchen and servants' quarters were in an annex at the back of the main house. On the second floor, my parents' and Qinpo's bedrooms flanked our everyday dining room; children's bedrooms occupied the third floor.

Three was a recurring theme, from the arrangement of rooms, porches and windows to the family itself: three generations under one roof, dominated by three intractable adults. Though three made for harmony in design, the home's inhabitants were not destined to enjoy the same concord.

Growing up, we rarely saw our parents together. Muma had quickly embraced big-city life upon moving to Shanghai, becoming a devotee of popular culture. She was sociable to a fault, loving mahjong, shopping and other amusements, as well as frequent social outings with her many girlfriends. She and Diedie were the epitome of *cimu yanfu,* "loving mother, strict father"—polar opposites in every respect.

My parents' differences were manifest in the very scent of their rooms. Muma's bedroom smelled of sweet French perfume and face powder;

Diedie's study, of dusty books and wet ink. Beauty and refinement consumed them both, but in disparate worlds and to divergent ends. Muma's activities leaned toward the frivolous; Diedie disapproved of senseless pastimes. She was spontaneous; he methodical. Muma embraced all the latest fashions; Diedie immersed himself in classical pursuits. She flitted blithely from place to place; he was solitary and anchored, usually clasping a book wherever he went.

Their lack of closeness was probably less a matter of their having grown apart than of their barely having known each other in the first place. They had each been at a pivotal point in their lives when they met, looking toward the next milepost and becoming enamored with the ideal that the other embodied. My parents' marriage was a case of opposites initially attracting and, in the absence of common ground, ultimately repelling.

Other challenges made their coupling less than conducive: their fifteen-year age difference and, perhaps most significant, a stern resident mother-in-law.

When my father moved to Shanghai in 1913, Qinpo had accompanied him. Diedie was her only child; his inheritance enabled her to walk out on her philandering husband and dedicate herself to protecting her son. In our household, Diedie was the patriarch and Qinpo, our dowager; Muma was a distant third in the hierarchy. The fact that Qinpo and Muma both suffered from their husbands' infidelities did not make them allies. Indeed, unless it was a conflict or criticism of some sort, the women's relationship was one of mutual disinterest.

Muma rarely awoke before noon. During lunch once, she shuffled into the family dining room in embroidered slippers. Qinpo, who had already started to eat, fixed a withering look on her daughter-in-law's feet. Muma turned around without a word, returned to her room and changed into a pair of proper shoes.

The family shared its meals in the second-floor dining room at a rosewood *baxianzhuo*, "eight fairies table." Designed for eight, with two on each side, it was just right for our family—my parents plus Qinpo and five children. I loved its symmetry.

During meals, four servants stood at the corners of the table, ready to help with tasks like shelling our shrimp or picking fibers from our oranges. Ceiling fans that provided relief in the muggy summer months were turned off at mealtimes so our food wouldn't get cold. On hot nights, the servants swung palm-frond fans to gently circulate the stifling air.

We had so many rules during meals. They seemed restrictive at the time but were probably normal for a genteel family. Don't reach for food. Wait to be served. Do not swing your legs under the table. Be quiet while the grown-ups are speaking. No fidgeting. Sit up straight. Don't shovel rice into your mouth. Do not touch Qinpo's dishes.

Even Diedie was subject to Qinpo's reprimands. When he used his chopsticks to pluck the choicest pieces and place them atop our rice bowls, she chided: "Don't spoil those children—they'll have many chances in their lives to eat good things! Take them for yourself." Fortunately, he rarely heeded her; we savored the tidbits and loved Father for his indulgence.

Qinpo never raised her voice: one look was enough to freeze you in your tracks. As a teenager, my sister Virginia bristled with rebellion and impetuousness. One time, Grandmother admonished her for eating too quickly, like a peasant. "I hate living in this house," Virginia shouted. "You're much kinder to your maids than to your own grandchildren. The only time you ever pay attention is when you're scolding me!"

I held my breath, anticipating Qinpo's reaction.

Our grandmother was holding a pair of silver chopsticks, their tops connected with a chain, poised to pick up a slice of honeyed lotus root. Her delicate fingers, so pious when rosary beads clicked between them, stopped in midair. I watched as her hands quivered with such rage that the chain became tangled. She did not utter a word, but her fury was deafening.

After what seemed an eternity, Qinpo shook the chopsticks forcefully until the chain loosened. Her expression was stone-cold and without a trace of emotion. The rest of us continued to eat, our heads hung meekly. If chopsticks and porcelain spoons could tiptoe, that's how we finished the meal, in silence, careful not to make any noise.

Qinpo in her forties.

Nanjing Road, ca. 1907.

CHAPTER 7
NOW, THAT'S ENTERTAINMENT

Before Shanghai became Shanghai, it was a marshy fishing village, where Asia's longest river met the world's largest ocean. The city was born of vice—the offspring of unbridled commerce and colonialism, a treaty port where the illegal importation of opium shortened the lives of thousands and where Westerners were granted immunity to Chinese law.

In the 1930s, when Mom was growing up, no passport or visa was required to live there. Shanghai was a haven for the displaced: Russians fleeing Bolsheviks, Jews escaping Nazis, Communists in hiding and refugees seeking shelter from China's own political turmoil. With life in such peril, it's not surprising "the Paris of the East," as it was known, became a place of indulgence and excess. Shanghai's residents seized every opportunity to feel alive—or merely to escape—be it by taking a puff from an opium pipe or waltzing the night away in the arms of a taxi dancer.

Shanghai was a place where glamour and opulence brushed shoulders with poverty and squalor. Its streets were as diverse as its denizens. In the foreign settlements, neoclassical office buildings and art deco skyscrapers rose above shops and cafés on elegant tree-lined boulevards. A few blocks away, Shanghai's mostly Chinese inhabitants eked by in cramped, mazelike row houses. Luxury Packards and Rolls-Royces glided down the city's grand boulevards alongside barefoot rickshaw pullers and horse-drawn "honey carts" loaded with excrement. Foreigners called the indigent people who filled the streets "coolies," adopting the Chinese term for "bitter work," kuli. Others were referred to as biesan—*Shanghainese slang meaning "empty three"—a beggar who lacked life's three necessities of clothing, food and shelter.*

No other city crammed so much of the world into such a tight space. Grizzled Russian men met at the Cosmopolitan restaurant over piroshki and steaming bowls of borscht; European businessmen savored cocktails at long bars in gentlemen's clubs while their wives sipped Darjeeling tea at luxury hotels on the Bund. Chinese had their own places, such as Qinpo's favorite Buddhist restaurant that served entirely vegetarian fare made to resemble pork, chicken and seafood.

If one spot epitomized Shanghai it was the Great World, once described by the Austrian American film director Josef von Sternberg as a "circus fairground, theater, casino, spa, brothel and the Folies Bergère rolled into one."[13] Owned by the infamous gangster "Pockmarked Huang," the Great World had its dark side, but for a little girl it provided a memorable and exhilarating adventure.

It was Qinpo who took me to Shanghai's grand pleasure palace, the Great World. The first time I accompanied her there, I clutched her hand tightly as we emerged from our black Buick and walked toward the wedding-cake tower. Our assistant driver, Shengtong, pushed ahead to clear the way through the jostling crowd at the entrance. I was only seven and had never been in the midst of such commotion—ladies in stylish qipao and men in tailored Western suits mingling with coolies in sweat-stained rags. I crinkled my nose at the overwhelming aromas of perfume, incense and perspiration. Shengtong handed several coins to the attendant and stepped aside for us to enter. "Be careful, Third Miss, it's only two *jiao* a ticket—who knows what kind of riffraff are inside? My friend was pickpocketed here last week!"

---

13. Josef von Sternberg, *Fun in a Chinese Laundry: An Autobiography by Josef von Sternberg* (New York: Collier Books, 1973), quoted with permission from Nicholas von Sternberg. Some of the descriptions of the Great World's contents are paraphrased excerpts.

On the first floor, we navigated past gambling tables, singsong girls, slot machines and acrobats; every inch of space was occupied by crickets in cages, herbs in jars, ice cream cones and earwax extractors. As it was teatime, we stopped at one of the many restaurants on the second floor for red bean *tangyuan* rice balls.

The Great World in a 1957 poster depicting traditional entertainment.

Afterward, Qinpo headed toward the *shuoshu* stage to hear traditional storytelling, but I pulled her into a maze of fun-house mirrors, where we bobbed our heads, grimaced and stuck out our tongues. I thought how aptly they were named—*hahajing*, "haha mirrors"—because I'd never seen grandmother laugh so hard, throwing her head back and rolling her eyes with mirth.

On the fourth floor, we saw men in Western suits and polished wingtips press up against wavy-haired girls in high-slit qipao. Qinpo tugged at my arm to move away from them. "Come, Third Daughter," she said. "Leave those girls to their fate." I hoped it would be a good fate, because tucked in a nearby corner was a love-letter booth with scribes who guaranteed results.

Later, while Qinpo sat spellbound at her shuoshu performance, I managed to sneak away to the far end of the hall, where a troupe of magicians performed in bright brocade robes. I wove my way between the spectators until I reached a small platform where a conjurer had placed on a table two tall stacks of chips, one of them all white and the other all red.

In the blink of an eye and the swish of a silken sleeve, the two columns were suddenly identical, comprising perfectly alternating red and white chips. I looked up, awestruck, to discover that the magician with the amazing sleight of hand was a slender boy of seven or eight. When our eyes met, he seemed as surprised as I was to see a child his age in this mostly grown-up playground.

In the evening Qinpo and I watched a jumble of tightrope walkers and jugglers on the roof. In the sky above, a fireworks display exploded into the form of a Chinese princess. As exhausted as I was when we returned to Zhenning Road, I'd never had such a thrilling day and couldn't wait until my next visit to the Great World.

With Muma out socializing and playing mahjong nearly every day, some of my best memories were of time spent with Qinpo. As serious as she was about her devotional practice, one diversion gave my grandmother unbridled joy: shuoshu storytelling, or "speak book," a form of folk theater that originated in Suzhou. From the late 1930s through the '40s, Qinpo had season tickets at one of Shanghai's top venues, the Cangzhou Shuoshu Theater, not far from the Nanjing Road department stores.

Since none of my siblings was interested, it was always me who accompanied our grandmother to shuoshu, which was performed as serials every afternoon for several weeks every summer. As with Shakespearean plays, aficionados already knew the storylines—the pleasure was in the players' interpretation of the roles.

There were two broad genres: one set to music, the other relying on voice alone. I was delighted by the sound of the *huqin*, a Chinese fiddle, and the *pipa*, a Chinese lute. Great versatility was required of the performers, who each spoke and sang the parts of up to ten characters.

My favorites were the romances; Qinpo loved tragedies. A classic that we both enjoyed was *Legend of the White Snake*, which recounts the adventures of a tortoise that transforms into an evil monk and a man who dies of shock after finding out his drunken wife is a snake. The plots could be difficult to follow, but the charismatic storytellers bewitched us with their imaginative portrayals.

On a typical afternoon, Qinpo and I sat at our front-row table, watching a legend at three o'clock, a drama at three thirty, a comedy at four and so on, returning to the house at dinnertime. We seldom had much of an appetite by then, thanks to the delicious Shanghainese snacks that we'd nibbled on throughout the afternoon: five-spice beef; *guoba* (scorched crispy rice); duck wings, tongues and gizzards; and *congyoubing* (green onion cakes). Qinpo had a sweet tooth, so our outings also included fragrant plums, candied almonds and sugarcoated lotus seeds.

One reason I loved shuoshu so much was that it made Qinpo relaxed and happy. On those rare occasions when I saw her mouth curve into a smile, it pleased me that she'd forgotten her sadness for a while.

KAFEI, TEA OR ME?

China has as many different dialects as it has villages. After the national Mandarin dialect, the two most widely spoken versions of Chinese are Wu, used in Shanghai and the surrounding region, and Cantonese, used in the South. Guttural, rolling Mandarin and clacky, hard-consonant Cantonese both have a lilting quality, with rising and falling tones within each syllable. In contrast, Shanghainese employs high or low tones for whole words. A profusion of s and z sounds and dragged-out syllables result in sibilant, breathy speech patterns.

Muma and Diedie had never studied English, yet they took it for granted that their children should learn it. As with many Shanghai people, transliterated English words peppered our conversations. The names of imported Western items quickly found their way into Chinese usage in the same manner that the French carotte *became the English "carrot." Not surprisingly, the most commonly Sinicized expressions related to food, entertainment and brand names.*

Here is something a Shanghai man might have said (shown in romanized Mandarin). Note "zh" sounds like j, q *like "ch," and* x *like "sh."*

"For lunch, I had a sanmingzhi *on* duoshi *with* qiaokeli buding *and* kafei*. Then I went in my* Bieke *to watch a* Haolaiwu *film called* Taishan*. Afterward, I relaxed on my* shafa*, smoking a* xuejia *with a small glass of* bailandijiu*."*

Here's the English version:

"For lunch, I had a sandwich on toast with chocolate pudding and coffee. Then I went in my Buick to watch a Hollywood film called Tarzan. Afterward, I relaxed on my sofa, smoking a cigar with a small glass of brandy."

Though borrowed, most of the loanwords are still in common use today.

sanmingzhi 三明治 sandwich
duoshi 多士 toast
qiaokeli 巧克力 chocolate
buding 布丁 pudding
kafei 咖啡 coffee
Bieke 別克 Buick

Haolaiwu 好萊塢 Hollywood
Taishan 泰山 Tarzan
shafa 沙發 sofa
xuejia 雪茄 cigar
bailandijiu 白蘭地酒 brandy

CHAPTER 8
POP CULTURE

SHUFEN AND I WERE TUCKING into our breakfast of *zhou* rice porridge and salted eggs when Diedie came in. "I am leaving soon to meet someone at a store on Fourth Road," he said. "If you like, the two of you can come and amuse yourselves there."

It was a sweltering June morning, my last week in second grade. We jumped at the opportunity to go out even as steam rose from the sidewalks. Virginia, my usual playmate, had gone to visit a friend.

Our driver, Ah Qian, was already positioned at the Buick's steering wheel, waiting for us to clamber into the back. His apprentice, Shengtong, stood at attention alongside the car. He closed the door crisply as he winked at me with his broad smile and scuttled around to the front seat, where he was a fixture next to Ah Qian. As driver-in-training, Shengtong was responsible for keeping the car spotless and helping with its maintenance.

Ah Qian always wore a tidy brown changshan and sported a shaved head that shone as brightly as the Buick's chrome fittings. He drove with intense concentration, often correcting us if we became too boisterous. He had his work cut out driving around Shanghai—navigating a helter-skelter road system and deciphering foreign names that had been transliterated into Chinese, all the while dodging heedless pedestrians, pedicabs and rickshaws.

Roads and buildings in the settlements carried names honoring their colonial heritage. In the French Concession, you could live at Pension

Nouvelle on Rue Massenet; in the International Settlement, your home might be Norfolk House on Seymour Road. The streets near our home were the British-designated Jessfield, Kinnear and Edinburgh Roads.

The creek that originally separated the International Settlement and the French Concession was later filled to create Avenue Edward VII. No signs delineated the border between settlements; everyone just knew that at the opposite end of the intersection the street name would change from British to French, or vice versa—and you'd have to switch trams or driver's licenses in order to carry on. Even the electrical systems were different: 110 volts on the French side, 220 volts in the International Settlement.

Early on in the settlements, the British drove on their customary left side of the road, while the Americans drove on the right. Eventually the Americans prevailed: the traffic direction was standardized overnight, creating a period of confusion.

In our eyes, none of Shengtong's tasks was as fun or important as when we were nearly at our destination and he had to spring nimbly out of his seat onto the Buick's narrow running board, jump onto the curb and swoop the back door open for us the instant the car rolled to a stop.

That June day, Shengtong opened the back door with his usual flourish when we arrived on Fourth Road. Diedie stepped out and strode purposefully into an inkstone shop, leaving us in Shengtong's charge while Ah Qian waited behind the wheel of the Buick.

Shengtong had come into our household as a teenager; of all the servants, he was particularly close to us children because he was only two years older than Virginia. His quirky humor never failed to make me smile—like now, as his eyes gleamed appreciatively at the sight of two women strolling under parasols on the opposite side of the street. They looked like they were not yet twenty and were dressed to the nines in bright floral qipao. "Third Miss," he said, waggling his eyebrows playfully as if he wanted to attract their attention, "quick, call them auntie, call them auntie!" Although I never acted on his cheerful goading, it had been a joke between us for as long as I could remember.

The other time I'd glimpsed pretty girls like those was in Muma's bedroom. Muma had bought me a gift and asked me to retrieve it from where she'd hidden it in her armoire. I stood on tiptoes and stretched my arm past the papers and playbills, bending my neck in order to reach farther back. At last, I pulled the object into view: the Shirley Temple coloring book that I had coveted. Muma, always thoughtful about selecting toys and trinkets for us, beamed and patted my cheek affectionately. "Clever girl—my gift to you for winning the school writing contest!"

As I drew the book closer, something else dislodged from the back of the armoire and fell to the floor.

Muma's smile disappeared and she looked down with a strange expression that made me forget Shirley Temple for the moment. Was it a promotional booklet of some kind? It had fallen open facedown, so we could see both covers: on the front was a large portrait of a lovely young woman with dainty features; and, filling the back cover, were thumbnail-sized photographs of many other women, pretty but not as exceptional as the featured one. The red characters on top said *Escort Service*, words that I wasn't familiar with.

"Muma, what is that?"

Mother's brows puckered in a frown. "Nothing you need to know about, Third Daughter. Give it to Muma now, please."

It was unusual for my mother not to humor me. I wasn't sure what to make of it. "Those ladies are so beautiful. Especially the one in the big photo—are they actresses?"

"No, they're not," she answered. After a pause, she gave a wry smile. "But if I think about it, maybe . . . in a way, you could say so. Yes, that's exactly what they are—a certain kind of actress."

I might have forgotten the episode if not for what happened a few days later. My parents had four godsons, all in their twenties, who often visited and took us on outings. We had not seen their favorite godson, Li Gege, for some time, so it was a happy surprise when he arrived at the house in a brand-new Cadillac convertible, his black hair slicked back from his chiseled features and a smart striped ascot tied around his neck.

Li Gege took me window-shopping on Bubbling Well Road, and then to the popular Kiessling Café. I'd just taken my first bite of chestnut cake when the "actress" on the cover of Muma's booklet entered the café. She made her way past the glass counters filled with éclairs, macaroons and profiteroles, and sat down at our table between Li Gege and me.

I was speechless at first. Jinling was even prettier in person than in the photo I'd seen of her. I liked her name too: "Gold Tinkle," like a little bell. A dimple accentuated one side of her smile, endearing her to me all the more. She fussed over Li Gege in a way that suggested they were in love. When she saw that I was shy, she removed a pink polka-dot ribbon from her purse to play cat's cradle with me, and then used it to braid my hair.

On our way home, I asked Li Gege, "Can Jinling come to the house and play next week?"

Between clenched teeth, Li Gege said, "Third Daughter, you must promise me—don't tell a soul you met Jinling today. Promise Li Gege you won't breathe a word to anyone, all right?"

I wasn't sure why Li Gege would want to hide his relationship with someone so nice, but I was determined to keep his secret.

Reading excerpts from Shufen's writings made it clear to me how much the family revered books. When Diedie arrived in Shanghai after the death of his fourth uncle, he studied law at Dongwu University, but his first job was as an editor at Commercial Press, one of the city's largest publishing houses. Scholarly pursuits came easily to him. The bigger challenge was his sudden responsibility to oversee several hundred residential and commercial properties. I suspect he was something of a rarity: a scholar-turned-landlord.

Fourth Road (Fuzhou Road) ca. 1910.

A sizable section of Fourth Road and properties on several neighboring streets were foremost among Diedie's land holdings. Originally called Mission Road and later renamed Fuzhou Road, Fourth Road ran laterally about a mile westward from the Bund, through the International Settlement, and ended at the public Recreation Ground. Locals knew it simply as Si Ma Lu, "Fourth (Horse) Road." Nanjing Road, the city's commercial hub, was called Da Ma Lu—"Big Road" or "Main Road"—and the roads to its south Second Road, Third Road and so on.

Diedie found a way to indulge his passion for art and literature at the same time that he expanded the family properties. In the 1920s, a combination of his own interests and good timing led him to develop Fourth Road into a cultural area at precisely the moment that a growing middle class was discovering an unquenchable thirst for the arts. Fourth Road became the hub of China's publishing industry; book emporiums like Commercial Press and Zhonghua employed thousands of staff to handle editing, translation and printing. In specialty stores barely larger than a closet, customers could buy a Chinese classic or a Marxist treatise and have a silk scroll mounted or a stone seal carved.

Although Fourth Road was home to a few foreign entities such as the American Club, the majority of its occupants and clientele were Chinese, and their establishments ran the gamut from restaurants and bookshops to the settlement's police station—in all, more than one thousand stores and newsstands.

For Diedie, books were a link to the virtues and lessons of the cherished past, while for us children they were a window into distant lands and cultures. Diedie often came home from "meetings with friends" carrying armloads of books, including original Chinese works and foreign novels translated into Chinese. Among my favorites were *Jane Eyre*, *Anna Karenina* and *Madame Bovary*. I am certain Father would never have given those books to us had he known that they revolved around romances and adulterous affairs.

For all the hours he spent hunched over his enormous ledger, Diedie spoke little about his work. Years later, I learned that he had almost constantly been in litigation, chasing lessees for nonpayment. It makes me wonder whether the many books that lined every shelf of our house had been his tenants' way of apologizing for not paying their rent.

Back on Fourth Road that day, Shengtong accompanied Shufen and me into Commercial Press. We made a beeline for the comic book section, where Shufen used a week's allowance to purchase the latest issue of *Flash Gordon* and his space adventures. I had been in search of an issue of *Jinfa Nülang*, which featured the American "gold-haired maiden" Blondie—a particular edition about her wedding to Dagwood. The sales clerk told me they had sold out and that I should try again later.

Shufen lost interest when I moved over to the movie star photos. A Pekinese puppy had somehow found its way into the store, and my brother dashed from aisle to aisle playing hide-and-seek with her. Before long, I was running alongside him. Still under Shengtong's watchful eye, we chased the dog through an arched portal in a far corner of the store.

The sun shone brightly as we entered a hidden world behind the building—a small courtyard inside a stucco wall whose emerald tiles undulated like a dragon's spine. Men played Chinese chess at a porcelain table; above, several dozen terraced houses lined the alley and teemed with family life.

"What is this place?" I asked Shengtong.

"Hehe, Third Miss, you remind me of a songbird in an ivory cage. You live in your nice house with its own garden—how would you know?" He jerked his thumb at the alleyway. "Most people in Shanghai spend their lives in longtang like this. Your father built this compound a few years ago."

He chuckled. "See the sign over there, *Chongrang Li*? Your father named it. 'Yield Esteem'—who else could come up with a highbrow name like that?!"

"Who lives there, Shengtong?"

"Mostly people running from trouble in the provinces."

"What do you mean? What kind of trouble makes someone leave home?"

"It's dangerous in the countryside near Shanghai. People are fighting there. The city is safer, especially inside the foreign settlements. In the country there are no Ah Sans to protect them, you know."

Shengtong loved to turn serious things into jokes. "Ah San" was short for *hongtou asan*, "redheaded number three," our nickname for the Sikh guards who directed traffic and opened doors at luxury hotels. It was hard to imagine how the mild-mannered, often pot-bellied Ah Sans, with their florid mustaches and turbans piled high, would protect us in a hostile situation.

"Also, there are lots of jobs in the city—something else you'll never have to worry about, Third Miss," Shengtong continued. "That's why so many of your family's servants came here from the provinces. If they weren't so lucky to be working in your house, for sure they'd be living in a longtang like this."

Shengtong glanced at Shufen. "One day, Master Shufen will own all of this. What a thought!" For now at least, my brother was more interested in stalking the Pekinese puppy.

A short time later, we were back in the car with Diedie, cruising the length of Fourth Road en route home. Near its western end, we reached an alleyway whose sign identified it as Huile Li, "Will-Be-Happy Neighborhood." Dozens of cheerful red lanterns strung across the alleyway declared the residents: names like *xianglan* ("fragrant orchid") and *meizhen* ("beautiful treasure"). The little district was feminine and enchanting, in contrast to the scholarly shops around it.

Huile Li.

Shufen had had his face pressed against the side window. Suddenly he asked, "Diedie, look, isn't that Li Gege?"

Ah Qian slowed the Buick to a crawl, keeping pace alongside a young couple holding hands as they strolled out of the red-lantern alley. I'd never seen this kind of affection in public before. And indeed, it was Li Gege, my parents' favorite godson. I hadn't seen him in several months—not since the day we had gone to Kiessling Café—and when I'd asked Muma why, she had always changed the subject.

In the car, Shufen exclaimed, "Who's that girl with him?"

I nudged my brother to one side for a closer look. I was about to call out and say hello to Jinling, when I remembered my promise to Li Gege—a good thing, considering what Diedie said next.

"Idiotic godson, what a loss of face for his parents," Father muttered. "Drive on, Ah Qian." Li Gege turned toward us at that instant. His jaw dropped when he recognized us, as if we'd caught him in an embarrassing act.

Back at Zhenning Road in the evening, Virginia shrugged indignantly at my account of what we'd seen. "So, Li Gege found some strumpet that he wants to marry, and the grown-ups don't like it. Do you think Diedie's any bet-ter with those women in the photos that we found in his drawer—just because he doesn't bring them home? Good for Li Gege, I hope he's happy!"

I couldn't tell my sister I had no idea what a strumpet was. A form of explanation came after Virginia accompa-nied me to the magazine stall next to our lane. I found the *Blondie* comic that I'd been searching for and stayed up most of the night devouring it under the bedcovers with a flashlight.

Blondie Boopadoop had been a carefree girl who, before meeting her boyfriend, Dagwood, loved spending time in dance halls. Dagwood, the bumbling son of a tycoon, had once gotten lost in his own mansion. His society parents so disapproved of his marrying the "gold-digger blonde" that they disinherited him, forcing the young couple to make their own living.

I was impressed that Blondie's hair still looked like Marie Antoinette's even after she became a suburban housewife. The image that stayed in my mind was of the young couple's wedding and guests filling the church pews, saying things like "What a pity!" "She's only after his money!" "They'll never be happy! Mark my word . . ."

I hoped against hope that, like Blondie and Dagwood, Li Gege and his actress would find happiness too.

UP YOUR ALLEY

Shanghai is noted for its striking colonial mansions and art deco apartments, but in fact dense alleyways known as lilong ("neighborhood lane") or longtang (Shanghai dialect for "lane interior space") housed most of the city's four million inhabitants during my mother's childhood.

Following the lead of foreign developers, local entrepreneurs like Taiyeye generated a building boom with longtang compounds in the second half of the nineteenth century. They created a new type of housing to accommodate the thousands of refugees from neighboring provinces who were escaping the upheavals of the Taiping Rebellion.

Much of the lodging was in the style of gray-brick shikumen ("stone-framed gate"), named after the carved stone lintel adorning the top of each entry. The hybrid style combined elements of a two- or three-story British terraced house with a traditional Chinese courtyard. Even a small yard offered sunlight, ventilation and refuge from the hubbub of city life.

With several hundred units across a maze of lanes in a large compound, the developments situated businesses in the front and residences in the back. The alleyways teemed with communal life: a hodgepodge of workshops, newspaper presses and private schools operated alongside vendors selling everything from housewares to haircuts.

As the most affordable housing within the foreign concessions, shikumen were a sanctuary for struggling authors, artists and activists, and provided the setting for important historical events such as the establishment of the Chinese Communist Party in 1921.

An interior courtyard of Diedie's Fourth Road
longtang property, Chongrang Li.

CHAPTER 9
POSTER GIRLS

We moved into the Zhenning Road house soon after Diedie's financial losses in the early 1930s. Until then, my parents had made Uncle No. 4's Avenue Road property their home. Qinpo had exercised her right as our matriarch to take over the upbringing of her firstborn grandchild, and resided with Virginia in another house.

Diedie designed our new home so we could all live under the same roof for the first time. There were around thirty of us, including the servants—majordomo Ah Si, cooks, maids, drivers, the tailor, gardeners, maintenance staff, a nanny for each child and several helpers for Qinpo. I was thrilled to learn that I would be sharing a room with my oldest sister. Our *tingzijian*, "pavilion room," was tucked onto a mezzanine level at the first turn of the stairs, set back from the formal rooms and the bustling kitchen below. We moved in when I was three and she was seven, and it was the beginning of our close lifelong relationship. As Shufen was a boy and our as-yet-unborn little sisters would be five and six years younger than me, Virginia and I were together much of the time.

A few months after we arrived, Muma bought me a poster at a nearby magazine stand. The image showed a pair of smiling Chinese girls in Western dresses standing side by side in a lush garden. They looked like sisters, possibly twins, one in a pink dress with an apple-green ribbon in her hair; the other wearing a green dress, with a pink ribbon. How perfect, I thought, to hang the poster in our bedroom.

I'd barely unrolled it from the wrapping when Virginia said, "If you want that on the wall, put it on your side of the room!"

I was crestfallen. She must have noticed, because she explained, "It's just so childish. I don't look anything like that, and I don't want to have to stare at it every day."

Virginia and I each had a four-poster bed with a mosquito net canopy, and I hung the poster on the wall inside mine. How I loved to clamber in, draw the gauzy net around me and daydream in the company of my imaginary companions. In the summer months, I'd linger in bed and watch the sun rise over the neighboring rooftops. The poster girls felt like my closest friends. I loved how they always smiled, unlike my real family members.

Virginia both dominated and loved me in equal measure. It wasn't malicious. It's simply how she was. To her, everything was black or white: there was no place for indecision or mediocrity. I attribute Virginia's brashness to our birth order and age difference. Our second sister died as a toddler, so I wound up next in line. Though Virginia and I slept next to each other, at times it was as if we were being raised in separate worlds. As the third daughter, I had none of the pressures Virginia endured as firstborn, nor the responsibilities of Shufen, the only son.

In the garden with our house in the background, 1937. Left to right: Shufen, five years old; me, six; Shuquan, one; and Virginia, ten, in her usual qipao.

Qinpo, detached from Yeye for years, wielded unquestionable authority over our household. I'm not sure if Muma very much minded the loss of control over her own children; if she resented it, she had little recourse. Diedie's deep-seated filial piety, a Confucian moral foundation, would never have permitted him to deny his mother.

While I and my younger sisters led a happy-go-lucky existence with virtually no parental supervision, Virginia spent her first seven years under Qinpo's strict tutelage. Our grandmother's interpretation of Buddhism held that if you enjoyed life too much, you risked using up your allotment of good fortune, and only misery and suffering remained. The only way to avert this was to exercise austerity early in life, and that's how she raised Virginia and Shufen.

It even affected how we dressed. In contrast to the rest of us girls, who wore flouncy Western outfits selected by Muma, Virginia had to wear qipao made by our tailor using remnants from Qinpo's robes. My oldest sister's ankle-length qipao were rigid, with sleeves ending below the elbows, limiting any kind of movement that a child might consider fun. They gave Virginia the look of a miniature old lady.

This was hard on a girl attending the best private school in style-conscious Shanghai. At McTyeire the seven Kwok sisters, whose family owned the Wing On department store (Shanghai's equivalent of Neiman Marcus), arrived each morning wearing chic little European-made outfits complete with bejeweled hair clips, matching shoes and fur shrugs.

The only hues Virginia routinely wore were Qinpo's favored colors: dark blue, brown and gray. At the age of twelve, she was over the moon when a friend of Muma's asked her to be a bridesmaid. The bridesmaid's dress, a peach satin confection with lace trim, was color coordinated with the bridal gown. For weeks, Virginia indulged herself, leafing dreamily through the beautifully sketched designs the bride had sent over.

The day finally arrived for Muma to take Virginia to her first fitting. I got to tag along, brimming with curiosity. My sister's eyes sparkled with excitement as we passed through the arched colonnade of the Cathay Hotel and pushed open the glass door of Garnett, the city's finest boutique. The bride and her mother were already there, along with two other bridesmaids. The store owner, Madame Garnett, was a Russian émigré who had trained in France and the most elegant foreign woman I'd ever seen.

The boutique resembled the inside of a jewelry box, with gilded decor and silvery brocade. Virginia gasped when Shanghai's most famous actress, Hu Die, "Butterfly" Wu, sashayed through the front door in a golden sable coat. Just the day before, Virginia and I had spent the afternoon hand coloring a photo of this very actress for our film-star picture collection. With penetrating eyes and a girlish smile, she had been voted China's first movie queen by over twenty thousand newspaper readers.

Hu Die in a promotional poster.

The dressing room was furnished with plush velvet seating, large enough for an entourage to watch or assist. We all filed in and sat down— the bride, her mother, Muma, Virginia and me and Madame Garnett.

Virginia was mortified at having to remove her brown qipao, in itself an embarrassment. Worse, she was forced to expose her wretched undergarment in front of all the women: a peculiar patchwork sweater Qinpo's servant had knitted out of leftover wool, saved under the orders of Qinpo, who wasted nothing. It had no rhyme or reason: the size, color and texture of the patches had been determined by which yarn the servant had happened to grab from the top of the remnant basket.

At the height of Virginia's red-faced misery, just as a shop assistant was opening the door of our dressing room, Butterfly Wu emerged from the room opposite. Splendidly attired in Garnett's latest creation, the movie queen fluttered a manicured hand over her mouth to cover her chuckle at the sight of the girl in such woebegone underwear.

The nuptials took place a few weeks later, but the Garnett humiliation must have tainted Virginia's enjoyment of the wedding, as she hardly spoke of it afterward.

On summer evenings, soon after dinner was finished, the heavenly scent of night-blooming jasmine floated indoors. I would join the servants gathered outside the kitchen on rattan lawn chairs to gossip and savor the breeze. I can still hear the cicadas grinding their songs to the rustle of plane trees and glimpse the fireflies flitting to and fro, as though connecting the stars in a velvet sky.

Most of our household staff came from our parents' hometown of Changshu. Their hierarchy was based on individual responsibilities and years of service. With so many living under one roof, there must have been plenty of behind-the-scenes drama, even if I didn't grasp all of it at the time.

We named my nanny San-naima, "Third wet nurse"—Third Daughter's nanny. She had given birth around the time I was born, and left her husband and baby in Changshu to look after me. It was a common circumstance in those days, as jobs in Shanghai paid more than in the countryside.

San-naima's sweet face was the first and last thing I saw every day for seven years. In prosperous families, day-to-day child-rearing duties fell to nannies. So it was that San-naima, with her pink cheeks, full upturned lips and unconditional kindness, was the constant in my life. I've always had a hard time waking up—Shanghainese affectionately call it *beitoufeng*, "blanket madness." San-naima was patient with my morning grumpiness, brushing my straight hair with long, soothing strokes while I fussed and complained.

One afternoon I came home early from school with a tummy ache and was surprised when San-naima did not greet me downstairs. Ah Si was equally taken aback when he let me in the front door. "I will find her for you, Third Daughter," he said reassuringly. "You go on upstairs and she'll come shortly."

At the landing, I pushed open the door of our tingzijian. My eyes must have opened wide when I saw one of our cooks, Ah Xing, sitting at the end of my bed with San-naima. It was rare to see a cook outside the kitchen, let alone in a bedroom. Ah Xing had joined our household several years before with his wife, a cleaner. She had gone back to their village a year earlier to have their baby and had not returned to work for us. I liked Ah Xing. Even when the cooks were hustling and bustling about, he always found time to chat or give me small tasks. The previous week he'd asked me to help pluck weevils from the rice bin, and it had entertained me for hours.

In the bedroom, Ah Xing and San-naima seemed to have been talking seriously about something. A deep frown had replaced Ah Xing's usually cheerful demeanor, and my nanny's eyes were red and swollen, as if she'd been crying.

San-naima stood up. "Third Daughter, why have you come home early? Are you all right?" She placed her hand on my head, gently brushing a stray strand behind my ear. "Third Daughter, please don't tell anyone you saw Ah Xing in here. It's very important. Do this for San-naima, please. Promise?"

I would have done anything for San-naima. But before I could respond, the tingzijian door swung open and Ah Si stepped in. Things escalated quickly after that.

As majordomo, Ah Si supervised virtually everyone and everything in our household. He exuded a sort of unflappable competence and can-do attitude that gave you a profound sense of security; even the smallest detail did not escape his scrutiny. Once inside, his eyes efficiently swept the tingzijian. Pulling at the white collar of his changshan, he addressed the helpers angrily: "Both of you, come to the kitchen and explain yourselves. Third Daughter, I am sorry, San-naima can't take care of you right now. I will arrange for another nanny to help."

I became worried when there was no sign of San-naima that evening. She'd never been absent for long, other than her occasional days off. Had I somehow gotten her into trouble? Virginia spoke to me in a confidential tone after dinner: "San-naima's in big trouble. Ah Si was talking to Diedie in the study. Ah Xing went to bed with San-naima and they made a baby. That's why she's so fat—the baby's growing inside her tummy."

It was too confusing. How could San-naima have a baby with Ah Xing if they both already had babies with their spouses back home? As was often the case, Virginia was telling me something I couldn't fully understand, and I was too embarrassed to admit it. I worried all night.

When San-naima came to my bedside the next morning, I was alarmed to see her crying.

"San-naima, why are you so sad? You told me grown-ups shouldn't cry."

"I'm going home to Changshu today," she whispered. Her sniffling tickled my ear.

"What do you mean? You said you'd always stay, even after I get married. When are you coming back?"

"I can't come back . . . I'm going to have my own baby."

"But who's going to wake me up every morning? Help me bathe? Walk to school with me?"

She stroked my hair soothingly and we sat quietly.

"Third Daughter, be happy like your friends in the poster. Try to forget San-naima."

I cried for several nights afterward, missing San-naima and nervously awaiting the arrival of her replacement from Changshu. I was just beginning to learn English; as my new nanny was the second child in her own family, I called her "Two-two."

In our new house, Virginia continued to wear qipao but was occasionally permitted to wear a Western skirt. Now that we were all living together, Qinpo turned her thrifty intentions on two-year-old Shufen. When he enrolled in McTyeire's primary school a few years later, our grandmother was supervising his attire in much the same way that she had Virginia's. Like their female counterparts, the boys at McTyeire were from Shanghai's best families and wore smart Western outfits to classes. Shufen was the only student with a crew cut, a changshan—coarse cotton in summer, padded flannel in winter—worn with long, baggy pajama pants inside, and rough black cloth shoes. Whenever classmates called him *tulaotou* ("old country bumpkin"), Shufen got into fights with three or four boys at once.

Many a time, when Shufen came home with his hateful clothes torn and bloodied beyond repair, Qinpo personally spanked him with a bamboo feather duster. It was such a regular occurrence that the servants set the duster aside for this specific purpose and routinely replaced its worn-out stick.

Qinpo's efforts to tame her grandchildren produced questionable results. Shufen was expelled from high school six times, and Virginia consistently received a *ding*, the equivalent of a D, in manners class.

If the unsettling changes gripping China in the 1930s penetrated the bamboo fence that surrounded our home, I wasn't aware of it. My siblings might tell a different story, but I recall a pastiche of carefree memories. Our fence filtered much of what I experienced as a child. During the day, I'd peer through to see who was passing on Zhenning Road. Inside, the shafts of morning sun pierced the lattice, spotlighting the dewy grass. From outside, coming home after a day away, I looked through the chevrons to see whether Diedie's study lights were still on.

In the afternoons the cheerful chants of street vendors floated in through the open windows: "Fresh roasted gingkooo—fragrant and soft ooo-ooo-ooo!" The wonton peddler never failed to whet our appetites with his high-pitched warble of "Aawwwhhh! Aaawwwhhhhh!" and steaming bowls of transparent wonton.

The inventive peddlers carried their kitchens all around the city. One clever contraption was slung over the vendor's shoulders, with a coal burner for boiling or roasting; cupboards and drawers for raw ingredients; and pots, bowls and utensils—all that was needed to serve up a mouth-watering delight.

On a balmy spring day, a vendor arrived at our gate with two baskets bouncing jauntily from a bamboo pole balanced across his shoulders. A chirping yellow blur of fluffy chicks hopped around inside the baskets. We chose five as our pets, representing us five children. Virginia and I learned to recognize their different personalities as they roamed around the garden, tumbling over each other in their rush to greet us.

Shanghai's most famous department stores were the "Big Four"— Wing On, Sincere, Sun Sun and the Sun. I didn't need to go that far for my first shopping adventure: our favorite *dingdongdan* ("dingdong stand") rumbled right into our garden. The cart overflowed with shiny baubles, rings set with a rainbow of stones and earrings dangling like gumdrops. My pudgy fingers couldn't get enough of them.

At school, everyone tried to imitate Shirley Temple's curls; Virginia and I slept with long strips of cotton wool rolled in our hair. After I watched *The Wizard of Oz*, I used ribbons and trinkets from the ding-dongdan to copy Judy Garland's pigtailed look.

In my *Wizard of Oz* hairdo.

Diedie didn't like us to play with typical toys. He preferred for us to read or engage in purposeful activities, such as raising silkworms in the spring. Virginia sometimes pooh-poohed my pastimes as little-girl games, but she enjoyed helping with my silkworms. First, we poked air holes in shoeboxes and lined them with shredded newspaper, where we scattered dozens of silkworm eggs about the size of sesame seeds.

After a week, our eyes would be glued on them, so we wouldn't miss the moment when tiny black larvae broke through the eggs. Whenever I pried the lids off the boxes, the worms rose to attention, wriggling their heads in anticipation of their next meal.

My hatchlings ate around the clock; I fed them mulberry leaves at least three times a day. They could chomp a large leaf right down to its veins in minutes, leaving a bare skeleton.

Although mulberry trees were widespread in Shanghai, my superstitious father did not want any planted in our garden because the Chinese name for them, *sangshu*, sounds similar to the characters for "funeral," *sangshi*.

Perhaps Diedie saw it as a lesson in responsibility and economics. I was consumed with securing mulberry leaves for my caterpillars and was forced to barter with schoolmates who had mulberry trees. I paid them richly with my best comic books and film star photos. Most of the time my silkworms' insatiable appetites placed me in a weak bargaining position.

As my babies got bigger, their munching grew so loud that I could hear them in the still of night. The bristly black larvae went through a series of transformations, molting five times as they outgrew and shed their previous skin. They molted like tiny soldiers stepping out of old uniforms, becoming smoother and fleshier with each change. When a

worm was the size of my finger, with a taut translucent skin, it would spin its cocoon of raw silk. The caterpillar's casing glowed with candy-floss hues—milky white, pollen yellow or dusky peach—hinting at the color of its silken strands.

The worm made nonstop figure-eight movements for a few days until it was fully encased in silk filament. The final product of all this intense labor was surprisingly unassuming—more like a blanched peanut than the miracle of nature that it represented—but the industriousness of these dedicated little creatures was amazing.

To prevent them from being ruined by the moth's escape, we gave the cocoons to our cook to boil. I couldn't bear to watch the ignominious end to the larvae I had so carefully raised. My siblings and I then unraveled the silk by rolling the fibers repeatedly around a

pencil, up to a mile in total. For all the effort, I don't recall doing anything with the glistening silk thread that we had so painstakingly produced.

We did spare a few of the largest cocoons from the cooking pot. Breaking out from their silken chambers, the pale, plump moths were doomed never to fly; their singular duty was to reproduce. After mating, the females laid several hundred eggs each. All the moths would be dead within a day or two, and we had an ample supply of eggs for the next growing season.

At school, our teacher told us that silkworms grew to ten thousand times their original size in a month and that it took two hundred pounds of mulberry leaves to produce a pound of raw silk—just enough for one dress.

No wonder my hobby required so much work.

Starting from when I was about eight, the Japanese occupation led to many shortages, and our meals were sparser than before. Diedie ordered that everyone in the household face the adversities together: family and servants, regardless of position, ate the same food. Only Qinpo received better dishes.

In the mornings I was still served a bowl of steaming zhou, perhaps with a few peanuts instead of the richer condiments I loved, like *rousong* pork floss and dried shrimp. The cooks were adept at making the simplest ingredients taste delicious—for example, pickled crunchy watermelon skin, turnips or bamboo shoots.

Nanny Two-two sang me a country ditty in consolation: "Eat plain, get fat, raise a son who'll open a pawnshop."[14] In those challenging times, pawnshops were one of the few businesses that prospered.

When World War II and the Japanese occupation ended in 1945, Virginia was eighteen, living at home while attending St. John's, the city's top university. In her late teens, she embraced qipao in a reincarnated form—a more flattering, fitted silhouette that was in vogue among Shanghai women. Discarding the drab dresses and patchwork underwear

---

14. *Baichi baizhuang, yang ge erzi kai diandang.*

of her childhood, Virginia adopted a sleek modern look that was perfectly aligned with the popular art deco style of the times. Her original designs earned her the title of Best-Dressed Student at St. John's.

Despite ongoing shortages, Virginia had a grand time searching for interesting fabrics to create one-of-a-kind outfits. It took patience and resourcefulness; the money situation was chaotic. We had grown up using *yuan*, Shanghai-minted Chinese dollars, as our main currency. However, with inflation out of control, many people preferred US dollars, silver and gold.

One day Virginia went out to buy a pair of new shoes. She made her selection, came home and got a small trunk full of cash from our father. When she returned to the store the next morning, the price had doubled. She came back with a larger trunk of banknotes the following day, but the shopkeeper now refused to sell the shoes. His rationalization was that he couldn't afford to replace them, and then he would have nothing to display.

In her youth, Virginia stole the hearts of many admirers. Decades later, I ran into one suitor who recalled how he'd been smitten with her in university: "I arrived at your lane to take Virginia to a movie. At the time, I was reading *Romeo and Juliet*, and had this romantic vision of her standing on your bedroom balcony, waiting longingly for me. When I looked up, all I could see was you—jumping up and down like a plump monkey—and then Virginia emerged behind you like a *Vogue* model. She yelled down at me: 'This is my third sister. She's totally annoying and you should ignore her. Don't even bother to say hello or she'll pester you!'"

Although I irritated Virginia when we were kids, we complemented each other well as adults. We were the only two siblings who left Shanghai before the Communists took over in 1949. Even our Western first names, which we'd chosen for ourselves, set us apart; our younger siblings, who remained in China, went by their Chinese names.

Virginia and Shufen both exhibited nonconformist, at times combative, behavior in later life. To this day, I am not sure if the cause was their underlying character or Qinpo's strict practices.

Glorious dahlias from our garden.

THE TAO OF TOFU

Diedie didn't approve of my being in the kitchen, as he assumed I'd marry well and oversee my own household staff one day. But I enjoyed sneaking in to watch the cooks shell broad beans, fold a lotus leaf around glutinous rice or carve a squash into a chrysanthemum. I learned to appreciate how much time and effort it took to prepare my favorite delicacies.

I don't recall ever seeing either of my parents in the kitchen. Cooking, like raising children, was a hands-off exercise: you knew what you liked and entrusted the details to professionals. Before the Japanese occupation began in 1937, we had one cook specializing in Chinese and another in Western food, each with several assistants. The kitchen had iceboxes that were replenished from a longtang stall. In summer, the cooks cooled large items like watermelons in a wooden bucket suspended in the garden well.

Heavily influenced by the cuisines of bordering Jiangsu and Zhejiang Provinces, Shanghainese taste buds prized a blend of sweet, sour and salty flavors. A combination of soy sauce, vinegar, a pinch of sugar and a dash of Shaoxing rice wine produced the shiny red appearance of our region's signature braised or "red-cooked" delicacies.

Many dishes were presented in small mouthfuls to create a medley of tastes and textures, such as *xiaolongbao*, pork dumplings wrapped in translucent skin so their juicy flavors burst in your mouth, and *shengjianbao*, made in a breadlike casing and pan-fried until brown and crispy.

Perhaps more than any other culture, the Shanghainese have devised hundreds of ways to use bean curd, tofu (*doufu*)—coagulated soymilk that is pressed into blocks or sheets. We had wafer-thin, pliant *doufupi* ("skin") and chewy, sinuous *mianjin* ("tendon") as well as soft, oily, dried and frozen variations. A tofu named *baiyejie* or "hundred-leaf knot" was tied into nubby knots, while the dried *gansi* was cut into fine threads to mimic noodles.

Shengjianbao.

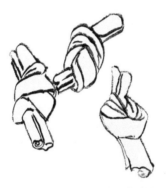

Baiyejie.

Gansi.

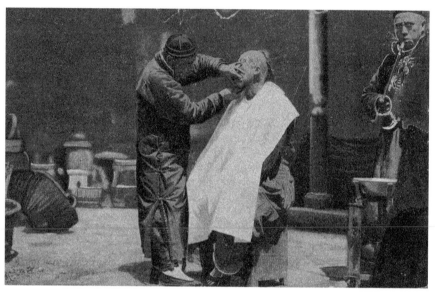

Was this the sort of street practitioner who removed Yeye's cracked tooth? (In this postcard image, the man to the right appears to be smoking opium.)

CHAPTER 10
KIDNAPPED

IF HE WERE A CAT, Yeye's nine lives, from his birth as No. 7 son to old age, would have looked something like this:

Prodigal son
Swindler
Detainee
Womanizer
Estranged husband
Heir
Entrepreneur
Kidnapee
Miser

After conspiring with No. 4 to steal their father's money from Hongkong and Shanghai Bank, Yeye found relief in the relative peace of house arrest under Taiyeye's purview. No longer partaking in the heady life of adventure with profligate No. 4, Yeye now had a simpler existence free of his older brother's crooked influence.

In middle age, Yeye made an unlikely about-face. Having relocated to Shanghai in the 1910s, he not only expanded Taiyeye's property, banking and shipping holdings but also made his own mark developing hotels in Shanghai and four other cities. By his forties, he had become a prosperous and respected entrepreneur in his own right and—to everyone's surprise—a thrifty, indeed outright stingy man.

Yeye's frugality bordered on the comical. He ate at lousy restaurants and once broke a tooth trying to chew an undercooked noodle. Too miserly to see a proper dentist, he went to a street practitioner who removed the cracked incisor without anesthetic—creating his trademark smile with a hole punctuating his mouth where his front tooth should have been.

More than business occupied Yeye. Though reformed in other quarters, he had not lost his appetite for the opposite sex. It was an era when a man of means could own any number of young women as easily as he could possess a collection of foreign cars. And he could also just as easily gift one of those women to a friend, or swap her for a woman belonging to someone else. Yeye had five acknowledged concubines, along with a bevy of mistresses. Qinpo, his first and only legal wife, had long since renounced him for his infidelities, so he was free to amuse himself in the company of young maidens, which he did with gusto.

Short and dark, he had large eyes that twinkled above a puckish grin. He always wore changshan, usually a brown floor-length robe, with a dark silk magua jacket, in the style of the Qing court. A black skullcap topped with a round jade bead completed his attire.

Yeye was extremely *keqi*—charming and courteous in a rather formal way. He seemed genuinely pleased to see us, his head bobbing heartily in greeting— *"Meimei, meimei, nihao, nihao!"* "Hello, hello, little girl!"—but it was always in passing. He was kind, yet remote, not taking the time to either scold or commend us.

Yeye enjoyed *zongzitang*, a hard confection of nuts and caramelized sugar. He would suck one for a moment or two and then put the candy back in a round tin to save it for a later sucking. Because of his missing tooth, not chewing hard things was practical as well as thrifty. Occasionally he offered us kids zongzitang, thrusting the container under our noses for an intimate view of several sucked, dried, resucked and redried candies nestled among a few not-yet-sucked specimens. "Meimei, try a zongzitang. They're delicious, sweet and tasty, Yeye's favorite, you know . . ." (The candy, not me. He wasn't close enough to any of his grandchildren to designate a favorite.)

Our response invariably came out as an overly polite, embarrassed whisper along the lines of "No, thank you, Yeye—it looks very nice but I'm full from lunch," followed by an eruption of uncontrollable giggles the instant he was out of earshot.

The jewel of our grandfather's enterprises was the Huizhong Hotel at the busy intersection of Third Road and Hubei Road in the Huangpu District, a short distance inland from the cosmopolitan Bund and one block from the thriving bookstores and scholar's shops that occupied Diedie's Fourth Road rental properties. Yeye had leased the land from Diedie and built the hotel in the 1920s, operating it under a license issued by the British settlement authorities.

In its heyday the hundred-room Huizhong was one of Shanghai's most modern structures. Its atrium lobby was a grand, eccentric amalgam of motifs: Greek columns and Moroccan mosaics with Spanish-style Baroque furnishings. The bold foreign decor notwithstanding, the staff and guests were almost exclusively Chinese.

My brother and male cousins were obliged to go to the hotel regularly and pay respects to Yeye, our family patriarch; my sisters and I joined them infrequently. One of my earliest memories is of a visit when I was three or four years old. Accustomed to Diedie's austere Chinese furnishings, I couldn't resist sitting on one of the florid carved sofas in the hotel lobby. The overstuffed burgundy velvet cushions were so deep that I sank into the billowy seat and was unable to stand on my own. Shufen and Virginia each had to take one of my arms to haul me up.

The five-story Huizhong was one of the first buildings in Shanghai to install elevators. How we loved riding up and down, standing in the back of the compartment and admiring the uniformed operator as he scrunched the brass accordion door shut and announced each floor in English and Shanghainese.

Our grandfather's spacious apartment occupied most of the penthouse floor, where dozens of curing ham legs hung incongruously from the high gilded ceilings. Friends had gifted Yeye with the hams and, as he was too frugal to eat them, they grew in number from year to year. Shufen and our male cousins spent much of their required visits racing up and down the wide terraces that wrapped all the way around the building, playing madcap games with no adult supervision.

Yeye was a man of regular habits. He rose at the same time every day and never failed to leave his apartment for lunch at twelve o'clock sharp. His routine, while no doubt reassuring, also made him vulnerable.

One day in the summer of 1938, Diedie was having lunch in a Chinese restaurant across the street from the Huizhong. He had gone on foot, leaving the Buick with Ah Qian in the hotel courtyard.

Back at the hotel, Yeye stepped into the elevator on the penthouse floor, barely noticing the two men who looked like well-off hotel guests entering with him. The operator bowed his white-capped head and swiveled the handle for the lobby. Hotel staff saw two unfamiliar men accompany Yeye past the front desk and out the main entrance. What the employees didn't see were the guns pointing at Yeye from inside the men's trench coats.

The men were kidnappers who had studied Yeye's regimen for several days. They ordered Grandfather into Diedie's car, pointed a gun to the side of Ah Qian's head and motioned him to drive off.

When Diedie finished lunch, he was surprised to see that his Buick was no longer in front of the hotel. A porter said Yeye had taken it with two men he'd assumed were business associates. He commented that it had seemed strange at the time, since Yeye's own car, with his driver waiting inside, had been standing by on the other side of the courtyard.

A British police inspector came to the Huizhong a few hours later to report to Diedie that our Buick had been abandoned on Columbia Road in the western part of the city. Mercifully, they found Ah Qian inside, knocked unconscious but still alive. He soon recovered. The kidnappers left a letter on the back seat demanding that our family prepare funds to pay Yeye's ransom. They did not specify an amount.

I'd recently started third grade and hadn't heard the term "kidnap," nor could I deduce the meaning from the Chinese characters: *bang*, "to tie," and *piao*, "slip of paper," shorthand for bank notes. The furrowed brows and fearful silence in our household revealed nothing more. All I knew was that Yeye had been taken by strangers, and no one would tell me the details. I slept restlessly, dreaming of my charming grandfather with a long filthy rope coiled round and round his torso.

The weeks wore on with no sign of my grandfather. Reports of the abduction hit the newspapers. The servants spoke in hushed tones that were markedly different from their usual idle prattle. At school, the children eyed me with serious expressions that made me feel uncomfortably isolated.

It was years before I learned the full account of Yeye's ordeal. Diedie's initial negotiations with the captors went nowhere; their demands were so high as to be unaffordable. He did not contact the authorities, as many abductees had perished when the police were involved. In 1930s Shanghai, the best chance to secure a victim's freedom was to appeal to the underworld. Diedie reluctantly called on the city's top mobsters, Huang Jinrong ("Pockmarked Huang") and Du Yuesheng ("Big-Eared Du") of the notorious Green Gang.

The gang's followers numbered in the tens of thousands and had a hand in every aspect of Shanghai vice: opium, brothels, gambling and extortion. But that wasn't all. Pockmarked Huang, so-called because of the smallpox scars pitting his face, also served as the French Concession's police chief—the perfect cover for running unlawful enterprises with impunity. His organized-crime network was the embodiment of corruption at the highest levels of government.

Du and Huang introduced Diedie to another gangster, Zhang Xiaolin. Zhang, whom we will nickname "Pipa Zhang," had a reputation for unpredictability. People likened his face to a *pipa* leaf, one side smooth and shiny, the other hairy and rough: a two-faced man with a violent temper. After a month of failed negotiations, Diedie had nowhere else to turn.

So it was that my scholar father became the unlikely associate of one of Shanghai's most ruthless mobsters. In all, the bargaining over Yeye's ransom went on for two nerve-wracking months. When Pipa Zhang and the kidnappers finally reached an agreement, Father dispatched his two most trusted aides to a riverbank outside Shanghai, where they exchanged two trunks for our malnourished Yeye. The trunks contained the agreed ransom of gold taels weighing over one hundred pounds and worth more than US$100,000—a Herculean sum in those days, far more than most people saw in a lifetime. (And that didn't include the finder's fees Diedie owed his new underworld protectors.)

On the day of Yeye's release, Ah Si summoned the entire family to the salon. Only Qinpo was missing; she had chosen to stay upstairs and practice nianfo. Grandfather was seated in a straight-backed *zitan* chair with Diedie standing beside him. I was much relieved to see no traces of the thick rope that I'd imagined tied around Yeye.

Father spoke to us: "Yeye would like you all to know that the kidnappers kept him in a village house and did not treat him badly. As you can see, he has lost weight, but he assures me he is feeling fine." Yeye did look skinny, his cheeks sunken with bristly gray whiskers that I'd not noticed before. He nodded and gave us a lopsided smile, exposing the familiar gap in his teeth.

"He needs to rest quietly and will stay with us for a while before he goes back to the Huizhong." Diedie cleared his throat. "Fourth Popo will be staying with us too."

Fourth Popo, Yeye's concubine, was standing behind Yeye. Her head was deeply bowed, so I couldn't see her features other than her small pearl earrings and a bun coiled neatly at the nape of her neck. I asked myself if she was the reason Qinpo hadn't come downstairs. This was going to be interesting.

Virginia and I moved to our younger sisters' bedroom so Yeye and Fourth Popo could stay in our tingzijian. The servants said Fourth Popo had been a teenaged singsong girl in a brothel when Yeye met her. By this late stage of his life, Yeye's first three concubines had died and the fifth had abandoned him. Though not a great beauty, Fourth Popo had an agreeable nature and was the only concubine to remain with Grandfather in his final years.

Qinpo had reigned over Diedie and our household since she had walked out on Yeye twenty-six years earlier. In homes of that era, it was not uncommon for wives and concubines to cohabitate and even become friends—but we'd never seen our estranged grandparents together, let alone at our baxianzhuo with his concubine. After Yeye's recent calamity, meals with our houseguests provided unexpected comic relief, if not to the adults, to us children.

Grandfather and his paramour often arrived at the table later than the rest of us. Instead of his usual enthusiastic salutation to us children, Yeye muttered a sheepish greeting to Qinpo. "*Taitai, taitai, nihao,*" he said, his eyes downcast and lips drawn so thin that we could no longer see his missing front tooth.

Qinpo totally ignored him. As far as she was concerned, this philandering husband didn't exist. She sat through our meals in stony silence, directing an occasional crisp comment at Diedie or Muma, her eyes piercing our hapless visitors like pitiless icicles. She ate her vegetarian dishes slowly and deliberately, as if to declare that she, and only she, was the ruler of this domain.

Despite Yeye's weight loss during his abduction, he was now even more abstemious. Food supplies had been disrupted by the war that had broken out the previous year between the Nationalist government of Chiang Kai-shek and the Japanese, who now occupied a large portion of eastern China. Our meals were modest compared to before the conflict. Even so, Yeye said repeatedly that the food was "too fine, too extravagant, too wasteful." The astronomical ransom Diedie had paid appalled him, and he pledged to be even more frugal to make up for it. No one could imagine how he could possibly be more frugal!

Everyone in the household tightened their belts. With gasoline becoming prohibitively expensive, we retired the Buick and turned to pedicabs for everyday transport. The *sanlunche*, "three-wheeled cart," resembled a large tricycle with a passenger's seat in the back. Diedie had a standing arrangement with a pedicab driver to come to our house every day.

I must say we breathed a sigh of relief when Yeye moved back to the Huizhong a few months later, and Virginia and I returned to our tingzi-jian. Though I bore him no ill will, Grandfather's presence had unsettled the routine rhythms of our household.

Kidnappings of acquaintances and public figures were increasingly common in this period. A friend of Diedie's quipped, "If you've never been kidnapped, you must be a nobody." A few years after Yeye's abduction, Diedie received kidnap threats targeting Shufen. This time, it was Muma who solved the problem. She asked her friend, the daughter-in-law of the mobster Pockmarked Huang, to intervene. Huang had stepped down as police chief, but the family must have still had influence because we were never threatened again.

We were fortunate in that regard. For many families, abductions ended in tragedy. One such case was the father of a young beau who courted me and took me riding on his Harley-Davidson during my last year of high school. Although the family negotiated with the kidnappers for weeks and seemed to be nearing an agreement, something went dreadfully wrong, and the father was killed.

Yeye had a great weakness for his concubines, and none more so than Fifth Popo. She was pretty and sassy, and had been a highly admired courtesan. After becoming our grandfather's concubine—an exclusive arrangement as far as Yeye was concerned—she had an illicit affair with a top shuoshu storyteller. The storyteller's enraged wife ambushed Yeye and Fifth Popo in the Huizhong lobby, yelling obscenities as they emerged from the elevator. Yeye was so infatuated with beautiful Fifth Popo that he forgave her for even this public humiliation.

Unchastened, Fifth Popo then took up with Yeye's married chauffeur, packed her jewelry and US bonds and ran away with him. It turned out that the driver and his wife had conspired to steal Popo's valuables and blackmail Yeye for their return. Grandfather paid off the driver and forgave his favorite concubine once again.

Eventually, Fifth Popo repaid the old man's indulgences by hiring Shanghai's fiercest British lawyer to sue Yeye for divorce on the grounds that she was entitled to a settlement as his common-law wife. No precedent existed in the Shanghai courts, and the case garnered newspaper headlines every day for months. It concluded with Yeye doling out a large sum, which Fifth Popo split with her lawyer. The settlement was seen as a substantial validation of the status of concubines and a legal victory for women.

Fifth Popo might have laughed all the way to the bank. But after she left Yeye, she lived the high life with countless lovers until an addiction to opium left her bankrupt. She had only one place to turn.

Everyone was stunned when Qinpo—still Yeye's official wife—took Fifth Popo in. The former concubine could live in our Zhenning Road home on Qinpo's condition that she give up opium, which she did. With Diedie's financial support, Fifth Popo was Qinpo's live-in companion for several years. Diedie continued to provide for his father's wayward concubine until her passing.

It was a strangely logical morality that insisted a man's first, official wife be from a respectable background so she could continue the family bloodline, while concubines and mistresses could be utter trollops. At least away from Qinpo's dinner table, society deemed Fifth Popo acceptable as Yeye's concubine—yet Jinling, the lovely escort, wasn't suitable to be Li Gege's first wife. Surprising twists and contradictions filled Qinpo's life. Serene and dutiful in her Buddhist practice, she was domineering in her conduct toward others. She could be severe with her daughter-in-law and her own grandchildren Virginia and Shufen, yet absolve a concubine of the same ilk that had caused her to leave her husband in the first place. She came of age during the waning decades of the Qing dynasty, and even as a girl she had rebelled against the convention of foot-binding. Virtually all her actions in life, good or bad, had been in the interest of protecting and perpetuating her family line.

Perhaps Qinpo was a feminist before her time.

In the end, my grandmother sheltered a recalcitrant concubine but could not forgive her husband. When Yeye died in 1950—at which point he and Qinpo had been separated for nearly four decades—a friend asked her, "Are you sad?" Her reply: "Not at all, we were strangers all our lives."

In a 1932 telephone directory, the Huizhong (romanized as Wei-Chung) Hotel charged $0.45 to $1.70 a night.

No one spoke much of politics in my mother's family, though China was immersed in political foment throughout Mom's life. The Chinese Communist Party, founded in Shanghai in 1921, initially cooperated with the Nationalists, who were known as the Kuomintang, but relations between them soured as they vied to gain leadership of the nation.

Building an army and vanquishing one's political rivals requires mas-sive funding. Kidnappings were a fast and easy way to extract money in a largely lawless city whose citizens had limited recourse. One historian estimates that the Kuomintang leader Chiang Kai-shek's links to the Green Gang contributed some US$50 million to his party's war chests from the proceeds of kidnapping ransoms alone.[15]

In the turbulent late 1920s, the Kuomintang were hunting down a revered Communist revolutionary named Zhou Enlai. Zhou was in hid-ing in Shanghai and wore varied disguises, moving constantly to avoid the ever-present threat of arrest or assassination.

By 1928, conditions were so hostile that the Chinese Communists held their Sixth National Party Congress in Moscow. Zhou, still wanted by the Kuomintang, returned to Shanghai as a newly elected Central Committee director. At thirty, he was embarking on a path that would lead to his appointment as the first premier of the People's Republic of China when the Communists eventually came to power.

Historical records from October 1928 show that Zhou Enlai stayed at Yeye's Huizhong Hotel, where he secretly met with trusted Communist colleagues on matters of security and intelligence. I like to imagine that Yeye met Zhou Enlai then and offered him a half-sucked zongzitang.

Occupation, civil war and revolution eventually took their toll on the Huizhong. Barely any trace of it remains since its demolition in the 1980s. Like many buildings favored by capitalists such as our family, the hotel suffered chaotic looting during the Cultural Revolution, which began in 1966. The Red Guards and military took what they wanted and destroyed what they did not. Afterward, they flung open the main doors, allowing people to help themselves to what remained.

A cousin told us that some years after the Cultural Revolution, he paid a social visit to the home of a friend's friend in Shanghai. As our rel-ative entered the cramped apartment for the first time, he was surprised to see that the man had outfitted his entire living room with furniture from the Huizhong Hotel lobby. Though clearly worse for wear, the ornate burgundy velvet sofas were immediately recognizable and, according to our cousin, still very comfortable to sit on.

---

15. Parks Coble Jr., *The Shanghai Capitalists and the Nationalist Government, 1927–1937* (Cambridge, MA: Harvard University Press, 1980).

Diedie in his customary changshan.

Menjiao Guniang.

CHAPTER 11
A HOUSE DIVIDED

FOR MY SIBLINGS AND ME, it wasn't the war that changed everything, but our parents' growing disaffection. Their turning point followed hard on the heels of our grandfather's kidnapping, when I was eight. I came home from school a few days after Yeye's return to the Huizhong to find that Diedie had arranged for a bed to be moved into the zhongjian.

I never worked out if there was a defining moment that pushed my parents to the edge, or whether it was simply the natural progression of an ill-matched marriage made worse by family crises and financial strain. Either way, Diedie's new arrangement dashed my hopes of life returning to normal.

It also created a shift in our home dynamics. The configuration of the original layout, from the first floor up to the third, had been formal area, adults, children. Diedie's abandonment of his conjugal bed changed the division of space to man, women, children. When Diedie moved downstairs, the ground floor became his alone, an extension of the study. Muma's sanctuary was her bedroom; she was there primarily to sleep and to prepare for her next engagement.

Father's sensibilities were evident in the austerity and refinement of our public rooms. Unlike the more casual parts of the house, which freely mixed Eastern and Western styles, the salon where he now slept was completely Chinese. The zitan chairs had no cushions or padding whatsoever. They were so tall that even as a teenager I had to sit bolt upright in them, my legs barely touching the ground.

The dining room adjacent to the zhongjian was furnished in the European style: a long table for twelve with an assemblage of crystal decanters, sterling flatware and candelabra intended for formal entertaining. The room was rarely occupied, however. My parents each met people outside the home—Diedie's literati colleagues and Muma's socialite friends. They had no common interests, and I don't recall a single occasion when they had guests over for a meal.

Around the time that my parents' relationship was at its worst, Diedie and Qinpo took Virginia to Changshu for Chinese New Year. Muma remained in Shanghai, but she was out most of the time.

One night I joined the servants in an occult session of *menjiao guniang*, "the girl in the corner," a game that involved a spirit board similar to the Ouija board. We were in the upstairs living room, near the altar where we honored our ancestors. About ten of us sat at a table where the helpers had placed candles, fruit and scattered rice grains to appease our girl spirit. I sat next to my nanny, Two-two, who had recently replaced San-naima.

Standing at the head of the table in his starched blue changshan, Ah Si took charge, first carefully poking a long silver hairpin through the edge of a woven bamboo bowl. He then turned the bowl upside down and balanced it on the hairpin in a way that allowed it to hang and slide across the table. After Ah Si covered the contrivance with a chiffon square, two servants each rested two fingers on the bowl's inverted base. The group chanted unintelligibly, then rose one by one and approached the door to welcome the spirit.

"There she is—do you see her? She's coming to the table," Ah Si whispered hoarsely, his eyes shifting from the door to an empty seat opposite me. As curious as I was to see the ghost, the prospect of it also petrified me.

Muma as a young woman.

The bowl swayed and bobbed, leaving a wake in the rice grains. Focused intently on the vessel's smooth movements around the table, our majordomo murmured, "Oh, you want to look at the candle." The bowl drew closer, grazing the flame as if bowing in agreement. I held Two-two's hand tightly and squeezed my eyes shut.

Ah Si addressed the group: "I want to remind you to ask only questions that have yes or no answers. We must show respect to Menjiao Guniang and not trouble her with long questions. Please remember Third Daughter is with us"—several heads turned toward me—"so be careful not to say anything unsuitable."

The participants took turns, always two at a time, positioning two fingers on the bowl. They asked the kind of questions that concerned grown-ups: "Is my husband going to find a job soon?" "Will my village have a good crop this year?" "Is my wife carrying a baby boy?"

With each question, the bowl teetered on the hairpin like a miniature seesaw, nodding once for yes and twice for no, gliding in smooth circles between questions. At one point Ah Si asked, "Menjiao Guniang, are you thirsty?" and the bowl slid across the surface to a teacup, dipping down as if taking a drink.

Ah Si partnered with me when my turn came. The query at the top of my mind didn't surprise anyone: "Will I pass my math exam next week?" Everyone knew it was my weakest subject. We held our breaths as Menjiao Guniang nodded once, paused, began to teeter . . . and then, as we let out a collective groan, nodded deliberately, a second time. "No."

I'd decided my second question met the criterion for a yes or no answer. My voice quivered as I asked: "Are my parents going to divorce?" Across the table, Ah Si raised an eyebrow but said nothing. The bamboo bowl, still with our fingers lightly atop it, started to move in measured circles and stretched my short arms to their limit as it arced wider and wider—not stopping, as it had previously, to respond. Perhaps Menjiao Guniang hadn't heard me.

I asked again, louder this time: "Will my parents divorce?"

No change: more large circles.

I asked a third time. The bowl, which until now had circumambulated the table at a steady pace, suddenly accelerated and sped round in an erratic path with no apparent intention of stopping.

Ah Si intervened: "Menjiao Guniang, forgive us if we've upset you. Are you tired? Would you like to stop?"

The bowl came to an abrupt halt, and nodded once: "Yes."

The game was over.

Two months later, in the autumn of 1939, my parents' marriage was over too. Muma had given birth to six children in a decade and would divorce after twelve years of marriage. Her lawyer did his best to negotiate the settlement, but his powers were limited by the fact that women had virtually no rights. Custody of my siblings and me, ranging in age from three to twelve, was indisputable: children remained with their father. It was not only the legal requirement, it was the social norm. Diedie's agreement to permit Muma three weekend visits each month was considered a generous concession.

Virginia expressed her usual resentment toward our father: "Typical— every month has four Sundays!"

Muma's alimony of 250 yuan had to cover monthly rent and necessities; with rampant wartime inflation, she could run through the entire amount in days. (By comparison, Grandmother's monthly allowance of 300 yuan was all disposable income, as she lived with us.) Mother had no choice but to accept the terms. She moved to an apartment building next to Jessfield Park, a ten-minute walk from our house.

Virginia once said that neither Diedie nor Muma was qualified to be a parent. I find this unfair. Diedie may have been aloof and Muma absent, but hands-off parenting was normal then, and they did care deeply about us in their own ways, on their own terms.

For years, I pondered the unanswerable: which came first, the marital strife, or my father's lady friends, whose photos I'd found in his desk drawer? Had the marriage been happier, might Diedie have forgone other women? I observed with curiosity friends' families in which the first wives didn't seem to mind sharing their husbands with concubines. As difficult an idea as it was, I wondered if Muma might have tolerated, even welcomed, mistresses had she and Diedie felt some mutual affection.

This was a time when men routinely sold, gave away or tossed out women. Most women accepted their lot, whether as the wife of an inconstant husband, or as one of many concubines—it was still preferable to being a mistress or out on the street. Divorce was uncommon enough; one initiated by the wife was unheard of. Muma traded an unfulfilling yet materially comfortable marriage for an unknown future. She wasn't fool-hardy, and I don't believe she acted impulsively. Neither could I believe it was all the fault of my father. Diedie settled back into the bedroom after Muma left. He removed all the photographs of our beautiful mother from display. For the rest of my childhood, he never brought another woman into our home. It's a little surprising when I look back on it, because he was the sort of solitary man that many women find irresistible.

The divorce and ongoing wartime uncertainties likely sparked my lifelong habit of setting aside unhappy events. If I was sad and lonely at the time, I never admitted it, even to myself. I found happiness through my relationships with family and friends, and treated Shanghai's many diversions as just that: entertaining ways to divert my mind from worries.

Still, one memory tells me I must have missed Muma terribly. The day after her departure, I spotted a crumpled piece of clothing on the kitchen floor. It was Muma's gray qipao with its fine filigree of peonies and plum blossoms. "Your father asked me to throw it away," Ah Si said. He put down the vase he'd been cleaning and bent over so he could peer closely into my eyes. "Take it if you like, Third Daughter. It was your mother's favorite. You need something to remember her by."

Upstairs, inside the veil of my four-poster bed, I unfolded the qipao and discovered it was inexplicably torn at the waist. I mended the tear with my embroidery threads and hung the dress in my closet. When I yearned to be close to her, I nestled in the back of my wardrobe and pressed the precious qipao to my cheek.

FORTY-EIGHT ME'S

In the 1930s Polyfoto, one of Shanghai's earliest photo studios, introduced a new concept dubbed "Forty-Eight Me's." For a reasonable price, the photographer shot two sheets of twenty-four head-and-shoulders images. It was the first time that clients could be photographed in casual, spontaneous poses, rather than formal portraits.

Muma visited Polyfoto's Bubbling Well Road store shortly after the divorce. I don't know what motivated her to go at that particular time; perhaps she wanted to commemorate the momentous change in her life.

The two sheets of cells read as a time-lapse sequence, beginning with a hesitant Muma unsure of where to look and what expression to make. Before long she has progressed to striking a few uncertain poses, gaining confidence virtually frame by frame.

In the last image, my beloved Muma is relaxed and sports a natural, endearing smile. I daresay there's no longer even a trace of camera shyness.

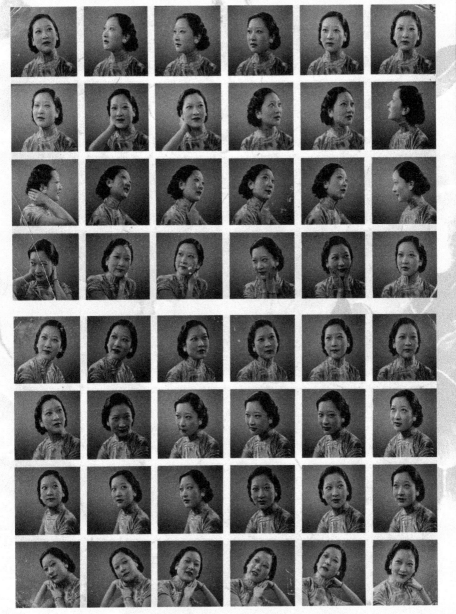

Muma's Forty-Eight Me's.

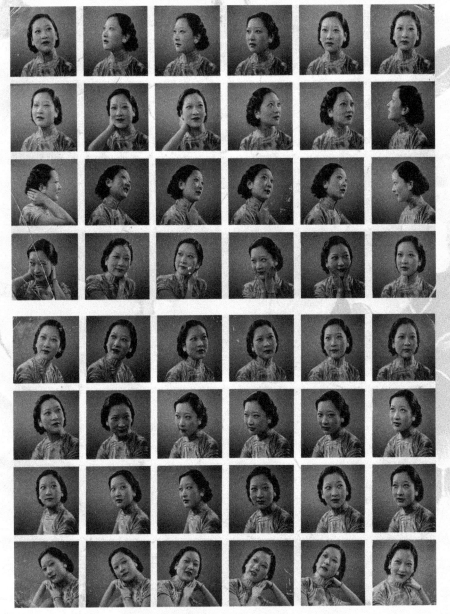

Muma's Forty-Eight Me's.

CHAPTER 12
SEAL OF APPROVAL

EDUCATION BEING OF THE UTMOST importance to Diedie, it was a given that I attended Shanghai's best schools—McTyeire and then St. Mary's Hall.

McTyeire's Gothic-style buildings occupied an impressive site on Edinburgh Road, an easy half-mile walk from home. Although the school educated the children of China's elite, Father didn't speak more than a few words of English, and might have hesitated to send us to a Southern Methodist Episcopal institution whose curriculum bore no resemblance to his Confucian upbringing. He must have concluded that if it was good enough for the famous Soong sisters, who became the wives of three of China's most powerful men, then it was good enough for us.

In Chinese, the name of McTyeire School for Girls combined the characters for "China" and "the West" to convey its hybrid education system. (Despite its name, the school did accept male students.) Classes in the first two years were taught exclusively in Mandarin and Shanghainese, with English-language textbooks introduced in the third year. Instruction in classical subjects such as Chinese literature was in Mandarin; Western arts and history were taught in English. The result was that my classmates and I spoke in a lively style that blended words from several languages or dialects within the same sentence.

In elementary school, my friends were all girls with the exception of my classmate Liang Ming. We weren't exactly pals, but we shared a sort of solidarity as top boy and top girl in Chinese composition. Liang Ming had received straight As throughout our first four years. Things changed when we entered fifth grade; friends whispered that his father had fallen ill and died. Liang's mother, who had never worked, had been forced to find a job.

Liang's grades slipped dramatically that year and did not improve in sixth grade, as worries weighed on him. He was soft-spoken and clever as always, but his clothes looked increasingly worn, their sleeves frayed and fabric patched. I felt sorry for my friend.

One morning, a teacher scolded Liang for not turning in his home-work on our reading of a Chinese translation of *Huckleberry Finn*. I approached him in the playground during our lunch break.

"Sorry you got into trouble with Teacher Jin this morning," I offered. "She's always in a bad mood these days."

Liang gave a half shrug. "It's not her fault. I didn't do the reading, so I deserve to be punished."

"Even so, poor you, having to write *Hakebeili Fei-en* one hundred times. At least the characters don't have too many strokes," I observed. "You didn't find it hard to understand, right? You're so smart. I like Mark Twain a lot—I read *Tom Sawyer* over the summer. Maybe I could help if you're having problems—"

I stopped midsentence, embarrassed that I was rambling. We both stared at our shoes—my patent leather Mary Janes and his scuffed loafers—until moisture from the grass seeped into my lace socks. I feared he was angry with me; perhaps I should have minded my own business.

And then it hit me. "Liang Ming, do you not have the *Huckleberry Finn* book?"

Saying nothing, Liang squinted at me through his Coke-bottle glasses. That was it: he couldn't afford to buy books!

He accompanied me home in the pedicab after school and waited in the study while I went to retrieve the book. That's when I noticed him slowly taking measure of everything, as if drinking in the paintings and the porcelains and the gongshi. His expression reminded me of my own father as he unfurled a favorite scroll—a look of deep gratification, as though art sustained his very soul.

I came back down a few minutes later, arms laden with books. "Here you go, no need to return these," I said. Liang, perhaps ashamed that I'd

Japanese secret police headquarters. His wife, Lilian, had to sell her jewelry to pay off his abductors and secure his release.

The Thousand-Year Society disbanded in 1948, a symbol of national pride as the country stood on the brink of revolutionary change.

Diedie (first line from right) was one of the twenty members to sign the Thousand-Year Society's signature sheet.

Society members created many artworks featuring horses, like the ones painted on these fans.

Jessfield Park with Xiyuan Apartments in the background.

CHAPTER 14

THE GODFATHERS

On a Sunday afternoon, my godfather slept in his usual position on the chaise longue of his apartment, his tummy rising and falling to untroubled snores.

"Jidie,[16] please help me!" I shook his arm to wake him. "I can't find Sanmi. I've looked everywhere." I often brought Sanmi, Muma's Persian cat, to visit.

My godfather stood and crossed the living room, stroking his mustache. "Don't worry," he said, peering down at the dense canopy of the garden. "The windows are all closed—she must be here. How about asking cook for a piece of fresh fish—"

That's when we heard a squeaky *meeew*. It seemed close by but had an odd muffled quality. We turned our heads toward the massive Tudor-style fireplace. Though normally I took time to admire the portraits of Jidie's warlord father in his military regalia, today my eyes moved past the splendid plumes and shiny medals.

Sanmi sounded like she was inside the hearth. Jidie slid the fireplace screen to one side. *Meooooooooooow!* We still couldn't spot her. My godfather, the son of a mighty general, got on his hands and knees and crawled onto the charred hearthstone. I heard jiggling and clicking as he extricated the cat from the flue.

"Jidie, you found her! Is she all right?"

---

16. Jidie: "godfather," pronounced *jee-dee-eh*. Jiniang: "godmother," pronounced *jee-nee-ang*.

He was shuffling backward out of the hearth when a brassy clang reverberated up the chimney, setting off a cloud of soot.

Hearing the commotion, Jidie's valet rushed in just as my godfather emerged from the fireplace with Sanmi cradled in his sturdy hands. Jidie's face was covered in so much soot that his only discernible features were the whites of his eyes. The cat's normally silky white fur resembled a blackened rag.

"Shaoye, what happened?" the valet exclaimed. "Why didn't you call me to help?" My godfather caught sight of his servant's look of utter astonishment, and the three of us erupted into gales of laughter.

After the divorce, Muma moved to Xiyuan ("West Garden") Apartments, an avant-garde address outside the foreign concessions. The building had been designed by a Russian architect and was considered one of Shanghai's more luxurious residences. It was at the western end of Yuyuan Road overlooking the greensward of Jessfield Park and a short distance from McTyeire. Notwithstanding the terms of the divorce that allowed only three meetings a month, we walked to Xiyuan to meet Muma after school several days a week.

I yearned for companionship during that period. At home, my father had retreated deeper into his literary pursuits. Virginia, now a teenager, had lost interest in playing with me. Shufen preferred the company of his male school chums, and my two younger sisters were still toddlers. I visited Muma every chance I could, but my mother was still enjoying a busy social life. On weekend visits, I might catch her for just a few hours before she went out.

To pass the time, I rode the elevator up and down. The attendant didn't seem to mind. As each of the eight stories had only two apartments, it wasn't long before I'd met most of the residents. One couple entering from the floor below Muma's was particularly friendly. They were small in stature, were around the same age as my parents and had a dignified air: he statesmanlike in a flowing changshan; she exquisitely serene in a tidy chignon.

"Well, good morning," the husband said. "It appears we have a lovely new neighbor. Who are your parents then?" I had to listen carefully: he sounded as if he'd swallowed a bag of marbles. He was speaking Mandarin with an accent that I later learned was from the northern province of Shandong.

His square jaw and bushy mustache would have been intimidating had it not been for the upturned brows and twinkling eyes that gave him a look of mild amusement.

"My mother lives one floor above you. Our family name is Sun," I replied, embarrassed to mention my parents' recent divorce.

The wife said, "Could that be the same Mrs. Sun from the mahjong party a few weeks ago?" Her big eyes met mine. "She was charming . . . and you look like her. She mentioned she was moving, but I had no idea it was here! I wish I'd known—we would have given her a proper welcome."

As it turned out, she and my mother were soon playing mahjong regularly. I saw her again when I arrived at Muma's apartment after school a week later. She was one of the four mahjong "legs"—fresh-faced with no makeup over her flawless skin, and wearing a loose blue changshan that must have been her husband's. I had never seen a woman wear a men's garment—it was so chic.

My mother introduced her: "Third Daughter, say hello to our neighbor, Mrs. Helen Lu."

"Ah, I was so hoping we would meet again," Mrs. Lu said, her eyes sparkling in a lovely round face. Her soft-spoken words rolled with the guttural r's of the North. Other than my teachers and servants, grownups rarely focused their attention wholly on me. It felt nice.

Muma was surprised. "Oh, you two have met before?"

"In the elevator," I responded. "Mrs. Lu and her husband live on the third floor."

"Yes, we had a nice conver—"

One of the other ladies laid open her tiles to show she'd won the hand. The players tallied the score and paid the winner with chips from the built-in drawers on each side of the table. I watched silently as they "washed" the mahjong tiles, moving the bamboo and ivory pieces around the table in a click-clacking shuffle. They'd forgotten about me for the moment.

When the ladies stood up for tea a short time later, Mrs. Lu asked if I'd like to go downstairs and keep her husband company. "He is listening to his friend Mei Lanfang sing Beijing opera on his new gramophone. He'd love a companion."

That's how I came to spend many weekends and afternoons in the company of Lu Xiaojia, oldest son of a warlord. I am still not sure what he did for a living, but I was accustomed to men who, like Diedie, didn't go out to work every day. Ah Si once said Lu was one of the Si Gongzi, the "Four Lords": the sons of two different warlords, the son of China's president and the son of its premier.

Helen Lu was born in Qingdao, the Shandong seaport that had been colonized by Germany and had become famous for its brewery. When she was a young woman, her community voted her Qingdao Meiren, "the Beauty of Qingdao."

Mr. and Mrs. Lu did not have children together. That was my good fortune, as they took a liking to me just at the time that my spirit needed nurturing. They asked Muma if she would *ji* me to them—if I could become their goddaughter. With Diedie's approval, we held a small ceremony in which I served tea and kowtowed to my new protectors.

I use the title "godparents" loosely, because there is no English equivalent. *Ji*, meaning "to send, entrust and depend," was a customary way of cementing a friendship between families. Chinese godparents are essentially surrogate parents, but without legal or religious responsibility for the child.

The vital role of Jidie and Jiniang in my life was singular and simple: to cherish me.

Though not unkind, my own parents were self-absorbed. It wasn't in their nature to flatter lightly or express love openly. Hindsight tells me they immersed themselves in their respective pastimes to lessen the anguish of their divorce. It probably didn't occur to them that I was in anguish too, feeling neglected and alone.

My godparents enfolded me in their embrace, introducing me to friends as their *gan gui nü*, "precious foster daughter," and giving me the kindness that I needed to feel safe and loved.

figured out his penurious state, took them from me and hurried from the house.

That night, after nine, Ah Si stood at the door of my father's study. "Shaoye, a Mrs. Liang is here with her son. She apologizes for coming at this hour, but says she has something urgent to discuss." It was unusual enough to hear our door buzzer so late; extraordinary that it should be my friend, and a boy at that. Soon, mother and son and father and daughter formed an odd quartet around Diedie's desk. Mrs. Liang was plain-featured and dressed tidily in a matching qipao and jacket. Her puffy red eyes worried me: the last time a grown-up had cried in front of me, my beloved nanny left me forever.

Mrs. Liang looked up at the painting on the wall behind the desk. Diedie had hung it just that morning to mark the change of season to spring. Our eyes followed hers to the scene of swallows beneath a curtain of willow branches—two large and two small birds, like parents with their children. When Mrs. Liang finally spoke, her voice was so hushed I couldn't tell whether it was her sigh or the rustle of the willows.

"You probably remember my husband," she began. "He was in the same art circles as you."

My father nodded. "Of course. Allow me to extend my condolences. His hometown wasn't far from mine." He straightened an inkwell on his desk. "We both collected early Qing paintings from the area. I was sorry to hear of his illness. It's a blessing his suffering was not prolonged."

"I'm afraid our son has been deeply affected," Mrs. Liang said. "He was his father's protégé. My husband was mentoring him in classical studies. The boy was so keen . . . he took it upon himself to catalog all our paintings."

Diedie leaned forward and appraised Liang Ming. "In this day and age, how unusual for a boy to embrace our old ways. Young people of his generation tend to be more interested in American movies and music."

"We had to move out of our house after my husband died," Mrs. Liang continued, looking down at her calloused fingers. "Over the last year we've been selling his art pieces to pay bills. I recently had to let the last painting go. It was my husband's favorite." She sighed. "Liang Ming took it especially hard. Your third daughter—such a kind girl—gave him some schoolbooks today. I never realized he wasn't doing his homework because he didn't have the books."

"If that is your concern, please don't worry," Diedie assured her. "I'm glad my daughter is trying to help."

"Your family's kindness makes what I must tell you more difficult." Mrs. Liang took a deep breath. "When I returned home this evening, I found Liang Ming at our table, admiring a handsome jade seal. Apparently, this afternoon your daughter asked him to wait here for her, in your study."

She withdrew a silk pouch from her purse, passing it to Liang Ming, who presented it to Diedie in both hands, with his head deeply bowed.

"I can only surmise that this belongs to you," Mrs. Liang said. "I am wholly to blame as an inadequate parent." She placed a caring hand on Liang Ming's arm. "I should have been more attentive to my son's needs."

Diedie removed an object from the pouch. Indeed it was one of his most cherished pieces, a Ming dynasty jade seal carved in the shape of a lion. Surveying the desk, his eyes stopped at the empty spot where he normally kept it.

My father looked at the boy sympathetically. "Do you see these small holes in the lion's head? They were for the owner to thread a cord and tie the seal to his waist—a safer place than the top of my desk, wouldn't you say?"

I gave my friend a sidelong glance. His shoulders slumped and he buried his face in his hands.

"Different seals are for different purposes. Thankfully, this isn't my official seal for legal documents," Diedie said. "I keep that one locked away. This is for my pleasure: a studio seal to mark paintings in my collection." His eyes twinkled with amusement. "If someone wanted to forge a document in my name, it would have been useless."

Looking up at last, Liang Ming stammered, "No, no, I never thought of anything like that. It's just . . ." His eyes met Diedie's. "The carving is so beautiful—it reminded me of my father and all the things he loved."

It was awhile before Diedie spoke again. "Liang Ming, what you did was wrong, but you've been through a difficult time." He was reflective as he rubbed the top of the lion's head. "Your passion for scholars' art is honorable. Being obsessed with it is not."

"I know this because when I was a few years older than you, I too did something foolish. I do not want to punish you. And I certainly wouldn't want to cause your mother more worry."

Liang's eyes widened in surprise and relief. "Thank you, thank you very much. It was wrong of me to take it."

My father gave Liang Ming a smile of forgiveness. "As it happens, I've been wanting to organize my art collection. Do you think you might help me with that?"

Liang Ming and I attended different high schools, but he paid Diedie regular visits for years. Soon after the seal incident, Father took over Liang's classical instruction, and within a few months my friend's school grades returned to their previous excellence.

CHAPTER 13
SAVAGES

DURING THE OCCUPATION, JAPANESE MILITARY police confiscated shortwave radios to stop people from listening to programs like *Voice of America,* which the Japanese regarded as Western propaganda. The fact was, no one in our household was interested in those broadcasts. We favored harmless cultural programs: Qinpo's shuoshu serials, Father's Beijing opera and Virginia's and my American music. Nonetheless, Diedie warned us to keep the volume down on our radios and to hide them when we weren't using them.

On a balmy autumn day when I was ten, I was on my own in the zhongjian reading comic books. I had tuned my Zenith portable radio to Bing Crosby singing "Stardust," when the doorbell suddenly buzzed. When I reached the vestibule, I saw that Ah Si had already hustled in from the kitchen and was opening the front door. I heard an unfamiliar gravelly voice on the other side but couldn't make out any words. Ah Si slowly swung the door open. I gasped when a Japanese military officer came into view, and I instinctively stepped back into the zhongjian.

The man was broad-shouldered and imposing in his olive uniform with a stiff high collar, brass buttons and shiny black boots. He spoke Mandarin with a heavy Japanese accent: "Who is the owner of this house?" "How many rooms?" "How many people live here—family, servants?" A bead of sweat appeared on Ah Si's temple, but he answered the barrage of questions with his usual composure.

Bing had been crooning away by my side all this time. After the announcer chattered briefly, the sweet voice of girl-next-door Deanna Durbin began to sing "The Last Rose of Summer."

From the vestibule, the officer barked, "Is that a radio? Take me to it."

His powerful steps strode quickly in my direction. From the corner of my eye I glimpsed the little gray radio on a table mere inches from me, but it was too late to hide it. The horror stories the servants had told about Japanese gendarmes' brutality flashed in my mind. I froze as the officer crossed the threshold into the zhongjian.

He stood tall, scanning the room, taking in Diedie's prized artworks on their tables and stands. His eyes made a full circuit of the room before they finally dropped to where I was standing. He seemed surprised at first to see me. His face was impassive as he looked me over in a slow, meticulous sweep.

"Turn off the radio, please."

I jumped at the sound of his voice, which was like a loud machine gun echoing against the room's hard surfaces. We were close enough to touch now. The officer's face was chiseled and weather-beaten, but the skimpy visor of his kepi gave him an unexpectedly affable air. His eyes, an uncommon light brown, were far softer than the timbre of his voice. Though I was feeling less threatened, I was still anxious about what would happen next.

Ah Si was standing in the doorway of the zhongjian. The officer turned to our majordomo and said, "Would you kindly bring me a cup of tea?" Ah Si hesitated, looking uneasily from the Japanese man to me. The officer's voice was gentle: "It's all right. I will not harm her. I have twin daughters around her age in Japan."

The man turned to me. As he had with Ah Si, he asked a succession of questions, though this time it was less like an interrogation and more like a chat between friends. He listened with genuine interest to my Mandarin responses—a credit to McTyeire School, as most Shanghai natives spoke only Shanghainese. I wanted to learn more about his daughters: how old were they, were they identical, did he have other kids? But I was too shy to ask.

After a few minutes, the officer took off his kepi and sat in a zitan chair. "The Westerners are not going to be in Shanghai forever. It will help you to know about Japanese things. Would you like it if I taught you a Japanese song?"

I nodded. Why not? I enjoyed all kinds of music.

"Repeat after me: *Aru-ke aru-ke . . .*"

He enunciated each word with care, patting the armrest or tapping a booted foot to show me the rhythm while patiently correcting my mispronunciations. The time passed quickly and my nervousness melted away. Even Ah Si relaxed. After he'd brought the officer a pot of tea, he stood just inside the door watching and periodically topping up the man's teacup.

"*Aruke aruke aruke aruke, kitaminami tōzai, aruke aruke . . .*" "Walk walk walk walk, north south east west, walk walk!" The officer grinned broadly the first time I sang the whole verse on my own, but Ah Si wore a sober expression.

The officer patted my shoulder. "Little Miss, you have done something of great benefit to your family today."

I had no idea what he meant. How could learning a Japanese song help my family?

Ah Si apparently understood what I did not. A few days later, he addressed Father as we ate our breakfast of tea-leaf eggs. "Shaoye, I've just come home from the market. Do you remember I told you about the Japanese officer who came here last week?"

Diedie raised his eyebrows, folding his *Shenbao* newspaper. "Yes, Ah Si, I had hoped we'd seen the last of him. Has something happened?"

"He's going to confiscate the house at the end of the lane. I heard many Japanese officers are going to live there." Ah Si shook his head in disbelief. "He's given the family three days to move out. How on earth are they going to find a place on such short notice? Shaoye, we were lucky this time."

Both men glanced over at me. "We were *very* lucky," Diedie said.

The day began ordinarily enough. After attending classes at McTyeire, Virginia and I visited a friend's house in the French Concession. As it had rained on and off all afternoon, we opted to go home by tram rather than our usual pedicab. It was rush hour, and we found only one empty seat, in the front. Actually, it was barely half a seat, next to a chubby man in a gray fedora and ill-fitting pinstripe suit. Virginia's mouth twitched and

I suppressed a giggle—he looked just like a striped pig. The older and slimmer of us, she wedged herself into the narrow space, and I stood in front of her.

The tram stopped frequently. The conductor stood steadfast in the front; his hand dexterously controlled the speed while his foot pressed a treadle to activate a cheerful *ding-ding* to herald each stop and start. At one such stop, I let go of the rail to fish a glass jam jar from my schoolbag. Even though I'd punched air holes in the lid, I wanted to make sure my silkworm was all right. The fresh *shangshu* mulberry leaves I'd placed in the jar less than an hour before already bore large nibble marks.

"Lily's father is breeding a special kind of silkworm," I told Virginia. "She says it grows to double the size of ours. This one's only two weeks old and look how big it is! They eat and eat and eat—you can practically see them growing in front of you!"

I was filled with pride for my fat new larva but worried I couldn't procure enough mulberry leaves for it. "I had to swap my favorite hair ornament for this baby," I told Virginia. "You know, the clip Muma bought me from Wing On—"

"*Aaaiiiiiii!*" An anguished hiss arose from the street in front of the tram.

Virginia and I turned our heads in unison with the other passengers toward the rain- and dirt-streaked windshield. A few feet ahead, a van stood with its back doors flung open. Soft rain fell steadily, the drops splattering on the asphalt roadway. We strained our necks to see out. I barely discerned the shadowy silhouettes of two men just inside the van. One stood and the other knelt before him, his head hanging in defeat.

The sun shone through a breach in the clouds as the rain continued unabated. A sunbeam, white and sharp, reflected off flinty metal in the instant that the captor's pistol exploded into the kneeling man's temple. The tram window was awash with hundreds of crimson droplets that reminded me strangely of frilly peony petals. In a split second, the world as I'd known it changed forever.

The horror of the act didn't register immediately. I couldn't tear my eyes away, reaching for Virginia's hand and finding the tension in her slim fingers. Rain pummeled the windshield, washing it clean as the killer kicked his victim. The body toppled in an oddly balletic motion before hitting the pavement with a thud.

A crash of glass slashed the air. I had dropped the jar with my precious silkworm inside, shattering it on the cold timber floor.

"*Yeman*," our chubby companion muttered, "*Yeman* . . . savages." For the adult passengers, that single word was an adequate explanation. The killer slammed the van doors shut and sped away. Virginia and I looked down at the scattered remnants of my jar: the silkworm's milky head had a deep gash, but it was squirming toward the mulberry leaf.

Ding-ding . . . the tram got underway and we trundled homeward.

I still have no idea who it was that lost his life that day—a Japanese collaborator? A Communist spy? A merchant who owed protection money to the Green Gang? At the age of eleven, I couldn't distinguish the good guys from the bad. Most adults were probably no better at it than I. The significance of the incident to me was less the poor fellow's identity than the fact that I'd witnessed for the first time the cruelty of the city that I so loved.

Mom almost never speaks of being afraid as a girl in Shanghai. Yet I have long been perplexed by her fear of sleeping alone; it's in stark contradiction to her usually sunny outlook and has dogged her all of her adult life. She attributes it to the servants' many ghost stories, and even some of the Great World's scarier exhibits, like the giant mechanized spider that had towered over her and given her nightmares. As much as she insists that she was unaffected by the harsh realities of 1930s and '40s Shanghai, what still lies beneath the surface is a mystery to me.

After the tram incident, she said Virginia scoured the newspapers but did not find any articles about it. Such occurrences were probably too commonplace to be reported. While the foreign settlements were home to Chinese families like Mom's, they also provided a haven for gangsters, radicals and spies.

The Nationalist Kuomintang was led by the elite and backed by the Americans; the Communists were inspired by the Soviet Union to unite China's peasants. After a decade of hostilities, in 1937 the rivals set aside their differences to form an uneasy pact against the Japanese invasion. Shanghai fell to Japanese occupation the  same year, and after the Japanese bombing of Pearl Harbor in 1941, the conflict became part of World War II. When that ended in 1945, China's civil war immediately resumed.

With the political situation and alliances constantly shifting, it must have been difficult for ordinary people to keep track of the twists and turns during those years.

At 76 Jessfield Road, a short distance from the apartment Muma moved into after the divorce, was a large property whose Chinese arched entry sat far back from the sidewalk. Mom says she was in the habit of walking past on the other side of the road, because "76" was the infamous secret police headquarters run by the Japanese and their Chinese hired guns, whom many Shanghainese viewed as collaborators with the enemy.

Kuomintang sympathizers and suspected Communists were interrogated, tortured and executed in the building's basement.

Organized crime flourished in wartime Shanghai. Gangsters posing as businessmen owned or influenced virtually every sector that offered a chance of profit, be it the police force, an opera house or a coffee shop. Some were unaware of it, but every citizen was touched by mobsters in some way and contributed to their coffers. Even the frivolous entertainment spots that Mom and her family enjoyed had a sinister undercurrent. Like a magic act on the Great World stage, it was all part of the city's duality and illusion.

TWENTY HORSEMEN

Created around 200 BC, the Chinese calendar is a sixty-year cycle comprising the twelve zodiac animals in combination with the five elements that make up the universe. The stock-in-trade of a fengshui ("wind and water") master is his interpretation of how the animals' interaction with wood, fire, earth, metal and water will influence events.

The year of Diedie's birth, 1894, was known as jiawu, the year of the horse and of yang wood. Its cosmological confluences portended conflict, instability and disaster—all of which occurred in spades during his lifetime. About two months before Diedie was born, a great fire in Shanghai destroyed over one thousand buildings. The First Sino-Japanese War broke out shortly after his birth, ending with the humiliating loss of Korea, formerly China's tributary state, to Japan. War, famine and revolution plagued China throughout his life.

In the summer of 1943, Diedie accepted the invitation of an old friend, China's former ambassador to France, to join a new fraternal society. Jiawu Tonggeng Qianling Hui ("The Thousand-Year Society") commemorated the fiftieth birthdays of its twenty founding members, all "horses" born in the same year. Their inaugural meeting, held during the Mid-Autumn Festival, was widely reported in Shanghai newspapers as a gathering of intellectual luminaries.

The society of writers, artists and collectors was in the main apolitical. Their patriotism was veiled behind the proliferation of the horse paintings they commissioned and idealistic poetry they wrote, as a response to the humiliation of the Japanese occupation and an expression of resolve not to submit to the invaders.

The two most famous horsemen were opera stars who suffered for their unwillingness to cooperate with the Japanese.

Mei Lanfang, one of the "Four Great Dan" (male performers who portrayed female characters), had introduced Beijing opera to international audiences and befriended celebrities like Charlie Chaplin. Mei refused to perform for the Japanese army, growing a mustache so he could no longer play the women's roles for which he was renowned.

Zhou Xinfang, an opera grand master, specialized in the roles of elderly men. Though slight in stature, his lavish beard and voluminous robes transformed him into a powerful performer. Zhou was arrested for refusing to perform at 76, the

As a girl, I saw Jidie simply as my kind godfather. I knew little of his past and was not aware of his ill-fated face-off with another type of godfather—Shanghai's biggest gangster. A feud that began over a trifling matter irrevocably changed the lives of both men, as well as the very leadership of the mob. Claire uncovered the story in her research.

The "trifling matter" Mom referenced took place in 1924, when her god-father, Lu Xiaojia, was a young man. We will refer to him as Junior Lu. He was the eldest son of Lu Yongxiang, whom we'll call Senior Lu—the military governor of Zhejiang Province, which bordered Shanghai. In the early years of the Republican era, after the downfall of the Qing dynasty in 1912, the government was so weak that warlords controlled the provinces. Senior Lu had a reputation as a fierce warlord; his success was said to be the result of superior soldiering and political acumen. Though Junior Lu had no official title, as his father's son he had the power to influence the provincial army.

Junior Lu's rival Huang Jinrong was another type of godfather: the kingpin of Shanghai's ruling Green Gang, a mobster of the highest order. The Great World was just one of his countless enterprises. Pockmarked Huang bankrolled many gang establishments, including his designated "office" at the Cornucopia Teahouse on the Rue du Consulat. Stocky in frame and authoritarian by nature, he conducted himself as if he were the emperor of the French Concession. So powerful was Huang, people said, that if he stamped his foot three times, all of Shanghai trembled.

On the night in question, Junior Lu, an inveterate Beijing opera fan, had gone alone to Gong Wutai, one of the city's most popular theaters, on Avenue Edward VII. Pockmarked Huang, in his fifties, a generation older than Junior Lu, was also in the audience, in a box near the stage. The star attraction was Huang's mistress, a young temptress named Lu Lanchun.

Lanchun was playing the lead role in the opera Wujia Po, *"Wu Family Slope," whose plot was similar to Homer's* The Odyssey. *While Westerners view opera performances in respectful silence, Chinese audiences openly express their exuberance or disapproval. Along with light snacks and con-versation, the experience is as social as it is artistic. Toward the end of the show, Lanchun's horsewhip slipped as she prepared to exit the scene. She caught the whip in time, but the audience hooted and jeered. A particularly piercing* yeooow *of disdain came from the balcony.*

Outraged over the insult to his mistress, Pockmarked Huang, jowls trembling, trained his bulging eyes in the direction of the loge. Unable to identify the catcaller in the darkness, he dispatched several henchmen upstairs. They were surprised to find that the culprit was a handsome man in his early twenties, wearing a fine changshan and sitting calmly as they approached. The catcaller was Junior Lu.

Huang's followers grabbed Lu and threw him to the floor: "Why would a young shaoye like you make trouble like this? Who do you think you are?" Lu endured their beating in silent defiance. "You chose the wrong person to insult tonight!" the gang members shouted. "These are gifts from Huang Jinrong," they said, punctuating each comment with a well-aimed kick. "Next time, don't expect to come out alive."

After his attackers left, Junior Lu rose, bloodied but able to stumble out of the theater.

A few days later, Pockmarked Huang was again in his box watching Lanchun perform when armed military police burst into Gong Wutai and arrested him. They had come at the behest of General He Fenglin, who was Shanghai's defense commissioner because Senior Lu had placed him there. The general could not refuse Senior Lu's order to help him avenge Junior's loss of face at the hands of Huang's flunkies.

Even Pockmarked Huang and his followers were no match for Lu's military machine: an army equipped with tanks, machine guns and tens of thousands of soldiers who controlled the entire Chinese city outside the settlements, as well as the adjoining province. The military police brought Huang to General He's garrison, suspended him from a rafter and lashed him with a horsewhip—the choice of which was, of course, not coincidental.

When news arrived of his capture, Huang's horrified wife looked to her husband's two deputies for help. Huang's closest disciple, the young and ambitious Du Yuesheng ("Big-Eared Du") approached General He. Huang's other lieutenant, Zhang Xiaolin ("Pipa Zhang"), who later negotiated Yeye's kidnap ransom, made his way to the Hangzhou headquarters of Senior Lu.

Recognizing that cash alone would not be enough to secure Huang's release, Big-Eared Du engineered a three-pronged approach and was confident the Lus would find it irresistible. First, he devised a plan to raise funds to pay off the captors; second, he used his charm to gather a group of Junior Lu's best friends to persuade him to stand down.

The day after Junior had tea with his friends, a military truck drove across the Chinese city to its border with the French Concession. A subdued Pockmarked Huang emerged from the back and hailed a rickshaw to carry him the rest of the way home.

Finally came the third and most elaborate part of Big-Eared Du's strategy.

The Lu Lanchun affair, as it came to be known, exposed the Green Gang's weakness in the face of military force. Big-Eared Du's solution was to unite the gangsters and the military to create not only a long-term coalition but also the mechanism for raising the substantial monies needed for Huang's release.

Du and Senior Lu met in Hangzhou, where the mobster and the warlord agreed to jointly oversee the transport and sale of opium in Shanghai in cooperation with a leading clique of opium importers. The gangsters would handle wholesale sourcing and distribution; Lu's army would provide protection from rival gangs and bandits in the provinces. The French authorities, for whom Pockmarked Huang served as police chief, and General He, as Shanghai defense commissioner, would turn a blind eye once the goods crossed into the city.

The opium wholesalers pitched in the princely sum of US$2.7 million to settle the kidnapping of Pockmarked Huang.[17] It was a masterful arrangement, with all stakeholders standing to make huge financial gains.

The deal also enabled Pockmarked Huang to gracefully step aside as Green Gang leader, opening the way for a collective gang leadership that placed Huang on equal footing with his two former lieutenants, Big-Eared Du and Pipa Zhang. In a culture that loved to lionize outstanding people and things in numerical lists, now Shanghai's underworld had San Da Heng, the "Three Big Bosses."

Big-Eared Du, the most charismatic of the triumvirate, amassed honorary titles that included company directorships, president of the Associated Chamber of Commerce and, of all things, supervisor of

---

17. Stella Dong, *Shanghai: The Rise and Fall of a Decadent City* (New York: HarperCollins, 2001).

Left: Jidie's father, the warlord Lu Yongxiang. *Right:* The Three Big Bosses
(left to right: Big-Eared Du, Pipa Zhang and Pockmarked Huang).

*the Association of Chinese Taxpayers. He maintained close ties with
Nationalist leader Chiang Kai-shek, using his connections to abduct or
kill Chiang's enemies.*

*Yet Big-Eared Du was also reputed to send coffins to the homes of his
enemies. In later years, even his façade of respectability couldn't cover up
his ruthlessness or the stigma of his own opium addiction, which left him
with glazed eyes and brown-stained fingertips.*

*Pockmarked Huang never forgot the loss and humiliation he suffered
as a result of the Lu Lanchun affair. The incident forever changed the
gang leaders' balance of power and the destiny of Mom's godfather, Junior
Lu. With the retirement of Senior Lu a few years later, Junior Lu lost his
military protection and was exposed to Pockmarked Huang's thirst for
revenge. For his own safety, Junior Lu moved back to his native province of
Shandong and settled in Qingdao, where he met and married the Beauty
of Qingdao—Mom's* jiniang.

*Having benefited immensely from his relationship with the Green
Gang, Chiang Kai-shek was keenly aware of the value of the region's
underworld activities. When Chiang and the Kuomintang lost Shanghai
to the Japanese in 1937, he urged the Three Big Bosses to leave, to prevent
them from helping the Japanese gain control of lucrative gang operations.*

*Big-Eared Du heeded Chiang's suggestion, living in Hong Kong for the
duration of the Japanese occupation. He went back to Shanghai for a few*

years after World War II but never recovered his glory days. Associates felt he had abandoned Shanghai during difficult times and gave him a chilly reception. He fled Shanghai on the eve of the 1949 Communist takeover and died in Hong Kong two years later.

Pipa Zhang remained in Shanghai. Always the volatile one, he had long begrudged being passed over for the gang's top position. Following Du's departure, Zhang's attempts to expand his power base by collaborating with the Japanese put him at risk, and he was assassinated by his own bodyguard.

Jidie's nemesis, Pockmarked Huang, stayed in Shanghai throughout the occupation years, but his refusal to collaborate with the Japanese cost him his former influence. This became Mom's good fortune, because the Lus deemed it safe to move back to Shanghai, and she soon met them in the Xiyuan elevator.

Pockmarked Huang regained power after the Japanese surrender. Jidie, again in jeopardy, moved permanently to Taipei with Jiniang in 1946.

Who could have imagined that Jidie's impulsive heckling of an opera performer would have such far-reaching consequences? If he ever harbored

regrets, Mom says she hopes Jidie was aware that the same incident also enabled him to meet Jiniang and, in fleeing to Taiwan, rescued them from an ignominious fate under the Communists.

Of the once indomitable triumvirate, Pockmarked Huang was the only one to remain in Shanghai after the

Huang Jinrong at eighty-four.

Communists' ascendancy in 1949. The firstborn of the Three Big Bosses, he managed to outlive both of his younger associates and died at eighty-six. A photograph taken two years before his passing clearly shows his reduced circumstances: an old man in a stained changshan, his arthritic shoulders squared over a twig broom, surrounded by rubbish carts on a dusty street.

DRAMA KINGS

The male opera star Mei Lanfang poses in dan costume with water sleeves, mid-1930s.

First staged in celebration of the Qianlong emperor's eightieth birthday in 1790, the repertoire of Beijing opera brings to life China's past. A rich cast of characters includes upright statesmen, mischievous maidservants, crafty ministers, ambitious scholars, spurned lovers and doltish buffoons.

With little more than a table and chairs, actors transform a stage that vividly evokes a kingdom, an ocean or a pitched battle. Not only accomplished singers, Chinese opera actors are skilled in dance, mime, martial arts and acrobatics. The work is physically demanding, yet requires poise and subtlety.

Beijing opera relies on stylized gestures to convey actions and emotions. Walking in a circle represents a long journey; holding a whip symbolizes riding a horse. Elaborate costumes and striking makeup establish characters' rank, occupation and personality. A well-trained actor can expertly manipulate his garment's "water sleeves"—which can be over a yard in length—to evoke joy, shyness or lamentation.

The roles that an actor may assume fall into four categories: sheng ("male"), dan ("female"), jing ("painted face") and chou ("clown"). A performer typically devotes his entire career to a single type of role. It is a rich irony that actors, who were mostly poor and uneducated, perfected one of China's most sublime and subtle art forms.

Taking a dim view of entertainment by female courtesans, the Qing imperial court banned female performers, so early renditions were delivered exclusively by men. The gender ban led to a class of dan—male performers who developed specialized skills for impersonating women. Great dan such as Mei Lanfang were possibly the most venerated entertainers of the 1930s, admired for their vocal vibratos, the arcing sweep of the eyes or tottering steps that mimicked those of a woman with bound feet.

The musicians do not rely on printed notation but play familiar melodies to the rhythm of their leader's hardwood clappers. For the uninitiated, the music is an acquired taste: high-pitched fiddles and at times relentless percussive drums and gongs.

Muma.

CHAPTER 15
NOT FOR SALE

IN 1909, MY MOTHER, FEI Baoshu, was born into the first generation in China that did not hobble girls with foot-binding. While this essential freedom dramatically improved women's lot, legally and financially their destinies remained largely subject to the whims of men.

Muma spoke little of her childhood. She was the youngest of three sisters in a well-to-do Changshu family; her father was the head magistrate of the *yamen*, or county office. She could read and write, which revealed her parents' somewhat modern outlook, but her school grades were so poor she drove her mother to tears. Her eldest sister entered an arranged marriage with the son of a wealthy local family that purportedly preferred for him to stay home and smoke opium rather than run around and squander their money.

Tragedy struck early: Muma's parents died when she was in her teens. It's unclear how, or for how long, she and her second sister, Baoqi, had to survive as orphans. While Muma was blessed with mellow looks and a gentle disposition, Baoqi, two years Muma's senior, was industrious and inquisitive by nature.

When Muma moved to Shanghai to marry Diedie, Baoqi, who had given herself the name Pauline, accompanied her from Changshu. Auntie Pauline set about mastering English and painting; she read everything she could get her hands on. Her stormy short-lived marriage to a customs officer concluded with her husband cutting up all her beautiful qipao.

In the 1930s Auntie Pauline met the man who would become her second husband and life companion, R. C. Chen, a senior executive with the Bank of China who moved in the Kuomintang's top circles and had the ear of Chiang Kai-shek himself. Chiang's wife was the youngest of the influential Soong sisters, who had all married well. The husbands of the older sisters were H. H. Kung, reputedly the richest man in the nation, and Sun Yat-sen, the founder of the Kuomintang. And just to keep it all in the family, the sisters' brother, T. V. Soong, was the minister of finance.

This became Auntie Pauline's milieu, where she rounded out her education by carefully listening and learning until she was as well versed in current affairs as she was in art and culture. She was remarkable for the era, a woman of erudition whose knowledge stemmed from passion and determination rather than formal schooling.

Auntie Pauline Chen.

Auntie Pauline and Muma were close, and they shared an enthusiasm for fashion and mahjong, even if they lived vastly different lives. Fortunately for my fun-loving mother, down-to-earth Pauline played the part of protective older sister naturally.

As a divorcée, Muma would have had a hard time surviving on her limited funds in the best of circumstances. The Japanese occupation of Shanghai, which had begun two years before my parents' breakup, made a difficult situation untenable. Muma found out runaway inflation made it impossible to budget: a simple outing for the day's groceries required a bagful of cash.

Until the divorce she'd lived well and been generous to a fault, but her life changed dramatically. She no longer went to her favorite restaurants and clubs; they had either closed or were being patronized by the Japanese military. Kidnappings continued unabated, and Muma often knew the families of the victims. Many of her closest friends and even her own sister had fled Shanghai, leaving her increasingly alone and vulnerable outside the protection of Diedie's home. She could not deny that Shanghai had become a dangerous place.

The stress of it all brought forth a nervous habit that stayed with her the rest of her life. She pulled her glossy hair into a neat chignon as before, but now she constantly pulled and twirled a loose strand forward and back behind her ear.

The Japanese Imperial Army launched a full-scale invasion of China in July 1937. After occupying Manchuria and several northern provinces, Japanese troops seized Shanghai and the capital city of Nanjing. Casualties among the Chinese were staggering: an estimated two hundred thousand deaths in the Battle of Shanghai alone.

In the aftermath of their defeat, the Chinese forces led by Chiang Kai-shek and the Kuomintang retreated to the remote western interior, where they established a provisional capital in Chongqing. In 1938, the representatives of more than fifty embassies and thousands of Nationalist sympathizers, industrialists and civilians joined the exodus to Chongqing. Among them were Pauline and R. C. Chen.

Muma's situation in Shanghai deteriorated further with the onset of World War II. She called it quits after four years in her Xiyuan apartment. Her natural haven was with her sister. In 1943 Muma—ill-prepared, lacking sufficient funds and in the company of a woman she barely knew—embarked on the same journey to Chongqing. The eight-hundred-mile trek across China was perilous on many fronts. There was the ever-present risk of being caught in the Sino-Japanese fighting or in skirmishes between local warlords, or being attacked by bandits or arrested by Japanese gendarmes.

The route Muma and her companion took mostly hugged the banks of the Yangzi River, where more populated areas meant they had a better chance of finding accommodation. The great river, the longest in all Asia, flowed across China from the Himalayan Plateau, nearly four thousand miles eastward, finally reaching Shanghai and the East China Sea. Steamer service was erratic and costly. Most ships, including Yeye's, had been conscripted by the Nationalist army to transport goods to Chongqing. As the women traveled upriver, they would have to journey by foot and hope to find transportation along the way.

Like Muma, Sheng Ayi was traveling to Chongqing to stay with relatives. When mutual friends introduced them, at first Muma asked herself whether the older woman was fit for the journey. Even Sheng Ayi's loose-fitting qipao couldn't hide her goldfish eyes, overflowing chin and bulky contours. But Muma set aside her apprehension: it was still safer than traveling alone. With limited cash, they chose not to hire a single guide for the entire trip. It would be cheaper to retain escorts for short distances, when they believed the difficulty of their passage required it.

They found that the farther they advanced from Shanghai, the more challenging it became to communicate with townspeople. Even neighboring villages a few miles apart had their own accents and idioms. Of China's hundreds of spoken dialects, Muma and Sheng Ayi were fluent only in the Changshu dialect, which is similar to Shanghainese. They spoke a smattering of Mandarin, derived from the more formal Chinese of the Beijing imperial court—not very useful in the rural South, along the Yangzi.

Sometimes, they resorted to scrawling what they wanted to say, as written Chinese is intelligible to all. Even this often proved futile, as local villagers were mostly illiterate. Discussions were then reduced to feverish pantomiming, which might have been laughable had it not been for the seriousness of their circumstances.

Their progress was far slower than Muma had anticipated. My mother, long accustomed to a leisurely existence, was taken aback by Sheng Ayi's lumbering pace and dependence on her to make all the arrangements. Every day Muma sized up strangers: whom could they trust, who was shady? Every day she evaluated the best route and mode of transport, and negotiated the best price—on foot, by mule, in sedan chairs, or shamefully piggybacked on the shoulders of sweating men.

When the river conditions were amenable, they boarded dilapidated sampans. For the price of a bowl of rice, half a dozen villagers harnessed frayed ropes across sinewy backs, straining barefoot along rocky shorelines to heave the boat upriver.

I try to picture my cosseted mother, her life until now almost exclusively focused on silk embroidery and mahjong tiles. I imagine her dewy eyes wide as she trudges her way through hardscrabble villages, past poor farmers and children with dirt-smudged faces. Do I sense in her a liberation amid the deprivation? Perhaps she is appreciating, for the first

Pulling a boat through the rapids.

time, the stark beauty of the countryside, rolling hills terraced with rice paddies and tea plantations, the simple homes of ordinary families nestled on the riverbanks—a family life she no longer enjoyed.

In the end, the calamity that nearly did her in was not military crossfire, rugged terrain or marauding bandits. Nearly three months into their journey, Muma and Sheng Ayi arrived in a small town in Anhui Province. They were less than one-third of the distance to their destination and had nearly depleted their cash.

It was dark when they checked into a small inn. They ate a meal of tepid zhou and sweet potatoes, and retired to their room. Despite her exhaustion, Muma lay awake on the kang as she pondered their financial predicament. Sheng Ayi did not seem to share her concern; she was already snoring lightly, a strip of damp cloth folded over her wide sun-burned forehead. Muma struggled to fall asleep as she mulled over her companion's shortcomings, which she had discovered included not only her sluggish pace but also poor judgment and a tendency to unkindness.

The sun was just rising, the room still dim, when my mother awakened from a deep slumber. She was surprised that Sheng Ayi had already left the room, taking her belongings with her. Muma hurried downstairs and found the innkeeper in the reception area cleaning a window with raw-knuckled hands. His face was bronze and leathery atop a wiry physique.

"Mr. Fu, did you see where my friend went? She's left our room with all her things."

The innkeeper shook his head, making no response. Muma asked, "What is it? Where did she go?"

"It's not for me to say. I've labored since I was five and finally saved enough money to buy this place. I can't get involved."

Even as the conversation stuttered with his reluctance and their conflicting dialects, it was clear something was terribly wrong. Muma continued, "We've been traveling for months. It's taken us much longer than I expected. I have enough money to pay for last night's room, not much more." She withdrew a pouch from her sleeve.

"Mr. Fu, I implore you to let us stay until I get help from my sister in Chongqing. I can give you my jewelry as security and pay you whatever I owe in a few days."

"I don't care if you do not pay for last night. I just don't want trouble." Fu's brow creased as he thought. "You seem decent. You don't deserve what that woman did to you."

Muma looked searchingly into his eyes. "What is it, Mr. Fu?"

"She came downstairs and met a man late last night—our village honcho, a big landowner. I bought my land from him, still pay him every month. He's an old, mean-spirited tyrant . . ."

"What does this have to do with me?"

The innkeeper pursed his lips. "He already has several concubines from the village. The youngest ones are half your age. He beats them."

"What are you saying?"

"Well, last night, your friend . . . she *sold* you to him."

Muma felt faint. "She what?"

"How could you not have heard her? She paid the bill and took off before sunrise." He laughed bitterly. "She's on her merry way to Chongqing right now, holding tight to that bag of taels she got for betraying you."

Muma's hands squeezed into fists. *"BUT I AM NOT FOR SALE!"* she cried.

Mr. Fu took Muma to the village's tiny cable office, which also served as post office and bank. He loaned Muma money to telegraph her brother-in-law R. C. Chen, in care of his offices at the Kuomintang Central Finance Division in Chongqing.

Muma waited at the inn for two nerve-racking days, worried that R. C. might not have received the telegram or that he might not find help in time; she was terrified that the sadistic landlord would arrive first.

It turned out R. C. had read Muma's SOS and had immediately appealed to his boss, China's minister of finance, T. V. Soong, who cabled Commander in Chief Gu Zhutong. The orders continued down the chain of command and out to the field.

The third day dawned cool and clear in Anhui. After another fitful night, Muma was awakened by clattering hooves and gruff voices. She pulled aside her curtain to view the courtyard below. A crimson bridal chair, silk ribbons flapping in the breeze, was parked on the cobblestone, its four bearers huddled alongside, muttering unintelligibly. They had arrived at the inn at the same moment that a cavalry of eight soldiers in crisp Kuomintang khakis pulled up.

The morning light played off the soldiers' rifles and bayonets. In her room, Muma watched as the bearers picked up the sedan chair and departed. She breathed a long sigh of relief.

R. C. had arranged for the men to procure a horse-drawn cart for Muma, and the cavalry escorted her to Chongqing without incident. Surely it wasn't the best use of China's military assets, but she traveled the rest of the way in relative comfort.

The Kuomintang remained in Chongqing until the end of World War II. Muma and Auntie Pauline did not waste time after V-J (Victory over Japan) Day; they boarded the first boat from Chongqing back to Shanghai in September 1945. My mother was amazed at how fast and effortless the return journey was, compared to her trek toward Chongqing. Of course, this time the sisters were traveling downriver, propelled by the mighty

Yangzi past the magnificent gorges of the interior, through the heart of China, into the fertile delta of their youth and all the way to Shanghai.

My siblings and I were overjoyed to reunite with Muma after two years apart. She rented an apartment in Liangyou Garden on Rue de Boissezon, about a mile from Uncle R. C. and Auntie Pauline's new place in the city's most prestigious building, Grosvenor House.

By now, Virginia was attending St. John's University, and Shufen and I were in high school. The war must have put things in perspective for Diedie, as he relaxed his earlier restrictions on our visits with Muma. Virginia, whose eighteenth birthday passed during Muma's absence, had especially missed her. The two made up for lost time, indulging in Shanghai's frivolities and dolling up in new designs.

A couple of years after returning to Shanghai, Muma received a surprise visit. Her erstwhile travel companion, Sheng Ayi, arrived on her doorstep, crying and apologizing for what she'd done in Anhui. My mother, never one to hold a grudge, was ready to forgive her. But Auntie Pauline, who was visiting at the time, berated Sheng Ayi in a way that Muma couldn't: "How dare you come here after what you did to my sister! She's not for sale and never was!"

Auntie Pauline threw the woman out, and they never saw Sheng Ayi again.

Thirty years passed before I learned the reason for Muma's unconventional actions, what had driven her to divorce our father and trek eight hundred miles into the fray of war. She was in love with another man: a Kuomintang general who was married to someone else and living in Chongqing. This piece of information also helps explain why Chiang Kai-shek would agree to dispatch a cavalry to rescue her from a little inn in Anhui.

The affair lasted for many years, but not forever.

Muma had to make drastic decisions for her own welfare. She moved to Hong Kong in 1948, a year before the Communists took over our homeland. More challenges lay ahead—for her and for our whole family.

CHAPTER 16
KNOCK THREE TIMES

THE SERVANTS SPENT DAYS PREPARING fresh delicacies and seasonal fruit to be placed on the long altar table. Lit candles and incense glowed between the porcelain-footed plates. Their smoky tendrils wafted up toward the life-size portrait of our grand-uncle, No. 4, seated in a resplendent embroidered robe.

At least from our family's point of view, Grand-Uncle's early death redeemed the transgressions of his youth. Though he'd cheated his own father, childless No. 4 bequeathed his estate to Diedie to ensure that a male descendant would honor him in his afterlife. That single twist of fate provided our family financial security for the next five decades.

Qinpo expressed devotion to her brother-in-law in her own way. As much as she had once blamed him for leading her husband astray, that was all in the past. For several weeks, we sat side by side at the baxian-zhuo, folding hundreds of paper squares in a precise origami pattern. The evening before Grand-Uncle's memorial offering, I asked, "Why do dead people need money, Qinpo? If Grand-Uncle isn't alive, how does he spend it?"

"Even after someone leaves us, we must honor him and make sure he's comfortable." Grandmother straightened a pile of silver squares. "You see, in the afterlife, if he has everything he needs, he'll still protect us. That's also why we must prepare special food for him to show our deep respect."

Qinpo's Buddhist companion, Gonggong, came in with a large cloth bag. This was my favorite part: it was my job to blow into the flat squares of spirit money until they puffed up into fat yuanbao. After we filled the bag with them, Qinpo fastened it with a loose knot. "Gonggong will bring them to the temple and burn them so your grand-uncle can buy whatever he likes," she said.

Qinpo said Grand-Uncle No. 4 had loved to play paigow, and I hoped he'd found a nice gambling parlor in his afterlife.

Diedie had a hidebound duty to honor our ancestors on the days of remembrance for No. 4's birthday and passing. As I entered my teens, even with food and supplies chronically in short supply, the family carried on these important traditions. When Shufen turned thirteen, it was time for him to step up and assist Diedie in the centuries-old rituals of filial piety.

On the appointed morning, with the rest of the family looking on, Diedie faced the altar to kowtow or "knock his head" three times, kneeling and prostrating himself so low as to touch his forehead to the ground. The deepest gesture of respect was *sangui jiukoushou*, "three kneelings and nine head knockings."

As the only boy in our family, Shufen bore a huge responsibility. Diedie was the only child of Yeye's official wife, Qinpo; if not for Shufen, the family name would have vanished in my generation. For Qinpo, Shufen's role at the altar was deeply significant on a spiritual as well as a practical level. She was determined to prevent him from growing up with the self-indulgent character of his grand-uncle and grandfather, No. 4 and No. 7.

In an era when good families brought up sons like princelings, Qinpo forged a unique solution: to raise Shufen with uncompromising strictness that bordered on deprivation. She believed it was our family's only chance of redemption. In Changshu, where Taiyeye's wealth awed the townspeople, it troubled Qinpo that many described our family as *juezi juesun*, "cut short sons and grandsons," meaning we had no heirs, which would lead to our family's extinction. Worse yet, the character for "grandson" is the same as our surname, Sun. Qinpo's desperate desire to reverse what she saw as a curse on our family further fueled her devotion to her Buddhist practices.

More than mere frugality made Qinpo dress her grandson like a country bumpkin: it was her mission to improve our family's karma. For years Qinpo gave Shufen copper coins to dole out to beggars on the way to school—until she found out many used the money on opium and gambling. Then she heard about an entrepreneur who'd opened a big zhou factory, and she purchased porridge coupons regularly so Shufen could distribute those instead.

When our brother joined Diedie at the altar for the first time, I was surprised at how distinguished he looked. Shufen's rangy bone structure acquired a certain elegance in his floor-length changshan. The mischievous schoolboy in peasant's clothes was now almost unrecognizable, bearing a newfound grace as if to substantiate his legacy.

We had been amused to watch Shufen practice his "kneelings and knockings" for months as he tried, clumsily at first, to tame the angles of his long limbs. At one point Virginia had teased, "Those clunky kowtows are going to scare away our ancestors!"

When the moment came, a hush fell over us as we followed the slow dip of Shufen's head and the fluid motion of his torso, his fingers gracefully lifting the corners of his robe with each genuflection. Even scary-looking Grand-Uncle should be pleased, I thought.

To my surprise, the rituals comforted me. It was the only time in my life that I was a little envious about something only boys could do. Though I was indifferent to history, it somehow connected me to a long line of relatives I'd never met. I hoped Shufen felt the same way I did, so he would carry on the tradition for a long, long time.

Shufen in his late teens.

TAP DANCE

Most people associate kowtowing with a loyal subject prostrating himself at the feet of an emperor or high official as a sign of respect or submission.

The kowtow has its roots in Buddhism. The number three reflects the Three Jewels: the Buddha, the Buddhist teachings and the Buddhist spiritual community. It is a common sight for the faithful to kowtow three times before statues and images in Buddhist temples.

Filial piety and respect for one's elders is a central tenet of Confucian moral philosophy and a pillar of good society. In Diedie's day, a full kowtow upon greeting an older friend or relative was obligatory.

One vestige of the disappearing custom is still seen in Chinese restaurants. According to lore, a Qing dynasty emperor, traveling incognito, poured tea for his servant in a teahouse. The servant did not dare prostrate himself as tradition required, for fear that he might reveal the emperor's identity. Instead, he placed two fingers on the table in a kneeling position, tapping the knuckles and nails of his bent fingers to show his gratitude.

Over time, the gesture evolved into modern shorthand for a kowtow: in southern China, when someone pours tea, the recipient expresses thanks by lightly tapping the table with extended index and middle fingers.

The ANEYRETA girls. Clockwise from front center: Esther, Charlotte, Margaret, Helena, Shirley, Mamie and me. (Susan was absent.)

CHAPTER 17
DO THE MATH

MY EARLY YEARS SPENT WITH strong-willed relatives contributed to my tendency to adapt to the needs of others. I came into my own during my last three years of high school, while a student at St. Mary's Hall. Before then, I'd always been defined by my relationships with everyone else. To my parents, I was Third Daughter. To my siblings, I was Third Sister. Even our servants called me Third Miss. At St. Mary's, for the first time, friends and teachers called me by my actual name—Shuying.

The influence St. Mary's had on me was enduring, both in the life-long friendships that I formed there and how it shaped the way I saw the world.

In addition to Chinese teachers, about one-third of the faculty was made up of unmarried American women associated with the Episcopal mission. One instructor, Deaconess Evelyn Ashcroft, was a legend at St. Mary's—an exceptional teacher who taught European history and literature with just the right mix of enthusiasm and exactitude. She had a tall, stately bearing, like a governess in a British film, and she wore a floor-length religious habit—white in summer, black in winter. She intimidated me at first, until I realized her headpiece resembled a giant wonton, immediately making her more approachable.

We became adept at reading her expressions within the compact area that wasn't covered by her veil. She had thick eyebrows and a long nose as straight as a ruler; blue eyes that widened like marbles and cheeks that glowed red when she was upset; and a radiant smile that lit up her face when she was pleased.

Deaconess Ashcroft was uncompromising about diction. She made us pronounce every syllable until our words were crystal clear. If a student mumbled, slurred, or, heaven forbid, spoke English using sibilant Shanghainese r's and z's, she had the student stand and repeat the phrase over and over, a dozen times or more, until it was perfect. With persistent repetition, "I vehrrr, I vehrrr" became "I will, I will," and "bahzz taa-verrr" transformed into "bath towel." She taught us so patiently that no one was embarrassed.

The shining star of the deaconess's efforts to teach impeccable English was a St. Mary's alumna eleven years my senior, Eileen Chang (Zhang Ailing), who became one of China's best-loved writers and my personal favorite for her portrayals of Shanghai life.

Not long after I began attending St. Mary's, the buildings were bombed by Japanese planes, and classes were suspended for several weeks. When I reflect back to that period, what comes to mind isn't the bomb damage but singing a capella with my friends on the Grace Hall stairs. As a teenager I wanted to simply enjoy life, and my privileged background certainly made it easier. That's why my most vivid memory of St. Mary's is not of the Japanese occupation but of my close-knit group of girlfriends—my "Gang of Eight." The school required seniors to board in its dorms, at which time we became truly inseparable.

With our embrace of Western culture, my girlfriends and I all wanted English names. I gladly took up the task of naming several classmates, taking my inspiration from books and films. I named one friend Mamie, after a character I came across in an American children's book, and years later I named her daughter Eugenie, after the French empress, a historical figure we learned about from Deaconess Ashcroft.

When I was fifteen, the Hollywood film *Devotion* enthralled me. It was a fictionalized tale of the writers Emily Brontë (played by Ida Lupino) and her sister Charlotte (Olivia de Havilland), who fell in love with the same man. We had studied their respective novels, *Wuthering Heights* and *Jane Eyre*, under Deaconess Ashcroft. The movie inspired me to choose Ida as my own name and Charlotte as the name of one of my eight pals.

But Ida didn't stick. A year later, I watched a rerun of the 1940 film *All This, and Heaven Too*, starring Bette Davis as a governess who becomes a murder suspect. Her employer, a debonair French duke, introduces his daughter: "This long-legged colt is Isabelle." And from that day on, I was Isabel Sun.

By combining the last letters of each girl's name I conceived an acronym for my group of friends, "ANEYRETA":

Id*A*
Susa*N*
Charlott*E*
Shirle*Y*
Esthe*R*
Mami*E*
Margare*T*
Helen*A*

On weekends home, I always watched two or three films, spellbound by epics like *Gone with the Wind* and *The Adventures of Robin Hood*. I can still vividly conjure Maria Montez as *Cobra Woman*, the court of Baghdad in *Kismet* and the lavish swimming sequences in *Bathing Beauty*. In the darkened theater, the dramas stoked my imagination, and I eagerly awaited Sunday evenings when I could reenact entire movies or perform my own invented stories for my friends late into the night.

Katharine Yang, two years my junior at St. Mary's, shared her memories of that time in the book *Looking Back at St. Mary's Hall*:

> I especially looked forward to nighttime, after everyone had gone to bed and Mrs. Jiang had made her rounds, and all the lights were off.
>
> Several of us would sneak into Isabel Sun's room and listen to her tell serialized stories. Her self-scripted tales of love were wonderful and moving, simultaneously happy and painful so they made us shed tears. (Isabel had this talent—it's a pity she didn't develop it. However, her brother Shufen became a bestselling modern Chinese writer.)

After telling stories all night long, in the mornings Isabel wanted to sleep in and skip the dining-room breakfast. Because she was petite, she could lay her body very flat in her bed. The teacher making the morning rounds never discovered her. We, her young listeners, smuggled *mantou* steamed buns from the breakfast table for her to eat.[18]

Chemistry wasn't my strong suit. Our chemistry teacher had a novel arrangement for reducing her workload. After a quiz, she would collect our test papers and redistribute them around the class. We were to mark the other students' multiple-choice answers as the teacher read out the correct responses. If we liked the classmate whose paper we'd received, we could improve her grade by marking an incorrect answer as correct. Once, Mamie signaled from several seats away that she had my paper and gave me a knowing smile to indicate that she would try to upgrade my answers. Imagine her surprise when she turned my paper over and saw that I'd left the page completely blank!

Of all my school subjects, I had a complete blind spot for math. A thoughtless mistake compounded my failing grades; one might consider it my version of a Mister Street comeuppance. On the first day of tenth grade, I accompanied my friend Katharine to the cafeteria in search of water. We assumed the homely woman at the tea stand, wearing a drab qipao and with her hair pulled in a tight bun, was an *amah*, a female servant. Her response to Katharine's repeated demands of "A-ma, A-ma, please bring me a cup of water" was merely to glare fiercely at us, making no move to help.

To my chagrin, I walked into my classroom a few minutes later and found that the woman in the cafeteria was far from being an amah: she was our new math teacher, Miss Chen.

Oh, how she had it in for me over the next three years. (She didn't like Katharine either, of course, yet somehow my friend managed to get passing grades.) After our first disastrous meeting, I could do nothing right. By my final year, my math grades were so bad that I was on the brink of flunking out. The passing mark for any subject was 70 percent;

---

18. Translated from *Looking Back at St. Mary's Hall*, edited by Xu Yongchu and Chen Jinyu (Shanghai: Tongji University Press, 2014).

at 60, students were permitted to retake the exam. My score was never higher than 59 percent.

Finally, the dean summoned me to her office. "In all my years, I've never had a student quite like you," she sighed. "I'd understand if you were average in other subjects, but you're top of the class in English and Chinese. Why do you keep failing math? Just promise me you'll try to pass. All you need is a D!"

Afraid that even a D was beyond my reach, I sought divine intervention. My first instinct was to attend morning chapel and recite a few Hail Marys, but I wasn't confident that my prayers would be sufficient. Instead of cramming for my dreaded math exam, I kept Qinpo company while she recited her Buddhist rosary; then, for good measure, I kowtowed and left three tangerines on our ancestor altar. I even contemplated appealing to Menjiao Guniang, "the girl in the corner," and then remembered my last unsuccessful attempt.

In spite of my last-ditch pleas for divine aid, I failed again. At our graduation ceremony, instead of leading the class in singing "Land of Hope and Glory" as I'd been nominated to do, I prepared to start math tutoring. My homeroom teacher arranged for me to meet with a Professor Tucker at St. John's—not an easy feat, because teachers avoided the unbearably hot classrooms over the summer. Nearly every morning for two months, it was just the professor and me by ourselves in a huge lecture hall. He had gray hair and a potbelly, rather like a beardless Santa, and was drenched with sweat from the moment he walked in.

I don't know if the torture was worse for him or for me; in late August he put us both out of our misery by giving me the D that I desperately needed. I would graduate from St. Mary's just in time to enroll in St. John's for the fall semester. St. John's was reputed to be the Harvard of China, and I hoped my lack of proficiency in math wouldn't lower the university's high standards.

St. Mary's allowed me to have a private ceremony to receive my diploma in front of Virginia and ten friends. In those days, parents rarely attended school functions. My Confucian father would have found such an affair shamelessly self-laudatory, and Muma had left for Hong Kong that spring. As it was two months later than the normal graduation, the summer dampness was now at full saturation: the girls carried fans, and the boys quickly sloughed off their jackets. I wore a qipao with dainty

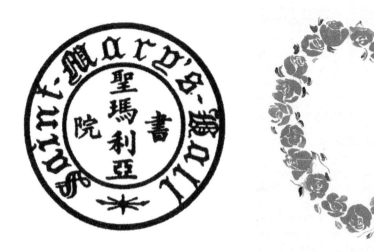

white eyelets and a lei of red roses. Lei are not a Chinese tradition, but the friend who made it was inspired by the Airline Club mural—the one with the Rita Hayworth look-alike in a grass skirt.

I could not have predicted that even more momentous changes would soon erupt. Within weeks, all my American teachers from both McTyeire and St. Mary's would leave Shanghai, never to return.

It was 1949, the year when everything changed irrevocably. On October 1, Mao Zedong declared the establishment of the People's Republic of China and took his place as its leader.

The second half of 1949 and early 1950 saw a mass exodus from China of virtually all foreign residents, including the bankers, missionaries, architects and merchants who had made Shanghai their home and helped transform it. Over two million Chinese fearful of living under a Communist regime departed too. The defeated Chiang Kai-shek and Kuomintang loyalists evacuated to Taiwan, where Chiang maintained a six-hundred-thousand-man army in the hope of eventually recovering the mainland.

Graduation, at last.

MAD ABOUT MULAN

Shanghai is as movie-mad as any city of its size in the world. The rest of China is oblivious to the energies of Hollywood, but this metropolis pays a huge annual toll cheerfully to feast its eyes on the antics of the silver screen. The theaters in Shanghai have improved in proportion to the interest shown in them, until today plans have just been announced for Shanghai's first "Cathedral of the Moving Picture"—the new Grand Theatre on Bubbling Well Road.[19]

—*China Press*, 1931

I was one of Shanghai's movie-mad citizens. War and occupation fueled the city's appetite for diversion, and scores of cinemas were built in the 1930s. None was more opulent than the Grand Theatre, whose architect, László Hudec, also designed McTyeire School and the city's first skyscraper, the Park Hotel.

My passion for Hollywood films made foreigners objects of fascination. As the Chinese film business blossomed, I also fell in love with Chinese stars. My all-time favorite was Nancy Chan (Chen Yunshang).[20]

Nancy rose to stardom in the late 1930s. At the age of sixteen she played the Tang dynasty heroine Hua Mulan in the film *Maiden in Armour*. My heart skipped a beat when Mulan's mare skidded to a halt and rocketed her heavenward. Still in flight, Mulan fired three arrows to impale three charging Mongol warriors. It was the first depiction I'd ever seen of a female warrior, albeit disguised as a man. The film broke box-office records, playing to packed houses for months, and making Virginia and me Nancy's biggest fans.

Previously, I'd never seen a Chinese actress in anything other than traditional qipao, but Nancy often wore casual Western clothes. Once, at a ribbon-cutting for a new swimming pool, Nancy arrived in a red floral bathing suit and white high-heeled pumps. Sweltering in the summer sun, frenzied fans charged the platform where she was standing. When she climbed a ladder to escape into a nearby building, the mob grabbed it with Nancy precariously clinging on.

19. Cited by *Shanghai Daily*, www.shanghaidaily.com, on November 7, 2014.
20. *A Movie Queen Chen Yunshang*, edited by Lu Yanyuan (Beijing: Xinhua Publishing House, 2001), by permission from Sherman Tang. The account of Nancy Chan's swimming pool story is a paraphrased excerpt.

Nancy Chan was often photographed in casual outfits.

Eventually, her bodyguards fought their way through the crowd and cleared a route to her car.

Afterward Nancy made public appearances only with a police escort and rode in a special car that gave electric shocks to anyone who touched the outside of it.

Me at eighteen, seated in the center of the Airline Club's six-piece ensemble. Moro is first from left; trumpeter Matthew Tayong is second from left.

CHAPTER 18
GOOD TIME HARLEY

Once I turned eighteen and was attending St. John's, I began to visit nightclubs with friends. Although Shanghai's largest ballroom, the Paramount, was only half a mile from our home, it had always been off-limits. As children, Virginia and I had been fascinated by how its curvy neon façade pulsated to the beat of the big bands playing inside. We also observed the gendarmes and bodyguards manning the club entrance on Bubbling Well Road, and grown-ups warned us that Japanese officers and gangsters patronized it.

That was in part why my university friends and I preferred smaller, lesser-known venues. By this time, the Communists were in power and most foreigners had fled Shanghai, but plenty of gangster types were still around.

For us, it was the music that mattered the most: when a favorite band moved from one nightclub to another, we followed. Indeed, we usually referred to the place by the name of its bandleader rather than the name of the club. The Paramount had Tino, the Metropole had Remedios, Ciro's had Lobing. From 1949 on, most of the musicians were from the Philippines.

I found nothing more exciting than live music—songs I'd heard on the radio and in movies, as well as those of local musicians. Mostly, we listened to jazz, popular Chinese songs and jazzed-up Western tunes, some with Chinese lyrics. I liked to think of it as "jazz with a Shanghai accent."

But we didn't simply listen. We danced! People knew how to dance in those days—the waltz, tango, rhumba, samba, cha-cha. I fox-trotted to "September Song," swung to "In the Mood" and waltzed to "One Day When We Were Young." One male friend was adept at tossing and flipping me to Glenn Miller's "Chattanooga Choo Choo"—not that I had any idea where or what Chattanooga was. The beat was infectious, and it felt so light and breezy when my partner pulled me through his legs and popped me up again. And later, when the band struck up another tune, it truly did feel like heaven dancing cheek to cheek with a handsome date.

At the Great World one afternoon, Qinpo and I passed a couple on stage performing a flamboyant tango. She shrugged and said, "Quite bizarre what young people do in public these days," never imagining her own granddaughter often jitterbugged the night away.

Mondays and Tuesdays taught me patience and tact, as those were the days when boys telephoned to ask me out for a Saturday night date. I did my best to put them off until Wednesday, in the hopes that the young man I liked best would call.

It is fitting that the last photo of me in Shanghai, in front of a Hawaiian mural, was taken at my favorite haunt: the Airline Club on Route Henry in the French Concession. Moro, the club's talented band-leader, had led an eighteen-piece orchestra of Filipino jazz musicians. With many patrons leaving Shanghai, Moro's big band became a small band, but I enjoyed the intimate setup. The ensemble of six, in the days I frequented the club, included Moro on the bass and his compatriots on trombone, trumpet, clarinet, Spanish guitar, piano and drums. The only non-Filipino was a Russian female saxophonist who sometimes doubled as a Hawaiian dancer.

The romantic ballad "Sleepy Lagoon" was my all-time favorite, and Moro's band played it for me often. That's until I was given my very own song, "Isabel." Moro's trumpeter, Matthew Tayong, composed it, and a St. John's classmate who had a crush on me wrote the lyrics. From then on, every time I entered the Airline Club ballroom, the band stopped whatever they were playing and launched into my song. Quite a thrill for an eighteen-year-old!

ISABEL

Each time I look at your eyes they seem to shine
Just like the few twinkling stars that I call mine
When you look at me still I feel
A warmth creep up from my heel

Each time you smile at me, dear, I seem to find
A kind of deep hidden love that's in my mind
But the happy moments were short for me
'cause you're in someone else's arms

I keep asking myself over again
Who's the lucky one kissing you now
As long as there is a chance I won't give up
Without your love I'm just like a wandering pup

But when the time comes you'll see my view
For Isabel, I love you

Matthew was blowing the last note of a trumpet solo one night when a coterie of unsavory-looking men entered the ballroom. Unlike the blazers with crisp khakis or linen trousers favored by my university friends, these men wore dark changshan and tight-fitting three-piece suits. The top frog knots of their robes were open at the throat, and their rolled-up sleeves exposed gaudy gold-and-jade rings on tobacco-stained fingers.

None deigned to remove the fedoras perched atop their slicked-back hair. These men talking loudly as they flashed wads of cash and flicked cigar ashes everywhere reminded me of James Cagney and his gangster cohorts in *White Heat*, which I had seen only a few days before.

The band struck the first chords of "Isabel," and my date and I rose to fox-trot. As he spun me close to the gangsters' table, I noticed one woman among them. She was attractive in a maroon qipao, with a slit cut higher than my girlfriends and I would have dared to wear. Her dainty features looked familiar, but soon my partner was guiding me back to where we'd started.

Not long after, I was in the restroom refreshing my lipstick when a voice called softly behind me. "Excuse me," the woman said. "Aren't you the Third Miss of the Sun family?" I peered at her reflection in the mirror as I daubed my lips.

"I'm sorry to be forward," the woman said. Her fine, sweet features were carefully powdered; yet, as she cast an appraising look over me, I couldn't help noticing her bloodshot eyes and the dark circles ringing them.

She stepped alongside me. "What a lovely young lady you've become."

I racked my brain but was still unable to place her.

"It's understandable you don't remember me," she continued. "When we met, you must have been eight, nine? I'm no longer the pretty young thing I was then." An embarrassed smile revealed a dimple in her cheek, and at last it dawned on me who she was.

"Ah—you're Jinling, the friend of Li Gege," I said, pleased to know it was her. "You were so kind. You gave me that polka-dot ribbon at Kiessling Café—I still have it tied to my bedpost."

While I refreshed my makeup, Jinling confided that her difficult marriage to Li Gege had ended after only a few years. "He couldn't bear being disowned by his family and friends. They put so much pressure on him." She closed her eyes, allowing the memories to wash over her. "After we broke up, he moved to America with his parents and I never saw him again."

When I reached Zhenning Road just before eleven that night, Diedie's study light was shining through the lattice fence. He was waiting for my safe return as he always did. I'd often taken for granted all the things that he'd provided me, and yearned for experiences beyond the tight cocoon of our home. The image of Jinling's tired eyes and her strained circumstances made me realize that my family's protectiveness might not be such a bad thing after all.

It was my last summer in Shanghai. I was still innocent, dating my first boyfriend, who was also a St. John's freshman. Michael's black leather jacket, combined with his thick hair and square jaw, lent him an air of confidence that set him apart from the other young men in their blue collegiate blazers. He picked me up at the house on weekends and took me out dancing, and to movies and restaurants. But the most memorable part of our evenings had little to do with Shanghai's nightspots: what I loved was the thrill of riding on the back of his Harley-Davidson.

Me in the garden at seventeen, looking grown-up in Muma's fur coat and heels, 1948.

I rode perched sidesaddle behind Michael. It sounds precarious and maybe even reckless, yet I'd never felt so safe or free as I did clinging to my beau on that streamlined leather seat. It was nothing like our rolling Buick or a swaying pedicab—when my beau revved the engine of that motorbike, its rumbling *baw-baw-baw-baaaaaw* and warm vibrations took my breath away. The speed and the loud roar were electrifying, with the pavement whizzing by inches below our feet.

The first time Michael drove up on the Harley, Shufen cocked his head and exclaimed, "Wow—who is this guy? That's a 1200-cc twin-cylinder FL. Wow! Don't let go of him, whatever you do!" He grinned cheekily and gave me a thumbs-up.

Shufen ordinarily showed no interest in Virginia's and my suitors. I had to ask, "What's so special about it, then?"

"It's one of the most expensive bikes available, that's all. Most people, like your poor brother, can only afford a 750-cc. The 1200 is the muscle version." He thrust his fists out to mimic twisting a throttle. "That's what gives you the *vroom-vrooooom!*"

It was a rare moment: I understood, and maybe even shared, my brother's passion for something.

Gas had been scarce for years. Any driver lucky enough to get a gallon of precious fuel painstakingly poured it into the gas tank one teacup at a time. Diedie warned us never to speak to strangers in automobiles, because the only people who could still get gasoline were gangsters and collaborators. I never knew how exactly, but Michael managed to secure enough fuel to take me on several long rides around the city.

The Grand Theatre and Park Hotel from Bubbling Well Road in 1937.

One afternoon, Michael escorted me to a Saturday matinee at the Grand Theatre. It was the biggest Hollywood film of the year, *Samson and Delilah*, with Hedy Lamarr and Victor Mature. The seductive story and glorious scenes seemed the perfect setting for *my* budding romance with the dashing man beside me.

After the movie, the sun's last rays warmed our backs as we zipped through congested city lanes, riding east toward the Huangpu River. In a short time, we arrived at that majestic curve of riverfront, the Bund, with its mile-long stretch of impressive buildings, each grander than the last. On the bike, no window separated us from the elements—it was just the wind in our faces carrying the briny aroma of the East China Sea.

We stopped to watch the sun's pastel rays fade into a deep-sapphire sky. In the evening, the outlines of the Western monuments along the Bund merged in a confection of Roman arches and Gothic turrets. The nighttime chill made me shiver, prompting Michael to pull over and wrap his leather jacket around me. He took out a camera, and, just for fun, I straddled the bike, posing with his jacket and sunglasses.

The glow of a full harvest moon and ten thousand twinkling lights turned the river into liquid silver. For a few blocks, Michael let me ride seated in front of him on the Harley, while he kept hold of the handlebars and steered. We zipped along the waterfront beyond the street lamps, where the cone of our headlight illuminated only a few feet into the darkness.

I'd never experienced this combination of exhilaration and uncertainty in the same moment. If Muma, Diedie or even my friends had seen

me on the Harley, they wouldn't have recognized me. Atop that motor-bike, I discovered a part of myself that had been hidden until now. The whirr of the engine and the wind at my back seemed to be hurtling me into the unknown, and I had nothing to fear.

The Bund in the 1930s.

GO THE EXTRA TILE

Mahjong, a quintessentially Chinese game, is a metaphor for life.

The tiles, 144 in total, form a symbolic universe. They depict, among other things, the four winds, the four seasons and Confucius's four noble plants (plum, orchid, chrysanthemum and bamboo). The three main suits, each numbered one to nine, are based on old Chinese money. *Tong* ("circles") are copper coins with a square hole in the center. *Suo* ("bamboo") sticks denote strings of one hundred coins. *Wan* ("10,000s") represent one hundred strings of one hundred coins.

Many variations of mahjong are played all over Asia. Starting in the 1920s, it was embraced by Jewish women across the United States. (I wonder if any of them had learned it in Shanghai.) Whether the setting is a folding table on a Hong Kong sidewalk or a game room in a plush hotel, the fundamental rules are the same.

The goal is to create combinations that are similar to those in gin rummy: triples of the same tile, such as 1-1-1, and consecutive runs, like 1-2-3, in the same suit. Rules and scoring can be complex, with points tallied according to the rarity of the combinations. Typically, players must memorize around one hundred patterns, some with quirky names such as *yitiaolong* "(dragon)," a run of 1-2-3-4-5-6-7-8-9 in the same suit, and *sanjiemei* ("three sisters"), the same run—for example, 5-6-7—in three suits.

Some people play mahjong boisterously, yelling out, slapping tiles on the table and clacking them noisily against each other. The Shanghainese ladies' game is serene, with the players connected by their calm concentration and the rhythm of play. We begin by building four walls of tiles; a roll of the dice determines where we draw the first tile. Then it's up to each individual to combine luck, skill, risk and defense to best effect. We draw tiles in turn, hoping they will transform our hands; afterward, we "wash," shuffling the tiles around in a "dry swimming" motion.

During more than six decades of regular play, I've found that what happens on the mahjong table reflects the inner self. I've seen it all: high-rollers striving for huge wins and losing everything; haphazard players with no discernible strategy; even a cheat hiding unwanted tiles in her Chanel jacket.

When I was young, I tended to lose a lot because I was often overambitious. Nowadays I play safe and settle for less, so I have a better chance of winning. It may not be a dramatic gain, but neither will it be a tremendous loss. Only when the winds are especially favorable—when I've had a string of wins—will I try for a big hand, and often I'll succeed.

Now that I'm in my eighties, my friends have noted my consistent earnings at mahjong. "What's your secret?" they ask. "Bend with the wind," I tell them. "Adapt."

Virginia in her early twenties.

CHAPTER 19
COME FLY WITH ME

THE 1930S AND '40S WERE *heady times for Chinese aviation, not only because newly formed airlines were developing commercial flights. China's earliest air transport companies had Nationalist government ties and foreign backing. Pan American Airways owned part of China National Aviation Corporation (CNAC), and the United Nations Relief and Rehabilitation Administration funded the Central Air Transport Corporation (CATC).*

When the Japanese closed the last remaining overland supply lines into China, US airmen joined Chinese civilian pilots to fly in desperately needed food and other supplies to aid the war efforts of Chiang Kai-shek and China-based US forces. The air route originated in northeast India and ended in Kunming, requiring planes to fly over peaks rising 16,500 feet. The so-called "Hump" over the Himalayas was fraught with danger, from brutal weather to a lack of accurate charts and the inability to navigate by radio.

With Japan's surrender in 1945, US efforts shifted to supporting Chiang Kai-shek and the Kuomintang in their civil war against the Communists. In the process of hauling in supplies and ferrying out refugees and wounded soldiers, the third and youngest air service, Civil Air Transport (CAT), earned a reputation as the "most shot-at airline." The American Central Intelligence Agency later acquired CAT to conduct covert operations in Asia.

In 1948, the summer before her final year at St. John's University, Virginia came across a CATC newspaper ad. The airline was launching commercial service to Asian cities and was inviting applications for stewardesses. Virginia was one of only six women hired from over three hundred applicants, partly thanks to the excellent education she had received at McTyeire and partly because, at five feet eight inches, she was the tallest candidate.

Diedie disapproved of his eldest daughter not completing university and taking on what he considered a servile job, but even he couldn't challenge Virginia's determination. During my senior year at St. Mary's, when I came home on weekends, I still shared the tingzijian with my oldest sister. Once a week, she rose at three in the morning and donned her chic CATC uniform designed by Madame Garnett. My sister had come a long way since she'd exposed her miserable patchwork underwear to Garnett and Butterfly Wu!

Virginia and her colleagues—pilot, co-pilot, navigator and one other stewardess—spent layovers at fine hotels like the Peninsula in Hong Kong and the Imperial in Tokyo. They flew in Curtiss C-46 and Douglas C-47 aircraft, mostly converted from wartime transports into forty-passenger civilian carriers. The engines were extremely loud, making polite conversation impossible, and the planes had no climate control—torture in tropical destinations. Worst of all, frequent turbulence inevitably led to vomiting travelers, passengers and crew alike. It quickly dawned on Virginia that it wasn't the glamorous job she had expected, something she'd never admit to Diedie.

While not flying, Virginia made regular use of her coveted French Club membership. The dazzling gold-and-crystal ballroom, indoor swimming pool and lawn tennis courts of the Cercle Sportif Français had been funded in part by the French government. Its nine-acre grounds were the focal point of the French Concession and the venue for the city's most sought-after social events.

The club was the first to admit Chinese members and, unlike its British and American counterparts, accepted women too. Still, it wasn't easy getting in, with hundreds of hopefuls on its waitlist. Auntie Pauline and her husband, Uncle R. C., who was now head of the Bank of China's Foreign Department in Shanghai, sponsored Virginia for membership. Our aunt and uncle frequently entertained at the club, and it was at a dinner hosted by them that Virginia met George Kiang. A thirty-year-old divorcé, he was a graduate of an American university and the top Chinese executive in a US-owned utility company. If our father was something of an archetype for his generation, then George was a poster boy for ours. He was well groomed in smart Western suits and gold-rimmed glasses—a man who worked and socialized easily with foreigners, but who was in character quintessentially Chinese.

George was smitten with my oldest sister, who proved to be as practical as she was stylish. Virginia had not stopped feeling resentful about her oppressive childhood at Qinpo's hands, and she had suffered a deep loss when Muma moved out after the divorce. At twenty-one, she was impatient to leave home and spread her wings.

I greatly admired Virginia's confidence and logic when she broke the news to Diedie with a series of questions: "Would you agree to George and me marrying? If I had gone to the United States to finish university, how much were you prepared to spend? How much if we had a big society wedding?" She finally led him to her desired conclusion like a trial lawyer. "I don't want those things when we get married. Please just give us the cash."

George formally asked our father for Virginia's hand a few days later. Diedie readily approved, relieved that his daughter no longer needed to serve drinks to strangers on airplanes. As modern as the marriage seemed—with the bride and groom choosing each other of their own volition, and everyone overlooking the groom's divorced status—Virginia in effect would leave home with a dowry, just as young Chinese women had done for centuries.

In the spring of 1949, Shufen carried a large box of gold yuanbao to the groom's home on Avenue Joffre, and Virginia commenced life as Mrs. George Kiang.

George continued his work as deputy to the American general manager of the Shanghai Telephone Company. The utility's owner, International Telephone & Telegraph (ITT), had constructed a new cable and wiring network for the foreign settlements in the 1930s. George was managing one of the world's most automated systems, one that handled an average of half a million calls a day.

In late 1949, a few weeks after the Communists had come to power, Virginia accompanied two girlfriends to a palm reader. The trio squeezed into the living room of a cramped longtang apartment and sat at a small table opposite a slender woman whose pallid complexion reminded Virginia of a wax mannequin. One by one they held their hands out to let the fortune-teller scrutinize their palms.

The first friend, one of a preacher's many children, asked if she would have money. "You will have a good, long life—uneventful and stable—and you will be well taken care of." This friend is still thriving in her nineties, and at latest count has sixteen great-grandchildren.

The second friend's husband, a Hawaii-born engineer, had been imprisoned by the Communists for his Nationalist affiliations. She was dancing hula at nightclubs to make ends meet. Her reading was encouraging too: "You are going through difficult times, but soon you'll leave China and your life will change for the better." Sure enough, her circumstances did improve dramatically after she immigrated to America several months later.

Virginia, the most skeptical of the three friends, was last. The palm reader began, as she had with the others, by taking a visual scan of Virginia's upturned palm. Then she pulled the hand closer, using her thumb to compress small fleshy areas to expose hidden creases. As the women patiently waited, the fortune-teller suddenly released Virginia's hand.

"I'm tired," the palmist said, rising unsteadily from her seat. "No more readings today. The first two ladies may put your payments on the table. Then, all of you please leave."

As the women emerged from the longtang, Virginia laughed off the awkward episode, dismissing the embarrassed glances of her friends.

"Who needs this superstitious stuff, anyway?" she said. "If things are good, why tempt fate? If they're bad, I'd rather not know."

During the first stages of their leadership, in 1949 through 1950 the Communist party's policies focused on ridding cities of wartime infla-tion, restoring order and rehabilitating the economy. While Mao Zedong enjoyed a strong base of peasant support in the countryside, hundreds of thousands of Kuomintang supporters and businessmen had fled overseas. In the cities, there were as many skeptics as there were intellectuals who viewed the Communists as reformers.

By 1951, the Communists' revolutionary agenda reached Shanghai as Mao launched a series of political campaigns to suppress capitalists and counterrevolutionaries. The "Three Antis" targeted corruption, waste and bureaucracy; the "Five Antis" aimed to eradicate bribery, theft of state property, tax evasion, cheating on government contracts and stealing state economic information.

The stated objective of the "Anti" campaigns was to root out corruption and waste, but they also served as tools for removing political opponents.

Despite the uncertainties, George and Virginia chose to stay on in Shanghai. Fueled by optimism and the invincibility of youth, the newlyweds were more naïve than idealistic about their prospects under Communism. At first, their lifestyle changed little. Indeed, the new authorities did their best to charm George. With the departure of his American boss, they needed him to keep the telephone company running.

The goodwill George had enjoyed lasted a year—just long enough for him to train a team of new Communist administrators. Overnight, the men who had begun as George's Communist liaisons turned into his minders.

The changes upended George's value system at its core. All the things that used to be worthy of admiration—studying to improve one-self, working hard to build an enterprise, basing rewards on merit—were now vilified. As the months passed, George's easygoing confidence could not mask his anguish. The Communists took over all the US-owned infrastructure organizations in Shanghai, the telephone company among them, and removed George from his position.

It was now out of the question for George and Virginia to leave China. Migrating would have required government permission, which most certainly would not have been granted. Even though the Communists had stripped George of his authority, they still wanted his expertise.

In the early 1950s thousands of zealous revolutionaries fanned out across the city to extract "confessions" from capitalists on charges of bribery and tax evasion. The once unabashedly capitalist telephone company was an obvious target. One of their first acts was to confiscate the Mediterranean-style home on Avenue Joffre that Virginia had decorated so tastefully. The young couple was forced to seek refuge in Diedie's home, the house that Virginia had been so desperate to escape. Unbelievably, she was back in the tingzijian where she and I had grown up.

The Communist cadres' denunciation of George and his managers started with harassment and humiliation, and culminated with four department heads, his direct reports, leaping to their deaths from the roof of the company headquarters. They were among an estimated two hundred thousand suicides resulting from the Three Antis.

My sister and her husband lived together in the tingzijian for only a few months, before George died of a heart attack in the middle of the night, at the age of thirty-three.

Rumors swirled that George had committed suicide. Fearing his son-in-law's untimely death might stigmatize and attract unwanted attention to the household, Diedie urged Virginia to move out as soon as possible. My oldest sister, a widow at twenty-four, saw his directive as yet another abandonment and never forgave him.

With George gone, Virginia served no purpose for the Communists. In 1952 she was permitted to leave for Hong Kong, never to return to Shanghai.

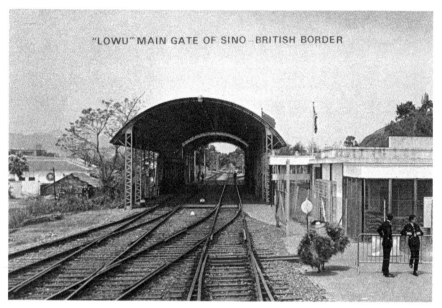

The Lowu border between China and the British colony of Hong Kong in the 1950s.

CHAPTER 20

NO TURNING BACK

THE RAIN WAS FALLING SOFTLY when I left Shanghai that morning in March 1950. I stood at the curb for several minutes after the pedicab dropped me at the North Railway Station, bracing myself for the crowd. A crush of people swarmed the terminal entrance, loaded down with wooden trunks, leather suitcases and grubby cloth bundles that seemed to contain all their worldly goods. I was just about the only one traveling lightly, with the small pink valise that I'd carefully packed with my prettiest summer qipao, anticipating three weeks of dances and parties while visiting Muma in Hong Kong.

Someone's hand on my shoulder made me flinch. I was relieved to see it was Ah Si. When I'd left the house earlier, the cook said our major-domo had already gone out on an errand, and I was sorry to have missed him.

"Just wanted to make sure you get off to Hong Kong all right, Third Daughter," Ah Si now said to me. In one smooth movement, he opened an umbrella over my head and picked up the suitcase. "All right, let's find Duan Ayi and get you both to the train, shall we?"

Duan Ayi was Muma's close friend and mahjong partner. Her daughter, Xiaoyu, whose English name was Diane, had been my St. Mary's schoolmate and had transferred to Maryknoll Convent School in Hong Kong. Duan Ayi was journeying there to attend Diane's graduation and had agreed to accompany me on the train.

We found Duan Ayi waiting in line at the ticket booths. She was slim and attractive, her hair pulled back in a neat chignon that accentuated her high cheekbones. "Ah, Third Daughter, you've made it at last," she said, her gaze resting on my pink valise. "Let's get a move on—I've been queuing for more than an hour already. We need to get our rail car sorted out. Wait here with Ah Si, please."

She spoke in a brittle staccato, eyes darting in all directions. I wasn't sure what was making her nervous. As if reading my mind, Ah Si said under his breath, "Duan Ayi has good reason not to linger. Now that you're traveling far from home, it's time for you to become a bit more aware of things." I looked at him searchingly, observing the furrows in his forehead. "Duan Ayi's husband was killed right in this station before Xiaoyu was born. His name was Tang Yulu—that's why your friend is called 'Small Yu' in his memory."

Ah Si explained that Tang had been secretary to China's minister of finance, T. V. Soong. A political enemy had ordered Soong's assassination. One day, Soong and Tang were disembarking from a train, and both men were wearing white linen suits and white panama hats. Xiaoyu's father got off the train first and was shot and killed in a case of mistaken identity.

"Don't worry, Third Daughter, just keep your eyes open. It's a dangerous world, but you'll be safe in Hong Kong." He thrust a white envelope in my hand. "Your father sent me to collect this for you from his friend—the taipan Mr. John Keswick. He's been your Diedie's friend for many years."

Ah Si tilted his head. "He's the most important foreigner in Shanghai—one of the few who's stayed behind since the Communists took over. Diedie says to show this to the officers at the border if you have any trouble."

Duan Ayi managed to secure the last sleeping car. Although it was comfortable, I slept fitfully during the overnight journey. I fingered the envelope that Ah Si had given to me, perplexed by his comment about my possibly having trouble in Hong Kong. What could he have meant? I tried to reassure myself that Diedie would never knowingly send me into danger.

I rose before dawn as the train rumbled southward past rice paddies and barren plains. Whatever exciting stories I'd heard about Hong Kong, the city's outskirts were bleak.

The train shuddered to a stop at the Lowu border zone. It was a blisteringly hot day. Through the dust-caked windows, I watched steam rise from the platform alongside a steel-truss bridge. Many passengers, restless after their uncomfortable night on hard seats, wasted no time detraining. Duan Ayi and I joined the end of a long line that snaked along the barbed-wire barrier separating China from the British crown colony where we were headed.

The sun's rays scorched my bare arms as we inched forward. People in the queue complained about how long it was taking the British immigration officials to interview everyone. A family ahead of us quietly rehearsed what they would say to the officers. Several people were escorted back to the train after being interviewed. That confused and worried me: was Hong Kong not an open border?

There was no shelter anywhere. Rivulets of perspiration made my silk qipao stick to my back. "Third Daughter, are you all right?" Duan Ayi's voice sounded as if it were coming from far away, and without warning my legs buckled. Duan Ayi reached around my waist to support me. "Your face is white as a ghost—let me call for someone."

Duan Ayi waved to a British policeman in starched beige shorts and knee socks. "Officer, officer, please help us." Even in my daze I was surprised by her words; I'd never heard her speak English before. When the officer didn't reply, Duan Ayi waltzed right up and handed him the letter that Ah Si had delivered to us. The policeman scrutinized it slowly, from the Jardine Matheson crest down to the neat signature.

"John Keswick," he said, his eyes wide as they shifted from Duan Ayi to me. "The taipan. The man bloody owns half of Hong Kong!" he mumbled, before waving over a Chinese policeman. "Ah Fung, get cracking, will you? Help these women to a taxi."

In Muma's apartment the next morning, I felt a twinge of nostalgia watching my mother apply her makeup with practiced precision. Scattered across her dresser were all the things I remembered—flower dew water, Pond's cream in a shiny white jar and her lacquered jewelry chest.

We hadn't seen each other since she'd left Shanghai two years earlier. I yearned to hug her like I'd seen families do in American movies, but Chinese didn't do that sort of thing. Instead, she gave me a long, appraising look with her dark-tea eyes, nodded and said, "Third Daughter, you look well despite yesterday's long trip—pretty as always. You've changed your hair, though. I like it very much."

We chatted for a while about my siblings and various old friends, hers and mine, who had moved to Hong Kong, and discussed shops and restaurants that she wanted me to try. I told her about my first term at St. John's but didn't dwell on it, since she'd never been much interested in academics.

Though we never spoke about money, Muma seemed to have settled into her new life. Later I came to understand that she'd received no income from Diedie after moving to Hong Kong and had learned to live on a tight budget.

Giving a sidelong glance to my little suitcase in the hallway, Muma asked, "Third Daughter, you don't really believe you're going back to Shanghai, do you?" Her tone was unexpectedly serious.

"I only have three weeks' vacation, and I need to get back for the spring term at St. John's."

"You really don't understand, do you? It's not safe anymore for people like us in Shanghai. Everyone who can is leaving."

That much was true: as many as half of my friends had left Shanghai in the last year. "But Diedie is expecting me back. And Virginia and George aren't leaving. Oh, Muma, you should see their apartment in the French Concession!"

My mother's expression hardened, and her next words sliced the air like daggers: "Third Daughter, listen to me. There's been a war. The Communists won. You can't go back to Shanghai. Your father wrote to me for the first time in ten years, insisting I make sure you stay here."

I thought back to Qinpo frozen at her window and Diedie's somber expression as we said goodbye. It suddenly dawned on me that I might never see them again and that I hadn't said a proper goodbye to anyone, not to them, or to my siblings or friends.

"If it's so terrible, what about Diedie and the rest of the family?" I asked. "Why don't they move here too?"

"Forgive me for saying this about your father: Diedie mishandled things. I can't say if it was the war, bad luck or poor decisions—somehow he's managed to run out of cash." Muma tugged the loose strand of her chignon. "First was the ridiculous sum the court ordered Yeye to pay that fifth concubine of his. Then after they paid Yeye's ransom, there was hardly any cash left."

Muma's voice was bitter. "Your father and Yeye still own the Huizhong Hotel, some buildings on Fourth Road and various stocks and bonds. A lot of good it will do them—everyone who could have bought them has long since left Shanghai. Basically it's all worthless."

I had left Shanghai gleefully expecting to have Muma to myself for the first time in my life. But this wasn't the mother I'd missed, with her embroidered qipao and carefree disposition. In all the years since she'd left our home, I had only considered my own loneliness. It hadn't occurred to me that behind the flurry of her social comings and goings, Muma might also have felt alone and vulnerable. Facing her now, I noticed something I'd not seen before—my mother's thinning hair and the crow's-feet crinkling the corners of her eyes.

Muma looked squarely at me. "Third Daughter, if the rest of the family came to Hong Kong, who on earth would support them? Of course, I want a better future for your brother and sisters. But what can I do? They're still in school, and Diedie would never let them leave him."

Mother sank into a plush armchair, her head cast down. In a minute, she'd banished her sadness, and her voice and demeanor were light and cheerful again. She rose and clasped my hands in hers. "Third Daughter, you are the lucky one. You're the perfect age to adapt—make a new life for yourself. We'll have to wait and see what happens to the others.

"You'll find that in some ways Hong Kong is even more modern than Shanghai. Many of my friends' daughters are working in offices. It's perfectly respectable. Your English is so good—you won't have any problems."

Muma was right. It dawned on me that I was eighteen when I left Shanghai for a new life in Hong Kong, the same age Diedie had been when he left Changshu for a new life in Shanghai. Although I still thought of Shanghai often, especially of Diedie, Qinpo and my siblings, I quickly felt at home in Hong Kong. Its natural beauty and urban amusements seduced me from day one: the verdant hills that rolled down to white

Hong Kong scenes: the harbor with Star Ferry in the foreground;
neon signs light up Peking Road, ca. 1970s.

sand beaches, Sunday tea dances at the Repulse Bay Hotel, catching a
walla-walla motorboat to cross the harbor after late-night parties at the
Ritz, when the Star Ferry had closed for the night. I grew fond of Hong

Kong's many delicacies: dim sum at Gloucester Restaurant, beef stroganoff at Jimmy's Kitchen and satay at the Peak Café.

Living in Hong Kong in those years was inexpensive. I easily found a job before I ran through the spending money that Diedie had given me. Despite my cosseted childhood, I found work rewarding. A foreign shipping company hired me on the spot when I was able to converse with the Australian interviewer in English.

In Shanghai, besides our American teachers, I had mixed only with locals; here, my new friends came from England, Germany, Holland and Portugal. My schooling had prepared me well to speak English. A bigger challenge was Cantonese, the dialect of southern China. I was accustomed to the guttural, rolling tones of Mandarin spoken by my godparents, but it took years to understand the clacky, nasal singsong of Cantonese.

Happily, many St. John's alumni and my ANEYRETA chums had also moved to Hong Kong, and we met regularly for mahjong and nights out on the town. Even a few of my favorite Filipino jazz bands and our jeweler and qipao tailors had arrived before me.

Me outside the Peak Café, Hong Kong, 1953.

Mahjong in Hong Kong with three ANEYRETA friends. Left
to right: Me, Margaret, Mamie and Charlotte.

Hong Kong's can-do attitude was in part spawned by the huge influx
of émigrés from Shanghai. Some brought capital and equipment to the
city, and developed substantial shipping, textile and industrial enterprises. Many were like me, starting from scratch. The flow of Chinese
immigrants to Hong Kong reached a crescendo after the Communists
rose to power in 1949, tripling its population in ten years. At the time
I arrived in Hong Kong in spring 1950, until the British colony finally
began to enforce border controls in June 1951, an estimated one hundred
thousand Chinese were streaming in every month.

Like the foreign settlement in Shanghai, Hong Kong had been ceded
to the British in the nineteenth century, after China's defeat in the First
Opium War. With increasing restrictions on the mainland, Hong Kong
quickly replaced Shanghai as a capital of capitalism, a role for which

it was well suited, with its blend of British discipline and Chinese industriousness.

It wasn't a conscious decision, but I adopted the view that to survive in a world of change, I had to face forward rather than dwell on the past. Besides, I was young and enjoying my new independence. When, in 1952, Virginia arrived in Hong Kong a young widow after the Communists' Three Antis campaign, I understood there was truly no turning back.

The cover of an elementary-school textbook shows child Red Guards clutching copies of the *Little Red Book*.

CHAPTER 21

BROKEN DREAMS

THE SHANGHAI WHERE OUR THREE younger siblings grew up was a far different place from the one Virginia and I had known. With the end of a Western presence in 1949, our brother and sisters did not speak much English and didn't even have English names.

Our fifth sister, Shuquan,[21] was thirteen when the Communists rose to power. She followed in our footsteps and enrolled in McTyeire, which had become a public school and been renamed No. 3 Girls Middle School. The only athlete in our family, she played basketball for the People's Liberation Army until a back injury sidelined her. She was accepted at the prestigious Beijing University and remained in the capital after graduation.

As a toddler, our youngest sister, Shujue,[22] had had the sweet nature and fair skin of a white summer peach. She had been only two years old when our parents divorced, and she followed me around everywhere. Shuquan was fortunate to be able to arrange for Shujue to join her at Beijing University. They both became educators—Shuquan a high-school teacher in Beijing, and Shujue a university professor in Tianjin—and both later married teachers.

---

21. Shuquan: pronounced *Shoo-chwen*.
22. Shujue: pronounced *Shoo-joo-weh*.

Shujue and Shuquan as students at Beijing University in the 1950s.

Mao Zedong initiated the Great Leap Forward in 1958, when my sisters were in their early twenties. The movement aimed to meet the challenges of the country's vast population by collectivizing farms and developing labor-intensive industries. However, agricultural disruption and flawed implementation, compounded by a series of natural disasters, led not only to its failure but also to the worst famine in history—an estimated twenty million deaths by starvation over three years.

Surrounded by deprivation, Shuquan and her husband managed to eke out a living as teachers at state-run schools in the nation's capital. For them, a far greater threat than hunger was the chaos and terror unleashed by Mao's Cultural Revolution in 1966.

Shuquan had become familiar with the scenes of madness that had begun over the summer: mallet-wielding Red Guards smashing cultural treasures, lighting up books in bonfires and parading intellectuals to the choleric jeering of children. It was distressing enough when the victims were strangers—and terrifying and mind numbing when Shuquan knew them.

On one particularly frigid morning, she was walking past the massive portrait of Chairman Mao that had recently been hung above the entrance to the Forbidden City, the former residence of twenty-four emperors inside the ancient walled city of Beijing. Months earlier, at the adjacent Tiananmen Square, Mao had led a rally of a million frenzied youths brandishing copies of his *Little Red Book*. Since then, Shuquan had gotten into the habit of walking on the far side of the wide boulevard, even if she had to dodge bicycles outside the massive square; she felt safer being a bit farther away from the chairman's watchful eyes.

Few people were out, no doubt because of recent Red Guard disturbances and the subzero temperature. In the distance, however, she saw that the biting cold had not deterred the teenage tormenters of a kneeling figure near the center of the square. The man was disturbingly still, as if his shins had become frozen to the pavement.

As she drew closer, Shuquan realized with a shock that it was her former coworker, a history teacher who had transferred to another school the previous year. He had always been on the chubby side, with a wide-eyed expression and a carefree swagger. The defeated man before her was almost unrecognizable. Snow crystals were melting on his matted hair and dripping down his sunken cheeks; a damp placard covered his chest, blaring his crimes in smudged, angry characters.

One of the students poked the teacher with a stick and shouted, "Look how this comrade is staring at you—she finds you pathetic."

All eyes turned to Shuquan.

She suppressed an impulse to run, having learned that people who drew attention to themselves, even unintentionally, often got into trouble. By expressing the smallest objection to the abusers or kindness to the victim in such a situation, one risked being tarred with the same brush. Shuquan thought fleetingly of the irony of such cruelty happening in Tiananmen, the gate named "Heavenly Peace" by a Qing emperor. As horrible as the pointless persecutions were, even worse was the profound sense of helplessness that she was left with. At times she felt it would destroy her soul.

Taking long breaths and clutching the collar of her thin coat, Shuquan willed herself to fix her gaze straight ahead and walk unhurriedly back to the teachers' dormitory.

In the afternoon Shuquan finally relaxed a little with the arrival of her friend, a Shanghai native who had grown up near our home. They met once a month, combining their rations to make dumplings. Though between them they had only a few small cubes of gristly pork, the women savored their dinner of wonton soup. Shuquan was accustomed to using cabbage—the only available winter vegetable—to stretch their meager supplies.

They ate in the grungy communal kitchen, standing in a dark corner far from the single suspended lightbulb. Neighbors came and went, preparing their meals while the two friends chatted quietly. The young women reminisced about old times and mutual friends; it was a rare chance for Shuquan to let her guard down. Though she was barely thirty, my sister's sweet upturned nose and girlish features were marred by many fine lines that creased her forehead.

Over their small tray of dumplings, her companion tucked something into the pocket of Shuquan's Mao jacket and whispered in her ear: "Shuquan, my brother brought this back from Shanghai this morning." The way in which she patted Shuquan's arm, ever so kindly, made my sister's head prickle with anxiety. "Look at it when you're alone. He saw the photo a few days ago in *Jiefang Ribao* [*Liberation Daily*] and smuggled it to Beijing."

Back in her rooms, my sister's apprehension grew as she unfolded the newspaper and peered at the grainy image. The photo showed a frenzied crowd of Red Guards, some no older than nine or ten, shouting at a man kneeling in their midst. He wore a tall white dunce cap (*daigao-mao*), and his body was contorted in an awkward *z* formed by bending his torso forward in the opposite direction of his legs. The man had a familiar uprightness despite his demeaning pose. Shuquan's blood ran cold as she read the sign hanging like a heavy yoke from his neck: *Sun Bosheng, evil landlord, collects millions in rent.*

Our father had become the latest casualty of the cult of Mao Zedong.

The Red Guards had dragged Diedie's zitan table, the one with the exquisite cloud carvings, onto the street and shoved him on top of it. How perverse that he should be prostrate like this—at seventy-two years of age, an object of ridicule to a sadistic mob—when in the past he had kowtowed only to honor his ancestors.

Shuquan's heart shattered at the idea of Diedie being turned into a caricature, as if he could possibly be an enemy of the state. Was he in prison now, injured, or dead? With no telephones and only sporadic mail service subject to censorship, she had no way of finding out for weeks, possibly months.

The ten-year Cultural Revolution was Mao's move to retain power after the disastrous Great Leap Forward, his call to arms for millions of young Red Guards, from elementary-school to university age, to wage violent class struggle in the name of revolutionary purity. Millions were so indoctrinated by the chairman's speeches and writings in his Little Red Book *that they committed the more than two hundred quotations to memory. The chairman's strategy to purge society of the "Four Olds"—"old customs, old culture, old habits and old ideas"—transformed China's youth into instruments of mass terror. By alleging that bourgeois elements had infiltrated the government and society at large, Mao outfoxed his political rivals and unleashed a period of lawlessness.*

Red Guards marched across China in a crazed campaign to eradicate the Four Olds. Classical books and art were destroyed, museums ransacked, temples and shrines desecrated and streets renamed with new revolutionary designations. Even the greenswards of parks and backyards were branded as "revisionist poisonous grass" and torn out.

Attacks on culture soon became attacks on people. Intellectuals and capitalists bore the brunt of the wrath. Mao took it upon himself to categorize nine kinds of enemies to be targeted for "class struggle." As landowners, our family was ranked at the top of the list, viler even than traitors and counterrevolutionaries:

> *Landlords*
> *Rich farmers*
> *Counterrevolutionaries*
> *Bad elements*
> *Rightists*
> *Traitors*
> *Foreign agents*
> *Capitalist sympathizers*
> *Intellectuals*

Millions were targeted in the anarchy that gripped China. No one was immune: partisan struggles gripped the military and Communist Party leadership itself, resulting in a mass purge of senior officials and the growth of Mao's personality cult to godlike proportions.

Mao's rhetoric was open to interpretation, enabling revolutionary factions and individuals to use his words to avenge grudges and to harass, imprison and execute alleged "enemies of the people." Many victims confessed to invented wrongdoings to halt their torture.

While she fretted for our father, Shuquan felt fortunate that her own class background had eluded attention. As the daughter of a landlord-businessman-scholar, she was conscious of how easily she could become a target of revolutionary zealots. And as a teacher herself, she fell into the "stinking ninth" category of intellectuals.

It was probably a combination of fate and her unassuming disposition that saved Shuquan. In contrast to Muma, Virginia and me—who set great store by our appearance—Shuquan came of age in Maoist China and understood that survival depended on fitting in and going unnoticed.

At the school where Shuquan taught, Red Guards branded the headmistress a public enemy by shaving her hair in a *yinyang* pattern—one half shaved and the other half intact. When the Red Guards stormed into Shuquan's classroom the next day, her eleventh-grade students formed a protective circle around her, defying the guards and shielding her from a similar fate.

Yet other perils and adversities sprang from the revolutionary upheaval. The economy was in shambles. Crowded living quarters and a dearth of childcare forced Shuquan and her husband to send their infants to be raised by relatives. Their younger daughter went to live with Diedie at our family home in Shanghai. Their son, who was being cared for by the parents of Shuquan's husband in Suzhou, watched in horror as Red Guards beat his elderly grandparents to death.

It would be several anxious months before Shuquan received word of Diedie's fate.

For almost twenty years, after Yeye's kidnap ransom and Fifth Popo's settlement depleted virtually all the family's cash, Diedie relied entirely on his rental income. In 1956, the government seized all privately held property and funds. They estimated the value of my father's remaining assets—the Huizhong Hotel, Fourth Avenue properties and the Zhenning Road house—at US$1.3 million (equivalent to US$12 million today), an amount greatly deflated from its earlier appraisals. Based on this, they determined a monthly allowance of US$530, on which my father would have to support himself and fourteen family members and servants. Seven of the household staff had chosen to remain in our home, which had been a haven for them as much as it had been for us. They had worked hard for our family in prosperous times; Diedie still felt responsible for them even when he could no longer afford it.

At the onset of the Cultural Revolution in 1966, the authorities ordered Diedie to move into the dining room—the room that had once housed etched crystal and silver candelabra—so some twenty strangers could live in the rest of the house. The last of our loyal household staff were forced to leave at this time. Ah Si, our loyal majordomo, had dedicated forty-two years to managing our household.

The government Cultural Relics Department confiscated Diedie's beloved art collection, which he had hidden away for fear of recrimination.

As Red Guard marches and attacks escalated across the country, someone reported to the authorities that our family had once had warehouses full of gold taels, and, since we no longer owned the buildings, a ton of gold must be concealed inside the walls of our house. A dozen Red Guards took turns drilling and pounding at the walls for days—of course to no avail.

Diedie's last debasement came at the hands of a seven-year-old boy whose family occupied my former bedroom in the tingzijian. The child slipped into Father's room, where he found a sheet of paper that Diedie had folded multiple times and hidden in a bamboo rice warmer. The boy brought the paper to his teenage Red Guard brother.

The incriminating paper was a letter that Diedie had written as an elegy of sorts to his former life. He had addressed it to no one in particular—indeed, he had never intended for anyone to read it. After providing shelter to four generations, from his kidnapped father to his infant granddaughter, Diedie himself in his final years had nowhere to escape, no one to turn to. The letter had been his way of threshing out his sense of powerlessness and confusion over a world turned upside down.

It was all the Red Guards needed to initiate a search of our home; within minutes they found several objects from Diedie's art collection that he hadn't had the heart to turn in or destroy, and which he had cached in various hiding places.

And so it was that a week later, Shuquan held a wrinkled newspaper under a dim fluorescent light, her legs collapsing beneath her when she realized the grainy photo of a contorted man in a dunce hat depicted our father.

In consideration of Diedie's advanced age and the overflowing prisons, the Red Guards incarcerated him at the Gonganju, the Public Security Bureau. Each day, he read the newspapers aloud to his illiterate wardens and, deprived of food, gradually starved. After several months, Diedie was skin and bones. Anxious that he might die under their watch, the wardens sent him home, placed him under house arrest and assigned him the job of sweeping the lane. "Consider yourself lucky we're not making you clean public toilets" were their parting words.

By then, Diedie's imprisonment and prior hardships had taken their toll. He suffered a stroke a few months later and was bedridden for two years until his death in 1969 at the age of seventy-five.

I received a terse telegram from Shuquan informing me of Father's passing. At the height of Maoist xenophobia, no one was allowed in or out of the country, so it was out of the question for me to come from Hong Kong to attend his funeral. And, after preparing all through his childhood to honor our elders, even Shufen, our family's new patriarch, couldn't attend Diedie's memorial services. Our brother was no longer living in Shanghai, nor was he a free man.

Shufen had become a target almost immediately after the Communists assumed leadership. Although he'd earned a law degree, his work unit would not permit him to practice law. He was instead assigned to teach middle-school government studies—an ironic punishment for our non-political brother. For the duration of the Great Leap Forward, he dug bomb shelters and stoked backyard steel furnaces in the countryside.

During the Cultural Revolution, Shufen's defiance resulted in count-less interrogations, torture sessions and solitary confinement in a cage for months at a time. As a boy, he had instigated fistfights nearly every day; as a man, he had no patience for the provocations of prepubescent Red Guards. While our younger sisters lay low through the worst of the mayhem, Shufen fought back, refusing to parrot Maoist slogans and pen the inane self-criticisms that had become part of daily life. Three times he survived being beaten to unconsciousness. As the decade of madness drew to a close, Shufen's natural grace morphed into a fierce defiance that shone forth from dark, feral eyes.

By some estimates, forced labor, violence and starvation claimed the lives of forty million people during Mao Zedong's regime. China's "Ten Years of Chaos" ended with Mao's death in 1976. When Shufen and thousands of others were finally allowed to return to Shanghai, hous-ing and jobs were hard to come by. Eventually the schools, which had been closed during the Cultural Revolution, reopened and Shufen began teaching again. But there was something else that he wanted passionately to pursue.

Shufen in the late 1970s.

During Chinese New Year of 1978, two years after his return from the countryside, my brother took the first vacation of his life and visited Suzhou—the fabled city of splendid silk and idyllic gardens. By day he rode a bicycle along the lakefront; in the evenings, in lieu of dinner he nibbled on watermelon seeds and peanuts and mingled with the locals. He listened to their real-life stories and the sort of tales that Qinpo had loved; indeed, Suzhou was the fountainhead of shuoshu storytelling.

And this is where the education that Diedie had provided us, and all the books we had read as children, became Shufen's salvation.

Back in Shanghai, every evening after work, Shufen wrote and wrote and wrote: 320,000 handwritten characters, to be exact. Within three months he completed his first full-length novel, *Springtime in Suzhou*, an adventure set during the Sino-Japanese War about an army doctor on a mission to buy medicine in Suzhou who, aided by guerilla fighters, confronts Japanese militia, mercenaries and collaborators.

The political climate in China was gradually liberalizing, as President Richard Nixon's visit six years earlier had ended twenty-five years of separation between the two nations. When it was published in October 1978, *Springtime* was one of the first books to break away from the customary propagandistic style. It became one of the bestselling works of fiction in post-Mao China, selling more than half a million copies in two years. Each copy earned Shufen the princely sum of 95 *fen*, the equivalent of 15 US cents.

Shufen not only survived but emerged from exile and persecution with vigor and creativity. He found a readership starved for entertainment after more than two decades of Communist literary fare. The book's overnight success changed Shufen's life: he quit his teaching job and became a full-time writer. *Springtime* was serialized on many radio stations and adapted into comic books, shuoshu and a film. It was on the recommended reading list of the Shanghai Education Department for many years.

Over the course of more than two decades, Shufen went on to publish fifty-five fiction and nonfiction books, most of which were set in the Shanghai of our youth. And although he wrote a trilogy relating the stories of our father, grandfather and great-grandfather, he never penned his own memoir, preferring nostalgia for what had once been over the bitter times he had had to endure.

By the 1980s Shufen was nationally renowned. He traveled frequently to domestic and international writers' conferences and took on leadership roles in Shanghai literary associations. His life had come full circle, from being denounced as a class enemy for his family background, to finally being able to savor his boyhood memories—and even, as he described it, benefiting from the remnants of our family glory. His rehabilitation coincided with a wave of nostalgia for Old Shanghai. He acquired a reputation as "Laokela," Shanghai's last "old-time aristocrat," known for his mane of white hair and his sensitive, observant nature.

Shufen was philosophical about our family's fate under the Communists. "When a tree gets big, it invites the wind,"[23] he liked to say—a rich or famous person attracts criticism. He also believed that wealth did not surpass three generations[24]—the first generation made it; the second generation, not fully appreciating their forebears' hard work, started to squander it; and the third generation, spoiled and apathetic,

---

23. *Shuda zhaofeng.*
24. *Fu buguo sandai.*

lost it. In fact, under Communism, everyone we knew who remained in Shanghai lost everything.

Never without a cigarette, Shufen died of lung cancer in 2005. He was seventy-three. Despite her intensive efforts throughout his childhood, Qinpo's consuming fear came to fruition: Shufen, her only grandson, didn't marry and had no children. There are no male Suns to pay respects to our ancestors.

Though his failure in this paramount duty had burdened him, Shufen found a way to preserve our family's honor. He donated first editions of all his books and several handwritten manuscripts to the permanent collection of the municipal hall in Changshu, our ancestral seat. Since our family's three generations of allotted prosperity had expired, surely Qinpo, who had died in 1958, would have accepted this as a legacy worthy not only of our family but also of a place lost in time.

GARDEN PARTY

樹瑩孫女　州拙歐園寄贈　丙申四月初三日攝於蘇　潤禪老人八十歲小影

Qinpo in 1958, with a tribute in Diedie's precise hand:
"Elderly Runchan, a candid photograph on her eightieth birthday
Third day of the fourth month 1958, the Humble Administrator's Garden, Suzhou
Mailed as a gift to her granddaughter Shuying."

Zhuozheng Yuan, the Humble Administrator's Garden, is a superb classical garden in Suzhou that dates back to the twelfth century. Its twelve acres comprise nearly as much water as land—large lakes, slow-moving brooks and intimate reflecting ponds. Along meandering paths and under sheltering pavilions, the scenery unfurls like a painted scroll, by turns imparting a sense of solitude and expansiveness. Here, in monumental scale, are the limestone rocks that scholars treasured, rising from the land like weathered sentinels.

In my eightieth year, I returned to China with my children and grandchildren. In Suzhou we visited Zhuozheng Yuan; Diedie had accompanied Qinpo to this very garden to celebrate her eightieth birthday in spring 1958.

In the Hall of Distant Fragrance, I pulled out an old photo to show my grandsons—Qinpo's birthday portrait, taken among bonsai in this same spot. She was the picture of calm and good health; it is hard to believe that she would pass away in her sleep only a few months later. I am glad she did not live to see the turmoil and tragedy of the Cultural Revolution, not to mention the cruel turn of events that befell her son.

The crabapple trees were in full bloom, and yellow forsythia exploded like fireworks against a backdrop of swaying willow branches. The idea of Qinpo spending her last birthday here, enjoying these same blossoms, gave me a feeling of deep serenity. It reminded me of how I'd felt as a child by her side as she slid her delicate fingers along her rosary beads. It was an apt setting in which to introduce her to our family's next generation.

Visiting the Humble Administrator's Garden. Left to right: Qinpo's great-grandsons, my sons, Lloyd and Leslie (first and second from left); Leslie's wife, Ann (fourth from left); and their sons, Alex and Garrett.

Raymond, my future husband, in Nanjing in the 1940s.

CHAPTER 22
SAFE HARBOR

I SPOTTED MY FUTURE HUSBAND on a crowded dance floor at the Savoy in Hong Kong in 1955. He was attractive and broad shouldered in a white linen jacket. It turned out Raymond was a St. John's graduate, eight years my senior, and we had many mutual friends in Hong Kong's Shanghainese community. Unlike my other suitors, he didn't adulate and pamper me, which made him perversely appealing.

His father had risen from poverty to manage textile mills and then, while Raymond was in high school, lost it all in a haze of opium. Raymond struggled to put himself through university. Once, he summoned his courage to invite an attractive girl out for tea, but he was so broke that after circling a pawnshop three times to sell his Parker pen, he had second thoughts and stood her up. How long, he worried, could he date her on the proceeds of a pawned pen?

While living in China, Raymond had many American friends, and at one time he worked as an interpreter for the US military. In the summer of 1949, the Nationalists were in steady retreat, and foreigners were evacuating out of Shanghai. Raymond was sure that once the Communists were in control, he would be in grave danger because of his American affiliations. The problem was he didn't have the funds to buy passage out of Shanghai.

One of his closest friends, John Roderick, a correspondent with the Associated Press news agency, asked Raymond to see him off as he boarded his ship on the Bund. John passed Raymond a crinkled paper package, saying, "I think you can use this." Inside was US$700, the equivalent of several months' salary—a lifeline that enabled Raymond to reach Hong Kong and start anew.

We married at St. Teresa's Church eight months after we met. Raymond's best man, John Roderick, and my maid of honor, Duan Ayi's daughter, Diane, were each connected to our final departures from Shanghai. My tailor, a fellow Shanghai émigré, created my dress from Belgian lace hand-beaded with seed pearls and fitted to my seventeen-inch waist. "Uncle John" later became a godfather to our oldest son, Leslie, and remained a close family friend for six decades before his passing in 2008.

Our wedding at St. Teresa's, 1956. John Roderick was Raymond's best man and Diane Tang was my maid of honor.

At the time of the wedding, I was working in reservations for Cathay Pacific Airways in the Peninsula Hotel. We held our reception in the hotel ballroom; my boss gifted us a round-trip ticket for our honeymoon to Taipei, Tokyo and Osaka. I was twenty-five, and it was my first time on an airplane.

Left: Looking relaxed on my first flight, 1956. *Right:* Honeymooning in Tokyo.

Later, while Raymond established and ran one of Hong Kong's first international advertising agencies, I found a job at the US Information Service (or USIS, the overseas arm of the US Information Agency) in the US Consulate General, where I worked for more than thirty years. Since the Communists allowed virtually no foreign presence in China throughout the 1960s and '70s, the consulate in Hong Kong served as a China-watching hub. The USIS had a reputation for being an American propaganda machine during the Cold War, amid concerns over the spread of Communism. The service's slogan was "Telling America's story to the world."

If my superiors had a political or intelligence agenda, I wasn't in on it. My primary responsibility as a cultural affairs specialist was to coordinate cultural and educational exchanges. The centerpiece was the Fulbright Program, created by the US Congress to provide funding for the best and brightest in academia. In addition to screening scholars' applications for research and teaching grants, I also coordinated a speaking program that enabled me to bring to Hong Kong speakers such as the actor Kirk Douglas; *Twilight Zone* creator Rod Serling; and Buckminster Fuller, the futurist architect who would become famous for his geodesic domes.

Years later, I learned that my US Consulate job had aroused the suspicion of my family's Communist interrogators in Shanghai. "A daughter

With Jidie and Jiniang in Taipei during our honeymoon.
I visited regularly until their passing.

marrying out of your household is like water spilling from a bucket—she has nothing to do with us," Diedie had said, trying to detach the family from me. I fully grasped the necessity of his words and would have been mortified if I'd caused them further hardship.

In the late 1950s, after the Chinese government confiscated Diedie's properties, he did the unthinkable: he asked me for help. I found a grocery in Hong Kong that sent monthly packages to Shanghai. It worried me that he lacked such basics as rice and soy sauce. I regularly mailed funds to him, tiny amounts equivalent to a few US dollars at a time, so as not to draw the attention of the Communist censors.

Censorship was a double-edged sword. As much as it curtailed exchanges of information and affection between me and my family in China, it also spared me the agonizing details of their suffering. Diedie

With Raymond and our children in 1965. Left to right: Lloyd, Claire and Leslie.

expressed how much our family depended on my deliveries, and his deep shame that I was supporting them. I always wrote back to say he should think nothing of it.

It didn't take long for Raymond and me to discover that in many respects we were polar opposites, and we drove each other mad. He was athletic and loved the outdoors; my workouts were confined to the mahjong table. Raymond had a very good heart but was self-admittedly "not a happy-go-lucky man," and told me my greatest virtue was my optimism. Yet nothing held him back from building one of Hong Kong's most successful advertising firms. The bond we shared was our love for and commitment to our children. Leslie was born in 1956, Lloyd in 1959 and Claire in 1962.

Besides motherhood, I was committed to my work as well—which surprised me, as I hadn't been known for my diligence in school. In spring 1968, I participated in a six-week US tour as one of about ten USIS specialists from embassies and consulates as far afield as Germany, India and Tunisia. The last city on the itinerary was Washington, DC, where the highlight was a reception with the senator from New York, Robert F. Kennedy. At forty-two, he had a boyish appeal and was by far the tallest person in the room.

I wore a green silk qipao that day, with a matching lace jacket. As he stooped to shake my hand, he said, "Well, China may not welcome the outside world, but you look like a gift of imperial jade!"

I was greatly saddened to learn of his assassination in Los Angeles two months later, while he was campaigning for the US presidency.

Left: On the steps of the US Consulate General in Hong Kong, where I worked for over thirty years. *Right:* At a reception with Senator Robert F. Kennedy in Washington, DC, spring 1968. I am at the far right.

I had a high regard for my American Foreign Service and local colleagues, and was immensely fulfilled by my work. I continued to share Muma's love of fashion and experimented with the latest trends—Jackie Kennedy–inspired skirts, culottes and wild geometric patterns, topped off with the requisite beehive hairdo. But for special occasions I always came back to my Chinese dresses. And while my Cantonese friends called them cheongsam, I still referred to them as qipao.

In the same way that I was raised, I've always relied on helpers to take care of our children and household. Having live-in servants and a driver made it relatively easy to juggle work with family life. Even if Raymond and I went out for evening engagements, we would first have an early dinner with the kids at home, and we always devoted our weekends to them. I never did outgrow my beitoufeng grumpiness in the mornings, though!

I like to think Raymond and I were complementary halves of a solid whole. As much as we delighted in our active social schedule together, we also had an ongoing détente when it came to indulging our own interests. I played mahjong regularly with my girlfriends, and he was often in the company of his buddies on the tennis court or golf course. To our own astonishment, in retirement we hit on a common passion, karaoke, which we enjoyed with many good friends—singing all the jazz and pop standards that I'd loved playing on my shortwave radio as a girl in Shanghai.

With Raymond in the 1980s.

Raymond fought valiantly to overcome cancer three times, until succumbing in 2012 at the age of eighty-nine. Like most couples, we'd endured our share of challenges and experienced great joy over our fifty-six-year union. We managed to combine his unerring sense of responsibility and moderation with my love of fun, in the process raising three wonderful children and prospering. It was a fine marriage, and it's been an excellent life by any measure.

At first I missed Raymond a great deal. It took time to adjust to being alone. In due course Claire was telling friends that in my eighties I'd

Karaoke at home.

taken on a new job, eight hours a day, five days a week. I had never had enough time for it when I was younger, and now I did. Of course, it was playing mahjong.

I have lived in the Repulse Bay area of Hong Kong for more than fifty years.

Destiny left Diedie's dreams broken; it blessed me with freedom and opportunity. As for my younger siblings, under Communism, their survival required an ability to *chiku*—"eat bitterness."

Our youngest sister, Shujue, lived her entire life in China. If there is such a thing as a personality somewhat suited for Communism, it might have been Shujue's. She was the timidest of us siblings and had always embraced rules and discipline. Although both she and her husband were acclaimed chemistry professors, they survived on salaries of about 60 renminbi, less than US$10, a month. Other than me, she was our only sibling to be blessed with a long marriage. Her husband was heartbroken when she died unexpectedly at sixty-three, after unsuccessful treatment for a medical condition. She was the first of my siblings to pass away.

I took great comfort knowing that our younger sisters had had each other for support during their difficult early years, and that even with their challenges they raised children who are all now leading productive lives.

Virginia's experiences proved more peripatetic and less stable than mine. That was unexpected, as she'd always been more driven and systematic, and she was a far better hostess and homemaker than I was.

Left: André Dubonnet onboard *Christina O*, Greek billionaire Aristotle Onassis's superyacht, in 1955. *Right:* Virginia in Paris in the 1960s.

Through the 1950s and '60s, my oldest sister's sojourns took her ever farther from our birthplace. After a short stay in Hong Kong, she moved to Taipei, then lived in Beverly Hills during a brief marriage, and went on to reside in New York, Geneva, Paris and Marrakech.

While working as a tour guide at the United Nations in New York City, she met the larger-than-life André Dubonnet, who was thirty years her senior, only three years younger than our father. Heir to the Dubonnet liquor empire, he was a member of the Paris beau monde, a former World War I flying ace, an Olympic bobsledder and a racecar inventor.

He was married four times—never to Virginia. They probably would have gone their separate ways sooner had Virginia not given birth to his only son, Anicet. The proud father installed her and the baby in a Paris apartment with a view of the Eiffel Tower, opposite the Hotel Plaza Athénée on fashionable Avenue Montaigne. But the relationship with Dubonnet came to an end, and Virginia won custody of Anicet when he was seven. As an only child, he was close to his mother and grew up to be an empathetic young man with a good deal of insight. In 2015, Anicet wrote his cousin Claire:

> My father had a great time flying planes, shooting, racing cars and boats, and trying to sleep with women. He had the means and vocation to do these things. He was a good father and friend, and had good friends.
>
> Things went wrong because he would not marry my mother. He was old fashioned, and he did not want a Chinese wife. (Growing up in Paris, I knew only one other Eurasian kid.) Instead, he married his long-suffering American socialite girl-friend to help him fight for custody of me.
>
> I have tremendous empathy for my mother because she had a tough life—but in a way she reproduced exactly what she had wanted to avoid. Her relationship with men was dictated by what she had heard from her parents, and she reproduced the same thing. When a child is caught in the middle of two people who want to hurt the other person, the child becomes a tool.
>
> My mother has been lonely since I went to boarding school. It made me suffer knowing that she was never happy.

To Muma's and my delight, Virginia moved permanently to Hong Kong with Anicet in 1970. Her relationship with André Dubonnet thawed when their son returned to Europe to attend boarding school in Switzerland. Having run afoul of the French tax authorities, Dubonnet had sold his Paris home to the king of Morocco, who gave him a piece of prime land in Marrakech. Virginia went to Marrakech for a time to assist Dubonnet in developing the property that never got off the ground. When he died in 1980, at the age of eighty-three, *Time* magazine reported that he was nearly bankrupt.

Anicet became a financier in Geneva with a beautiful family of his own, and was a loyal and loving son to Virginia in every regard.

Shufen used to say, "Do not have dreams. Have no expectations and you will not be disappointed." But even Shufen and Shuquan, despite decades of hardship, were able to dream and aspire again. Shufen spun dreams on the pages of his books; Shuquan began life anew at forty-seven, when she divorced and immigrated to Hong Kong.

Muma lived with Virginia in Hong Kong for more than a decade. In the 1980s she moved in with Shuquan, who had recently arrived from Beijing and was working hard as a Mandarin tutor, building a new foundation for herself and her two children. With all of us sisters helping, Muma had a stable and comfortable life until her passing, from undiagnosed gastric pain, in 1988 at the age of seventy-nine.

Though I'd annoyed Virginia through much of our childhood, as adults we were "telephonically" inseparable—talking on the phone daily well into our eighties. Virginia became increasingly reclusive as the years passed. During our chats, I knew that frequently I would be her only contact with the outside world that day. Since Anicet was overseas, the police called me early one morning in 2015, after they had found my sister unresponsive in her apartment. She was several months short of her eighty-eighth birthday.

As she lived on a distant island, I had not visited Virginia in many years. The young constable greeted me at the door and guided me to a neatly arranged dining table. Next to the loose pages that the police had set out for me to sign, I was stunned to see that Virginia had prepared a few things herself: about half a dozen tidy stacks of file folders, the top of each adorned with color-coded sticky notes containing numbered instructions for her funeral arrangements, banking, properties, subscriptions—and even a separate sheet detailing the removal of specific items from her fridge and where to dispose of them.

I can only surmise that it was Virginia's attempt to impose some form of order to her own passing—order that had eluded her when, more than once in her life, circumstances had spun wildly out of control. The life of my fiercely independent sister ended as solitarily as it had begun, back when Qinpo had separated her from the rest of our family. I hope she realized that, after a lifetime of searching for someone who would love her steadfastly and unconditionally, she needed to look no further than her third sister.

Only two of us are left now: Shuquan and me.

To the best of our recollection, this is the only photo ever taken of the five of us siblings together, in Hong Kong in 1992. Left to right: Shujue, Shufen, Virginia, me and Shuquan.

Soon after China reopened to the West in 1978, I returned to Shanghai after an absence of almost thirty years. Everything looked much smaller than I remembered. With all the families that had moved in and the filthy conditions, it was painful for me to reconcile the shabby setting with our once-splendid home, and I didn't expect to ever return again.

Japanese bombs had destroyed most of Taiyeye's estate in Changshu in the late 1930s. A large, modern hotel replaced the whitewashed pavilions where No. 4 and No. 7 had plotted to steal their father's fortune, where my teenage father had slapped an audacious antique dealer and where Qinpo had done the unthinkable and left her husband.

I visited the Changshu hotel to see if I could find some vestige of our family's past. I knew it was probably futile: the developer must have razed everything to make way for three hundred rooms, meeting facilities and even a bowling alley. Indeed, I found no trace of the lotus-filled lake, pagodas or serpentine bridge that had once been.

In the back of a blocky structure, I wandered into a drab concrete courtyard decorated with a hodgepodge of potted shrubs. I was preparing to leave when I became aware of a sweet scent wafting from a pair of white magnolia trees improbably wedged between humming air-conditioning condensers. The trees were in full bloom, magnificent twins with enormous flowers and glossy leaves that reached to the top of the four-story tiled wall. I had a clear image of Taiyeye in a floor-length changshan, his official seal dangling from his waist, supervising the placement of the two saplings more than a century earlier. They would grow into the largest and most beautiful specimens in the copse of magnolias edging the cobblestoned courtyard, where scores of carriage drivers and sedan bearers had awaited their employers during his grandson's full-moon celebration.

I read somewhere that the magnolia genus is many millions of years old. Scientists believe it has survived earthquakes, wildfires and ice ages. That these majestic trees are still here, and that I've stood next to them inhaling their fragrance, is enough for me.

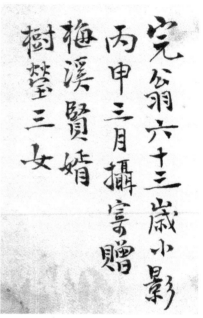

A photograph of Diedie with his handwritten inscription on the back:

"'Finished old man' sixty-three years old candid photograph
taken in March 1958
mailed as a gift to my good son-in-law Meichi and third
daughter Shuying (Raymond and Isabel)."

CHAPTER 23
HUMBLE TRANQUIL STUDIO

My FIRST VISIT TO MOM's *dilapidated childhood home, in 2008, was dispiriting. It pained me to see that the imprint of a Bakelite telephone on a wall was one of the only remnants of the family's presence. Since the Red Guards had ransacked the house forty years before our visit, no one in the family had had the heart to investigate what became of Diedie's lovingly curated art collection, which had included hundreds of objects as large as zitan tables and as small as a snuff bottle.*

Back home in Honolulu, I wrestled with the tragedies that had befallen the Suns. From a closet I removed Muma's torn silk qipao, left there for me by Mom, and ran my fingers over the embroidery. What few mementos remain of Diedie and Muma are of sentimental rather than intrinsic value.

As we entered a new millennium, I was gratified to witness China's rising prosperity and a robust interest in Chinese art. Indeed, China has surpassed the United States as the world's leading art and antiques market. That surely would have surprised and pleased Diedie.

A unique characteristic of classical paintings helped us make a connection with Diedie's vanished art objects. Traditionally, after an artist created and inscribed his painting, collectors would add their own calligraphed tributes to commemorate their ownership. Chinese paintings are thus inherently art-historical: as a painting's ownership changed, its surface might be covered with dozens of inscriptions and seals. Often poetic or philosophical in nature, the inscriptions, or colophons, reflected the artist's interaction with patrons and friends, and recorded centuries of ownership.

Though he acquired furniture, porcelain, scholar's rocks, classical books and objets d'art, Diedie was best known for his collection of landscape paintings. Because Diedie was the last owner to inscribe many of the paintings that were cropping up at international art auctions, his reputation as a collector would provide experts important proof of provenance to authenticate the works of art.

The seals of traditional Chinese painters and collectors reveal their inner life. Diedie selected his studio name in his twenties. It identified him for the first time as a collector and embodied a youthful dream: xujing-zhai *("humble tranquil studio")—an imaginary place of serenity inspired by a Confucian ideal.*

The sobriquets that he chose as the years passed record the derailment of a promising life: shengnian buque *("birth year not solid") in recognition of the inauspiciousness of his jiawu birth year;* pomeng *("broken dreams") and, finally,* wanweng *("finished old man") to describe a man who has lost everything.*

Several examples of Diedie's "Humble Tranquil Studio" seals.

For years, friends and relatives told us classical paintings bearing Diedie's seals and inscriptions were selling at auction for outrageous prices.

Though my siblings and I have virtually none of Diedie's possessions, I lacked the gumption to follow up on any of the leads. In the various sources that enumerated our family's major assets—the properties, banks, hotels and ships—Diedie's art collection did not even receive a mention.

I did not object when Claire suggested we search the Internet for Diedie's paintings. We sat together at her kitchen table in Honolulu, facing a computer screen dotted with dozens of images, mostly from China-based auction houses providing summaries of sold artwork. She randomly clicked on a landscape painting that was large in scale, yet its small houses were welcoming beneath a bower of leafy trees.

As I leaned in for a closer look, an image flooded into my mind of Diedie perched on a stool, hanging a painting on the wall above his desk more than seventy years earlier—a painting that had been owned by an emperor and nine princes. I reached for my daughter's hand.

Claire squeezed it back reassuringly, and together we peered into the monitor, reading the auction house description with intense concentration:

A painting by seventeenth-century artist Wang Hui. Painted in 1709. Entered the imperial collection in 1723. Acquired by the thirteenth son of the Kangxi emperor, remaining in the imperial collection and the ownership of nine princes for eight generations. Acquired by Sun Bosheng, Humble Tranquil Studio, who authenticated it after he was forty years old.

Painted when Wang Hui was seventy-eight years old and at the peak of his fame and fortune. Therefore, a sense of elevated peace and positivity, ease and openness is abundantly evident in the painting. Collected by Humble Tranquil Studio, a famous collector, and well preserved, in excellent condition. Opening price RMB4,500,000, estimate RMB6,500,000. Sold at Beijing auction on November 8, 2011, for RMB24,150,000.[25]

We saw that the final price was nearly quadruple the estimate, but couldn't convert the Chinese renminbi amount in our heads. I held my breath as my daughter punched the numbers into a calculator.

Claire's brows raised above wide eyes as she thrust the calculator in front of me. The selling price was nearly US$4 million.

---

25. Guardian Auctions: Accessed June 22, 2017. http://yz.sssc.cn/item/view/1791231.

The Wang Hui painting that sold at auction for US$4 million. The
painting measures 37 x 21 inches. The large square seal at the top is
that of Prince Yi, the thirteenth son of the Kangxi Emperor.

It is hard to describe the surge of emotions when I saw, for the first time, a tangible value assigned to something that had once been our family's: surprise at the amount; regret about not owning the artwork, yielding to acceptance; and, finally, an ironic, bittersweet sense of pride in Diedie's discernment to have collected such a fine thing.

However much you steel yourself to accept a sad truth, it takes effort to banish resentment. "Either you have it or you don't, and we don't," I said to Claire, and we did not speak of the painting again that day.

I returned to the auction website a few days later. In the bewildering intensity of our first reading, I had glossed over a critical fact that I now saw clearly—the name of the artist, Wang Hui. I had once known it well: I'd devoted a year to writing my senior thesis about this very painter at Princeton University three decades earlier.

As a way to spur independent thinking, every Princeton senior was required to write a thesis on a topic of his or her choice. I was majoring in art and archaeology, and had narrowed my focus to Chinese painting, but I had no ideas for a thesis subject. My adviser directed me to the archives of the university's small yet outstanding art museum, where I more or less stumbled upon the work of a seventeenth-century artist. The moment I saw two landscape albums painted by Wang Hui forty years apart—one during his prime, the other at the venerable age of eighty—I knew I'd found my thesis topic. Wang had produced the albums in a similar format, and each was handsome in its own right. But they showed distinct differences too, which I saw as an opportunity to demonstrate an evolution in the artist's body of work.

The life of Wang Hui spanned the long reign of the Kangxi emperor, who masterminded a golden age in politics, economics, science and culture in the late seventeenth century. When the artist was sixty, the emperor summoned him to Beijing to supervise the grandest art commission of the era: twelve enormous scrolls commemorating an imperial inspection tour of the southern provinces, replete with landscapes, architectural detail and thirty thousand inhabitants.

The senior thesis is the culmination of the Princeton undergraduate experience. For most students, it traverses uncharted territory and is marked by equal measures of angst and accomplishment. I can honestly say that, in my case, it was mostly a pleasurable undertaking. While I felt privileged to have firsthand access to the work of such a renowned painter, at the time I was completely unaware that Diedie had been a significant collector of Chinese paintings, let alone of this particular artist. Mom had never seen fit to tell me, probably because art hadn't been of much interest to her, and Diedie had lost his collection in such a heart-wrenching manner.

I don't have a rational explanation for why Wang Hui's paintings touched me so; I suspect the same qualities that had charmed Diedie so many years before captivated me too. And even if our family no longer possessed the physical pieces, I must have inherited his passion for them. It was my special, private connection to Diedie, something that even Mom couldn't share.

Just as unlikely was my odd affection for gongshi. I discovered them in a classical garden in Hangzhou, when I was studying as a teenage exchange student. My classmates teased me about my fondness for the "big old rocks." But I was unmistakably drawn to their plain yet playful character, like an ornery, weather-beaten old man with a good heart. I appreciate why they're also called "spirit stones" and how a scholar ruminating over one with a flask of good rice wine might attain a form of enlightenment.

Assuming she'd have the same response as my friends, I had not spoken of gongshi to Mom. It wasn't until we visited her childhood home and she pointed to four indentations in the floor that I learned my grandfather had collected them.

❖◆❖

Claire's scholarly considerations aside, there is another interesting connection between our family and Wang Hui. The artist was one of the Four Wangs, famous landscape painters from the Changshu area. At the time she was writing her thesis, Claire wasn't aware that Changshu was our ancestral home. (I hadn't mentioned it to the children when they were growing up; Shanghai, where I was born, seemed simple and sufficient.)

Not only was Wang Hui from Changshu, he had been born on Yushan Mountain, where Taiyeye built his estate.

I trust I am forgiven for not reading every word of my daughter's thesis, and for missing the uncanny connections for three decades. Claire once told me the Princeton University Art Museum has more than six thousand works of Asian art. What were the chances of her connecting with this particular painter?

One of my deepest regrets in life is that my children never met Diedie, so it comforted me that his gentle presence had somehow led my daughter to his favorite artist. She did her grandfather proud: Claire's thesis on Wang's two landscape albums garnered the Senior Thesis Prize from the university's Department of Art and Archaeology. She and her roommate tied for the award, splitting the $100 prize.

Claire and me at our hotel on the Bund, 2016.

CHAPTER 24
LOST AND FOUND

SHANGHAI, 2016

IT HAS TAKEN TEN YEARS to unearth details of our family's past and to pen this book. My daughter and I make an effective team: I talk; she organizes, researches and writes. We have enjoyed our respective roles immensely, as well as the journey of discovery that we've shared. We've passed a few milestones during these years. We have mourned the death of Raymond, my husband of fifty-six years, as well as that of my sister Virginia. I have celebrated my eighty-sixth birthday; Claire her fifty-fifth.

I treasure my time with my children and their families. Leslie, who lives with his wife, Ann, and two sons in New York City, is a property developer; Lloyd is a filmmaker and media executive in Hong Kong; and Claire and her husband, John, a retired physician, live in Honolulu.

In 2016 Claire and I returned to Shanghai again, I expect for my last time, and stayed in the magnificently restored Waldorf Astoria on the Bund. The English beaux arts building once housed the city's most exclusive gentlemen's club. On a 1929 visit, Noel Coward purportedly said of its 110-foot mahogany Long Bar, "Lay your cheek along the bar, and you will see the earth's curvature."

As we walk along the riverfront, the air is crisp against our skin, the hangover of summer humidity dissipated by an offshore breeze. Each building is a landmark in its own right: monumental in scale and extravagant in detail, representing the world's finest premodern architectural styles. My daughter and I stop about midway along the sweeping crescent of the Bund where, as a teenager, I posed for a photo perched on a Harley-Davidson. Nearby we gaze into the colonnade of the former Hongkong and Shanghai Bank headquarters, from which Yeye and his brother embezzled a cartful of gold yuanbao.

"That's strange," I mutter, peering up at the clock tower next to the bank. Old-world clock chimes are ringing from the graceful Customs House, which once controlled Shanghai port traffic. Though faint against the din of construction, the chimes don't sound right.

"The architecture looks so British," Claire comments.

Claire with husband John Falzarano on the Bund; the former Hongkong and Shanghai Bank headquarters and the Customs House are at left.

"Yes, it does—it was based on Big Ben." I turn my head to hear better. "The first time your father and I went to London, it was fun to see Big Ben ringing out the same tune that I grew up with."

The jackhammers pause, and the clock chimes ring out clearly.

Claire chuckles. "Then I guess there's been a changing of the guard, Mom. That tune is the Chinese national anthem, 'The East Is Red.'"

Bong... bong... bong... The chimes complete the hour, punctuating Claire's words like percussive exclamation marks.

The jackhammers resume their ear-splitting work. Much of the street is a construction site. At a nearby building, workers scale a tidy grid of bamboo scaffolding, resembling sailors on the rigging of a frigate. Above brightly decorated hoarding, pile drivers stand like stocky sentries at the water's edge.

The Western powers enjoyed their monuments on the Bund for less than a century, giving way to Japanese occupying forces. In the late 1960s, many of the buildings fell victim to the convulsions of the Cultural Revolution, remaining in a derelict condition for decades even as government offices moved in. Nowadays, after varying degrees of renovation, rooftop restaurants and designer shops once more beckon well-heeled customers.

Our eyes shift eastward across the Huangpu to the futuristic skyline of Pudong, developed in the 1990s as a new commercial district. While the Bund honors the past, Pudong unabashedly embraces the future. Amid the dense cluster of gleaming skyscrapers, three of the world's tallest buildings reach for the sky, and the Oriental Pearl Tower projects its space-age profile like something out of a *Jetsons* cartoon.

The two sides of the river remind me of my past and present, and the delicate balance it takes to hold one dear without destroying the other. Perhaps pain and loss are the necessary consequences of a nation's progress. That's why I've let go of my family's material assets. Yet I would have been crushed if bulldozers had razed the Bund in order to build glass-and-steel towers like those in Pudong. Be that as it may, my city is reinventing itself again. I've discovered a newfound pride in modern-day Shanghai—not merely the Paris of the East of my childhood, but a global economic powerhouse.

Claire and I set off for my childhood home a short time later. Eight years have passed since our first visit together, and we don't know

Top: The Bund in the 1930s. *Bottom:* Pudong skyline
across the Huangpu from the Bund in 2011.

what to expect. Inside the sealed windows of an air-conditioned taxi, we're glad to leave behind the noise and dust of construction. Our conversation with the Mandarin-speaking driver, who hails from the northeastern city of Harbin, reminds me how it is becoming less common to hear the Shanghainese dialect spoken in Shanghai. As job opportunities have drawn Chinese from all corners of the nation, people like us are akin to cultural relics in our former city.

We turn onto Fuzhou Road and drive due west from the river through the heart of what was the International Settlement. No longer called Fourth Road, locals now refer to it as Wenhua Jie, "Culture Street." People still read here: multistory bookstores line the street, as they did decades ago, and the sidewalk teems with shoppers. But there's no longer any sign of a red-lantern alley or courtesans strolling under parasols.

It is late afternoon when we arrive at Zhenning Road. The owners of the convenience store that has replaced Diedie's study have set out folding tables and plastic stools on the sidewalk for diners to munch on grilled snacks with a cup of tea or Coke. Where once our bamboo fence invited sunlight and moonbeams to shimmer through its slats, our soles now scrunch over carelessly tossed containers that litter the pavement like Styrofoam corpses.

As we approach the house, we're surprised to see the front gate, so intimidating on our first visit, flung wide open. Claire and I admire the scrollwork of the original iron grill and are amazed by how the grime has kept growing since our earlier visit—half a century's unadulterated dust suspended from walls and ceilings in thick woolly webs.

A middle-aged man in a checked sports jacket approaches us on the stoop. His voice is gruff, but his eyes are not unkind as he asks what we're looking for.

"Is the elderly Mr. Cheng still living here?" I ask. "We met him some years ago."

"Is your surname Sun?" We nod, and I'm surprised that he knows my family name. "I figured it must be you," he continues. "You're obviously overseas Chinese. Old Man Cheng went to a retirement home last year, so we can leave this gate open now. He was our oldest resident and insisted on keeping it locked."

"Now that he's gone, we all want to open up the house to light and air." He glances back into the dark vestibule. "Cheng told me about you. He found something of your father's when he was packing and hoped you'd come back one day."

The man leaves us for a few minutes and returns with a package wrapped in filthy newspaper. He eases it into the basket of a scooter that someone has parked inside the front door.

"Your father was some big art collector, right? Supposedly this was one of his most valuable pieces, but it was no use to anyone because it was already broken. Cheng said it was the only thing the Red Guards left behind."

The man looks at his watch. "I have to go now. Stay as long as you like—there are a couple of chairs in the hallway."

An image flashes of an almost imperceptible grimace and Diedie's unexpected restraint one morning nearly eighty years ago. I recall his exact words: "This isn't a valuable piece. It's just a stone after all, isn't it?" I again feel the distress that racked me when I showed him the gongshi that I'd broken, and it suddenly dawns on me what he did that day to calm an inconsolable child.

The stranger's words echo in my mind: the gongshi had been one of Diedie's most valuable pieces.

It was the same immutable discipline and empathy that enabled Diedie to make the ultimate sacrifice for me—the child who had taken the deepest interest in him—by sending me off to Hong Kong for my safety, knowing he'd likely never see me again.

Claire places one of the folding chairs next to the scooter so I can watch as she unwraps the bulky package. I immediately recognize the profile of the scholar's rock—the crescent-shaped one that I'd knocked off its pedestal. The two halves are detached, having lost their adhesiveness years ago.

I run my index finger across the weatherworn ridges, feeling the bumpy, dirt-caked line of glue. My finger stops at a slight protrusion inside a deep crevice. Using a nail file, Claire helps me remove a piece of rice paper so thin it's translucent, folded seven or eight times, tiny enough to conceal.

To our astonishment, it is a letter to Diedie from Mrs. Liang, the mother of my classmate, dated September 1967:

Dear Mr. Sun:

When Liang Ming and I first met you twenty-five years ago, I was deeply ashamed that he had taken your jade seal. You understood his grief over the loss of his father and turned a thoughtless act into one of kindness.

I have never known how to thank you for your financial support and careful guidance that helped Liang Ming become a man of good character. I confess I was uncertain in the beginning. I feared my son might not meet your expectations.

Due to your influence, Liang Ming earned his doctorate and was assigned a job as a professor of art and literature. He was so moved when you gave him the very seal that he had tried to take from you. My son treasured it more than anything.

With a sad heart, I must report that Liang Ming left us last month. Red Guards targeted his department for the crime of worshipping old things. They left my son drowning in a pool of his own blood.

I wish to return your jade seal. One of Liang Ming's most promising students removed it from my son's hidden pocket and brought it to me.

I heard you have had your own share of misfortune. May you find protection for yourself in these troubled times.

Claire pokes farther into the hole—a miniature tunnel gouged by moving water. Her file engages with a frayed cord, and a tattered silk pouch emerges, the same one that Mrs. Liang used to carry the seal back to Diedie. Inside the pouch is the jade seal—the stoic lion that crouched on my father's desktop and left its crimson imprint on his paintings.

Humility is a preeminent Confucian virtue. For much of my life I held the comforting delusion that Diedie was as kind to everybody else as he was to me. Now I see he was a princeling in a family that just as easily produced scoundrels. In youth, his arrogance sparked his public humiliation. Mister Street was his defining moment—a lesson in humility that transformed him, and that he carried the rest of his life.

When something cherished is broken, can it ever be made whole? In the 1960s, when news of my family in China left me heavy-hearted, I dreamed about returning home from work to find Diedie reading to my children. But it was never to be. It makes me recall the crack in his gong-shi, a jagged scar running through the lives of innocents.

His fate likely did not surprise Diedie. After all, his jiawu birth year had presaged instability and disaster—from the great fire that destroyed much of Shanghai when he was born, to his own degradation at the hands of adolescent Red Guards.

No wonder he'd found solace in art and literature. The classics he had read told of the rise and fall of China's great dynasties; art helped him understand beauty and loss, permanence and transience. In a cruel twist, it was the very thing Diedie treasured the most—his exquisite art collection—that caused him untold suffering and hastened his own demise.

Of course, a quirk of fate had brought my father wealth and privilege too, even if he had suspected it might not last forever. I marvel at how, amid war, occupation and revolution, and even as his wealth dwindled, Diedie maintained our sense of safety within the cocoon of our home. In the end, the bamboo fence that we'd believed shielded us from danger was no more than an illusion of security.

During the hardest years leading to my father's death, I felt frustrated that I could do no more than ship him a few groceries, and guilty that I could do nothing to console him. It angered me that his inability to let go of the past might have been to blame for him not leaving Shanghai. A sense of helplessness gnawed at me constantly.

It was only when I was raising three children of my own that I finally saw the reason why Diedie had misled me into thinking I was traveling to Hong Kong on a short holiday: he couldn't face saying goodbye. He had placed his hope for the family's future on my shoulders, and that lifted me from despair.

Diedie was a moral and dependable man in all matters except his marriage to my mesmerizing but frivolous mother. Muma's uncomplicated joie de vivre and love of beauty and glamour defined her character. I did not consider until I was much older the private anguish that might have lain beneath her mellow warmth, nor her inner strength from being orphaned at a young age.

As Muma was starting her marriage as an archetypal Chinese wife, Qinpo entered as the archetypal dowager mother-in-law. I have pondered whether my parents' marriage might have lasted longer had it not been for the constant tension between Qinpo and Muma. The conflict surely played a role in driving Muma to seek outside diversions and ultimately leave a home that may have been unpleasant for her, though it was an oasis of stability during dangerous times.

Muma's divorce and journey across the country exposed her to the plight of women with virtually no rights over their children or even their own being. Yet in that vulnerability she may have found her own power of survival.

Despite their opposition, Qinpo and Muma had more in common than they cared to admit: for one thing, their forgiving natures that bordered on the irrational (recall Qinpo taking in the intransigent Fifth Popo and Muma taking back Sheng Ayi). Perhaps this was also their redemption—their intuitive understanding that the loyalty of female friends empowers a woman to survive in a culture dominated by men. Survival still did not equate to independence, however; even after Qinpo and Muma broke the mold and left their husbands, they had to depend on their children for support.

My younger sisters, Shuquan and Shujue, had to rely on each other too. Later, Communism exacted a toll on my younger sisters, but they had known little else for most of their lives. Had Muma, Virginia and I not had the good fortune to leave China when we did, would we have faced our destinies as stoically as Diedie, or as tenaciously as Shufen?

For both Diedie and his protégé, Liang Ming, the struggle to preserve Chinese culture ended tragically. Standing here in the crumbling vestibule of Mom's former home, it strikes me that Diedie enigmatically guided me to Chinese art at Princeton in the same way that he'd mentored Liang Ming a generation before. My studies in pursuit of Chinese history, art and philosophy crystallized, making sense to me in a way they hadn't before.

The country that had produced a cultural legacy of such refinement, and then ravaged it, finally came full circle after three decades. Diedie's art pieces, albeit scattered, are treasured once again. China's cruel history broke our family, yet the sublime beauty of its culture endures.

It makes me believe that losing the ability to dream is a far worse fate than any material loss. And for all the suffering they caused to millions of people, even the agents of our family's adversity were victims themselves— that is the burden of history, change and the human condition.

After ten years pouring heart and soul into this book, I too have come full circle in my journey.

Growing up in Hong Kong, I was schooled exclusively in English. I began high school at the British-run Island School and then transferred to the Hong Kong International School, where I quickly traded my plummy English accent for an American one. A tutor came twice a week to teach my brothers and me Cantonese.

At home, we were exposed to several languages and dialects. Our grandmothers spoke only the Changshu and Pudong dialects. Our parents spoke Shanghainese to each other and English to us children. My brothers and I were raised by Cantonese and Filipina servants and fed by a cook from Changshu.

We were very Westernized. My father's advertising clients, many of whom were friends from our country club, were American and European expatriates; Mom, of course, had her US Consulate colleagues. When we socialized with Cantonese friends—by far the majority of the local population—I was an outlier of sorts, as my Cantonese wasn't perfect. I was more Westernized than our Shanghainese friends too. I had no shortage of friends of many ethnicities, but something was missing at a deeper level.

I had to go all the way to Princeton to learn Mandarin and to study Chinese history and art. I leapt at the opportunity to attend a summer language program at Hangzhou University, one of China's first such programs after reopening to Western students in the late 1970s. Besides the organizers, I was the only Chinese participant: the fact is, in those days few people like me pursued Chinese learning and culture. We were the children of immigrants building new lives, and China was an undeveloped Communist country that few in the industrialized world wanted to emulate.

Without being aware of it, I've grasped for connections to my heritage at every stage of my life. In 1987 my first employer in Hong Kong, the public relations firm Hill & Knowlton, sent me to manage its Beijing office—the first and, at the time, only PR company in China. It was fascinating work, building the public image and marketing the products of Western clients to Chinese consumers who'd had virtually no exposure to foreigners for more than two decades. Not that propaganda was an unfamiliar concept: at media conferences for local journalists it was standard practice to place a red packet of "lucky money" at the back of the press kits.

Many Chinese households then lacked running water, but mine was not a hardship posting. My expatriate benefits included a suite in the Beijing Hotel and a car with a full-time driver; I was deeply sensitive to my Chinese colleagues' living conditions and embarrassed about my own.

In the 1990s, after I had returned to Hong Kong, world stock markets were undergoing the dot-com collapse and its aftermath. Businesspeople were also turning their attention to China as a huge opportunity, which fueled a golden age of sorts in Hong Kong. I had a ball in those years, developing markets for Tiffany & Co. and reveling in my social life. I was the only one among my friends who wore qipao to formal functions.

My unrelenting schedule and urban lifestyle eventually wore me down. As much as I loved Hong Kong, when the company offered me a position in Hawaii, I accepted. I've lived in Honolulu for two decades and moved on to my own small enterprises. This is an excellent place for me—if for no other reason than its quintessential East-meets-West character. I've had a harmonious marriage to John, my Italian-American husband. The city is full of chameleons (or is it hybrids?) like myself—people of Chinese descent from all corners of the diaspora.

When Mom and I set out to write this book, I imagined the project would take a year or two. I'd expected a few interesting anecdotes and had no idea how they would be inextricably interwoven with the full sweep of Chinese history—nor how powerfully they would impact me. The stories have by turns enlightened, amused and unsettled me. If my destiny had been different and I'd been born inside China, how would I have reacted to my feet being bound, or my husband taking on five concubines, or someone selling me to a stranger in the middle of the night—let alone being sub-jected to the horrors of the Cultural Revolution?

Each one of us has a history and a memory, a past that weighs on successive generations. Here is my full circle: I am the first generation of women in my family who has the utter freedom to make my own choices. I've exercised that choice throughout my life, even if unconsciously at times, in search of my cultural origins.

My father is buried in the Shanghai suburbs about forty miles west of the Bund. Guiyuan Cemetery, "Returning Garden," provides prosperous overseas Chinese a final resting place back in their homeland. Though the

grounds are immaculately landscaped, a Westerner might find the dec-
oration bizarre. Sculptures interspersed throughout the cemetery depict
what the developers must have believed are worldly objects and experi-
ences that ought to be taken to the afterlife. A herd of elephants roams
across an immaculate lawn, within walking distance of bespectacled boy
monks, the Seven Dwarves (sans Snow White), a ten-foot-tall golfer and a
family of laughing pigs. My father purchased a plot with room enough for
our immediate family, so we may join him when the time comes.

My intention was to go back to Shanghai to find my memories. In the
end, it was my memories that found me.

Sometimes, when the night is especially dark, I dream of my father.
Although it's a cold day, he wears straw sandals and shuffles along outside our house, his gnarled hands clasping a twig broom. Above the sidewalk, dust roils in puffy clouds as if in slow motion. He looks so frail: I
ache to take the broom from him. My outstretched arms almost touch it
but do not reach.

Then I realize the scraggly broom is morphing into something else.
It becomes a giant paintbrush, a satiny horsetail, its strands white and
unbroken, free of entanglements. Diedie's hands are young, unblem-
ished as I remember them—fingers that can move with the fluidity of
long practice, the elegance of one unused to manual labor. Behind round
spectacles, his eyes crinkle as he smiles tenderly at me. He dips the brush
into the inkstone and prepares to write.

Nanjing Road at night, ca. 1930s.

SOURCES AND CREDITS

AFFECTIONATELY REFERRED TO as *Laokela* 老克拉, "old-time aristocrat," Isabel's brother, Sun Shufen 孫樹棻, often writing under the pen name Shufen, published fifty-five books over twenty-seven years. He served as administrator of the Shanghai Writers Association 上海市作家協會理事 and vice president of the Shanghai Community Literary Institute 上海大眾文學學會副會長.

His first full-length novel was *Springtime in Suzhou* 姑蘇春 (Shanghai: Shanghai Literature and Art Publishing House 上海文藝出版社, 1978).

We used the following of his books as primary sources for stories about the Sun family and Old Shanghai:

Shengsijie 生死劫 (Hong Kong: Cosmos Books Ltd 天地圖書有限公司, 1994)

The Last Dreams of Old Shanghai 上海的最後舊夢 (Shanghai: Guji Chuban She 古籍出版社, 1999)

Dreams of the Nobles 上海的豪門舊夢 (Shanghai: Zuojia Chuban She 作家出版社, 2002)

Shanghai Jiumeng 上海舊夢 (Hong Kong: Cosmos Books Ltd 天地圖書有限公司, 2002)

Shanghai Waltz 上海 Waltz (Shanghai: Wenhui Chuban She 文匯出版社, 2004)

The Last Mazurka 最後的瑪祖卡 (Shanghai: Shanghai Literature and Art Publishing House 上海文藝出版社, 2005)

Shanghaitan Fengqing 上海灘風情 (Shanghai: Shiji Chuban Gufen Youxian Gongsi 世紀出版股份有限公司, 2009)

Shufen also wrote a trilogy about our three patriarchs (Hong Kong: Cosmos Books Ltd 天地圖書有限公司):

Baofashijia 暴發世家, about Taiyeye (1995)

Fengyuyangchang 風雨洋場, about Yeye (1996)

Baizuzhichong 百足之蟲, about Diedie (1997)

A few of Shufen's book covers.

Unless otherwise noted, all photographs and illustrations are from the writers' family collections or in the public domain. Every effort has been made to locate the original rights holders for the photographs included.

Pg. xii–xiii, map legend, numbers 1–13, 15: Illustrations by Ming-fai Hui.

Pg. xii–xiii, map legend, number 14: Illustration by Sun Qian.

Pg. xiv, 5, 14, 28, 32, 35, 68, 83, 86, 93, 95, 96, 124, 132, 136, 138, 143, 150, 165, 170, 200, 245 and 291: Illustrations by Ming-fai Hui.

Pg. 7, 22, 56, 57, 60, 94, 104, 106, 107, 111, 144, 175, 182, 196, 197 and 291: Illustrations by Sun Qian.

Pg. 12–13, 26–27, 37, 58–59, 67, 85, 95, 110–111, 130–131, 146–147, 158–159, 175, 184–185, 196–197 and 229–231: Isabel and Claire's vintage qipao embroidery was photographed by Krista and Pete Mui and used as background designs for the sidebars of this book.

Pg. x–xi: Reproduced with permission from the private collection of Vince Ungvary, Sydney, Australia. The poster is fourth in a series of scenic illustrations published by Zhengxing Poster Company, 307 Guangdong Road, Shanghai 上海廣東路 307 號正興畫片公司.

Pg. 42: Map of the Master of the Nets Garden in Suzhou, photographed by Kanga35, via Wikimedia Commons. Accessed June 21, 2017. https://commons.wikimedia.org/wiki/File:2004_0927-Suzhou_MasterOfNetGarden_PaintedMap.jpg.

Pg. 45, 47, 48, 78, 112 and 166: From the New York Public Library.

Pg. 81: Stefan R. Landsberger Collections, International Institute of Social History, Amsterdam, the Netherlands. "The Great World in Shanghai" designed by Huang Shanlai 黃善賚, first published 1957; 1958 edition. Accessed July 7, 2017. https://chineseposters.net/posters/pc-1957-006.php. Although the illustrator portrays traditional entertainment, he also provides hints of the Maoist times, such as the red flag and star on the tower and the Maoist slogan that reads, *Baihua qifang, tuichen chuxin* 百花齊放, 推陳出新 ("Let a hundred flowers blossom, weed through the old to bring forth the new").

Pg. 121: Reproduced with permission from the private collection of Vince Ungvary, Sydney, Australia, *The Little Blue Book of Shanghai* 上海小藍本 (Shanghai: ISIDA,

1932).

Pg. 148: Photograph courtesy of Hugues Martin.

Pg. 158: Vandamm Studios, New York, New York, ca. 1930–1939. Lois Rather Papers, Museum of Performance + Design.

Pg. 185: Reproduced with permission from Chen Yunshang, *A Movie Queen Chen Yunshang*, edited by Lu Yanyuan (Beijing: Xinhua Publishing House, 2001).

Pg. 186: Photograph courtesy of Frank Chu.

Pg. 194–195: Reproduced with permission from the private collection of Vince Ungvary, Sydney, Australia. The illustration is part of a rare jigsaw puzzle set.

Pg. 205: Stefan R. Landsberger Collections, International Institute of Social History, Amsterdam, the Netherlands. "Advance victoriously while following Chairman Mao's revolutionary line in literature and the arts" 沿著毛主席的革命文藝路線勝利前進, designed by Central Industrial Arts College collective, ca. 1968. Accessed July 7, 2017. https://chineseposters.net/posters/e13-632_633_634.php.

Pg. 250: From Guardian Auctions. Accessed June 22, 2017. http://yz.sssc.cn/item/view/1791231.

GLOSSARY

OUR STORIES AND THE CHARACTERS in them are real or inspired by real events and real people.

In keeping with 1930s and '40s Shanghai, the glossary uses traditional Chinese characters rather than the simplified script used in China today.

There is no standard English spelling for the Shanghainese dialect. Instead, we provide Mandarin pronunciations in *pinyin*, China's official phonetic system since 1958. Where a non-pinyin version is in common use, for instance dim sum or mahjong, we provide it together with the pinyin version.

We use the most familiar spelling of individual's names. When Isabel was a child, Wade-Giles was a widely used romanization system, but many people invented their own Western-style names. Westernized Shanghainese men commonly abbreviated their Chinese given names using English initials. For example, 宋子文 called himself T. V. Soong or Paul Soong; his name is Sung Tzu-wen in Wade-Giles and Song Ziwen in pinyin.

Unless an individual was primarily known by a Western-style name, we use their romanized Chinese name in the traditional placement of surname first, followed by given name.

Chinese consider babies one year old at birth. We cite ages by the Western reckoning, unless it is a significant round-number birthday.

We've tried our best to include the former as well as current names for streets and places.

Wherever possible, monetary values are expressed in their US dollar equivalents.

PEOPLE

For Isabel's immediate relatives, please refer to the Family Tree on page 12.

Ah Qian 阿乾 driver in Isabel's household

Ah San 阿三 short for *hongtou asan*

Ah Si 阿四 "Ah Four," majordomo in Isabel's household

Ah Xing 阿興 cook in Isabel's household

amah 阿媽 female servant

Deaconess Evelyn Ashcroft European history and literature teacher at St. Mary's

Nancy Chan (Chen Yunshang) 陳雲裳 1919–2016, 1930s to '40s movie star who played Hua Mulan 花木蘭 in the film *Maiden in Armour* 木蘭從軍

Eileen Chang (Zhang Ailing) 張愛玲 1920–1995, popular modern writer, and a McTyeire and St. Mary's alumna

Miss Chen 陳小姐 math teacher at St. Mary's

Mr. Cheng 程 son of a Communist army officer who lived in Isabel's childhood home

Chiang Kai-shek 蔣介石, 蔣中正 1887–1975, president of China 1928–1931 and 1943–1949; leader of Kuomintang Nationalist Party

Cixi, Empress Dowager 慈禧太后 1835–1908, empress dowager and regent during the late Qing dynasty

Confucius (Kong Fuzi) 孔夫子 551–479 BC, Chinese philosopher whose teachings formed the basis of the national examination system

Du Yuesheng 杜月笙 1888–1951, "Big-Eared Du," Shanghai's top mobster, one of the "Three Big Bosses"

Duan Ayi 端阿姨 "Auntie Duan," Isabel's traveling companion to Hong Kong

André Dubonnet 1897–1980, father of Virginia's son, Anicet Dubonnet

Four Wangs 四王 seventeenth-century landscape painters based in the Changshu area and surnamed Wang, one of whom was Wang Hui 王翬

Mr. Fu 付先生 Anhui innkeeper

gan gui nü 乾閨女 "dry lady's-boudoir daughter," meaning "precious foster daughter"

gonggong 公公 "grandfather," also used to address imperial court eunuchs

Gu Zhutong 顧祝同 1893–1987, Kuomintang commander in chief

He Fenglin 何豐林 1873–1935, Shanghai defense commissioner from 1920 to 1924

hongtou asan 紅頭阿三 "redheaded number three," nickname for Sikhs

Hu Die ("Butterfly" Wu) 胡蝶 1908–1989, actress who was voted Movie Queen of China

Huang Jinrong 黃金榮 1868–1953, "Pockmarked Huang," one of Shanghai's "Three Big Bosses," a leading gangster

László (Ladislav) Hudec 1893–1958, Slovak architect who designed more than sixty of Shanghai's most noted buildings

Mrs. Jiang 蔣太太 teacher at St. Mary's

Jiawu Tonggeng Qianling Hui 甲午同庚千齡會 "1894 Same-Age Thousand-Year Society," fraternal society of twenty intellectuals born in 1894

jidie, jiniang 寄爹, 寄娘 (*ji:* "to send, entrust, depend") godfather and godmother; surrogate parents without legal or religious responsibility in caring for a child

Miss Jin 金小姐 teacher at McTyeire

Jinling 金玲 "Gold Tinkle," Li Gege's girlfriend

Kangxi emperor 康熙帝 1654–1722, fourth emperor of the Qing dynasty

Sir John Henry Keswick, KCMG 1906–1982, influential Scottish businessman in China and Hong Kong; taipan of the trading firm Jardine, Matheson & Co.

George Kiang 江晟 1917–1951, Virginia's husband; deputy general manager of the Shanghai Telephone Company

H. H. Kung 孔祥熙 1881–1967, financier reputed to be the richest man in China; husband of Soong Ai-ling, the eldest of the famous Soong sisters

Li Gege 李哥哥 "Li older brother," one of Diedie and Muma's four godsons

Liang Ming 梁明 Isabel's McTyeire classmate who became Diedie's protégé

Helen Lu (Lu Yuan Huixie) 盧袁慧燮 ca. 1908–1990, Isabel's godmother, Jiniang, wife of Lu Xiaojia 盧小嘉

Lu Lanchun 露蘭春 1898–1936, female opera star and mistress of Huang Jinrong

Lu Xiaojia 盧小嘉 ca. 1891–1968, Isabel's godfather, Jidie, husband of Helen Lu and eldest son of the warlord Lu Yongxiang

Lu Yongxiang 盧永祥 1867–1933, warlord, father of Lu Xiaojia; provincial military governor of Zhejiang from 1919 to 1924

Mao Zedong 毛澤東 1893–1976, Communist revolutionary, founder of the People's Republic of China and chairman of the Communist Party of China from 1949 to 1976

Mei Lanfang 梅蘭芳 1894–1961, popular Beijing opera star and one of "Four Great Dan," male performers who portrayed female characters

popo 婆婆 grandmother, also used to address one's grandfather's concubines

Puyi 溥儀 1906–1967, last emperor of China

Qianlong emperor 乾隆帝 1711–1799, sixth emperor of the Qing dynasty

Qingdao Meiren 青島美人 "the Beauty of Qingdao," title given to Helen Lu in her hometown

Lilian Qiu (Qiu Lilin) 裘麗琳 1905–1968, wife of Zhou Xinfang

John Roderick 1914–2008, Associated Press correspondent and Raymond Chao's friend

Ronglu (Guwalgiya Ronglu) 瓜爾佳榮祿 1836–1903, late Qing dynasty Manchu court official; cousin of Empress Dowager Cixi

San Da Heng 三大亨 "Three Big Bosses," triumvirate of Shanghai gangsters Du Yuesheng, Zhang Xiaolin and Huang Jinrong, which controlled 1930s and '40s organized crime in Shanghai

San-naima 三奶媽 "third (child's) wet nurse," Isabel's first nanny

shaonai 少奶 "young mother," polite form of address

shaoye 少爺 "young father" or "young master," polite form of address

Sheng Ayi 盛阿姨 "Auntie Sheng," Muma's traveling companion to Chongqing

Shengtong 生通 apprentice driver in Isabel's household

shiye 師爺 lawyer

Si Daming Dan 四大名旦 "Four Great Dan," famous Beijing opera performers, one of whom was Mei Lanfang 梅蘭芳

Si Gongzi 四公子 "Four Lords," the sons of two warlords (one of the sons being Isabel's godfather, Lu Xiaojia), the son of China's president and the son of China's premier

Soong Ai-ling 宋藹齡 1890–1973, eldest of the famous Soong sisters who married financier H. H. Kung

Soong Ching-ling 宋慶齡 1893–1981, second Soong sister who married Kuomintang founder Sun Yat-sen

Soong Mei-ling 宋美齡 1898–2003, third and youngest Soong sister, who married Kuomintang leader Chiang Kai-shek

T. V. Soong 宋子文 1891–1971, Kuomintang minister of finance; brother of the Soong sisters

Sun Bosheng 孫伯繩 1894–1969, Isabel's father, Diedie, whose studio name for his art collection was 虛靜齋 *xujingzhai* ("humble tranquil studio") and whose sobriquets included 生年不確 *shengnian buque* ("birth year not solid"), 破夢 *pomeng* ("broken dreams") and 完翁 *wanweng* ("finished old man")

Sun Yat-sen (Sun Zhongshan) 孫中山 1866–1925, first president of the Republic of China and founder of the Kuomintang; husband of Soong Ching-ling

tangsao 堂嫂 wife of the older son of one's father's brother

Diane Tang (Tang Xiaoyu) 唐小腴 "Small Yu," daughter of Tang Yulu and Duan Ayi

Tang Yulu 唐腴臚 1899–1931, secretary to T. V. Soong and husband of Duan Ayi

Two-two Isabel's second nanny

Wang Hui 王翬 1632–1717, renowned seventeenth-century landscape painter from Changshu

Betty Peh-T'i Wei, PhD 魏白蒂 1930–, historian and author, *Shanghai: Crucible of Modern China* (Hong Kong: Oxford University Press, 1987) and *Old Shanghai* (Hong Kong: Oxford University Press, 1993)

Xi Zhengfu 席正甫 1838–1904, Hongkong and Shanghai Bank's second comprador

Katharine Yang 楊其美 Isabel's St. Mary's schoolmate

Mr. Yang 楊先生 tailor in Isabel's household

Prince Yi 怡親王 (Yinxiang 胤祥) 1686–1730, thirteenth son of the Kangxi Emperor

yiniang 姨娘 "auntie (mother's sister) mother," one's father's concubine

yitai 姨太 "auntie (mother's sister) wife," concubine

Yuan Shikai 袁世凱 1859–1916, general who served briefly as the first president of the Republic of China

Zeng Guofan 曾國藩 1811–1872, late Qing dynasty military general and court official

Zhang Xiaolin 張嘯林 1877–1940, one of Shanghai's "Three Big Bosses," a leading gangster; we have assigned him the nickname "Pipa Zhang"

Zhang Yi 張翼 general under Empress Dowager Cixi whose ninth daughter was Qinpo

Zhou Enlai 周恩來 1898–1976, first premier of the People's Republic of China

Zhou Xinfang 周信芳 1895–1975, grand master and leading performer of the Shanghai School of Beijing opera

PLACES

Airline Club Isabel's favorite nightclub, on the corner of Route de l'Amiral Courbet and Route Henry

Anhui 安徽 province in eastern China, in the Yangzi River basin

The Bund (Waitan) 外灘 "outer shoal," riverfront area on the Huangpu along which foreigners built banks, trading houses and the port's customs authority

Cangzhou Shuoshu Theater 滄州書場 Qinpo's favorite *shuoshu* venue, on Nanjing Road

Cathay Hotel 華懋飯店 hotel on the Bund opened in the 1920s, now the Fairmont Peace Hotel

Changshu 常熟 "forever abundant," city in Jiangsu Province, about sixty miles northwest of Shanghai

Chongrang Li 崇讓里 "esteem yield neighborhood," Diedie's Fourth Road housing development

Dongwu University 東吳大學 university founded by Methodists in Suzhou

Forbidden City 紫禁城 "purple forbidden city," Beijing imperial palace complex built in the fifteenth century

French Club Cercle Sportif Français, social club in the French Concession on nine-acre grounds bounded by Avenue Joffre, Rue Bourgeat and Rue Cardinal Mercier; today the Okura Garden Hotel

Gonganju 公安局 Public Security Bureau, Communist organization similar to a police station

Gong Wutai 共舞台 "communal stage," opera theater on Avenue Edward VII

Grand Theatre (Da Guang Ming) 大光明電影院 2,400-seat theater designed by László Hudec and completed in 1933; located at Bubbling Well Road

Great World (Da Shi Jie) 大世界 China's largest amusement center, developed in 1917 and later owned by Huang Jinrong; located at Avenue Edward VII and Thibet Road

Guiyuan Cemetery 歸園公墓 "Returning Garden," cemetery near Shanghai

Hangzhou 杭州 capital and largest city of Zhejiang Province

Harbin 哈尔滨 capital and largest city of Heilongjiang Province

Heilongjiang 黑龍江 "black dragon river," province in northeast China

Hong Kong 香港 "fragrant harbor," territory on the South China coast that was ceded as a British colony in 1842

Huangpu 黃浦 name of district and Shanghai's largest river, at the terminus of which the Bund is located

Huiji 會稽 county in Shaoxing Prefecture, Zhejiang Province; location of Sunrui Township 浙江省紹興府會稽縣孫瑞鄉 where Taiyeye was born

Huile Li 會樂里 "will-be-happy neighborhood," red-light alley on Fourth Road

Huizhong Hotel 惠中旅社 hotel group developed by Yeye from the 1920s, located at the intersection of Third Road (Hankou Road) and Hubei Road in Shanghai, with additional locations in Hangzhou, Suzhou, Tianjin and Wuxi

Jiangsu 江蘇 province bordering Shanghai on China's east coast

Jiangxi 江西 province in southeast China bordering Zhejiang

Jingdezhen 景德鎮 town in Jiangxi Province

Kunming 昆明 capital city of Yunnan 雲南 Province in southwest China

Lao Jie Fu 老介福 fabric emporium on Bubbling Well Road

Liangyou Garden 良友公寓 apartment building on Rue de Boissezon

lilong 里弄 see *longtang*

longtang 弄堂 "lane interior space," Shanghai dialect for *lilong*, a "neighborhood lane" or alleyway of residential townhouses built behind shop fronts

Lowu 羅湖 or 螺湖 (pinyin: *Luohu*) border zone connecting China and Hong Kong

Maijiaquan 麥家圈 Diedie's Fourth Road development comprising about twenty street-front retail buildings and more than two hundred residential apartments

Master of the Nets Garden (Wangshiyuan) 網師園 a fine classical garden in Suzhou

McTyeire School for Girls 中西女塾 Isabel's elementary and middle school, located on Edinburgh Road, named for Bishop Holland Nimmons McTyeire

The Paramount 百樂門 "gate of one hundred pleasures," Shanghai's largest ballroom, opened in 1933 on Bubbling Well Road

Pudong 浦東 "east of Huangpu," commercial district on the east side of the Huangpu River opposite the Bund

Qingdao 青島 "green island," Shandong port city colonized by Germany from 1898 to 1914

Shandong 山東 province to the north of Jiangsu and Shanghai

Shanghai 上海 "on the sea," China's most populous city, at the mouth of the Yangzi River and the East China Sea, bordering Jiangsu and Zhejiang Provinces

Shaoxing 紹興 city in northeastern Zhejiang Province

St. John's University 聖約翰大學 prestigious university on Jessfield Road

St. Mary's Hall 聖瑪利亞女校 Isabel's school for the last three years of high school, on Brenan Road

Suzhou 蘇州 city in Jiangsu Province on the shores of Lake Tai

Taihu 太湖 "grand lake," Lake Tai, large lake in the Yangzi Delta, on the border of Jiangsu and Zhejiang Provinces

Taipei 臺北 capital of Taiwan

Taiwan 臺灣 island in the South China Sea to which Kuomintang loyalists fled in 1949

Tiananmen 天安門 "gate of heavenly peace," 109-acre city square in Beijing

Tianjin 天津 coastal city in northeastern China

Tianning Temple Lane 天凝寺巷 area in Changshu where Taiyeye built the Sun
  family compound
Wing On 永安 (pinyin: *Yong An*) popular department store
Wuxi 無錫 city in southern Jiangsu Province
Xiansheng Jie 先生街 "Mister Street," street in Changshu that was built using a
  municipal fine paid by Diedie
Xiyuan 西園 West Garden Apartments on Jessfield Road, designed by Alexander
  Yaron
Yangcheng Hu 陽澄湖 Yangcheng Lake, a lake in Jiangsu Province near Changshu
Yangzi Jiang 揚子江 Yangzi River, the longest river in Asia, flowing from western
  China to the East China Sea at Shanghai
Yuejiezhulu 越界築路 "road built across the border," the Outer Territories,
  Western Roads or External Roads area, west of the International Settlement
Yushan 虞山 Yushan Mountain, mountain in Changshu
Zhejiang 浙江 province on the southern border of Shanghai
Zhuozheng Yuan 拙政園 the Humble Administrator's Garden in Suzhou

ROADS

THEN	NOW
Lane 668 六六八里	Zhenning Road 鎮寧路
Route de l'Amiral Courbet 古拔路	Fumin Road 富民路
Avenue Road 愛文義路	Beijing Road West 北京西路
Rue de Boissezon 白賽仲路	Fuxing Road West 復興西路
Rue Bourgeat 蒲石路	Changle Road 長樂路
Brenan Road 白利南路	Changning Road 長寧路
Bubbling Well Road 靜安寺路	Nanjing Road West 南京西路
Rue Cardinal Mercier 邁爾西愛路	Maoming Road South 茂名南路
Columbia Road 哥倫比亞路	Panyu Road 番愚路
Rue du Consulat 公館馬路	Jinling Road East 金陵東路
Edinburgh Road 憶定盤路	Jiangsu Road 江蘇路
Avenue Edward VII 愛多亞路	Yan'an Road East 延安東路
Fourth Road 四馬路	
(formerly Mission Road 教會路)	Fuzhou Road 福州路
Route Henry 亨利路	Xinle Road 新樂路
Hubei Road 湖北路	Hubei Road 湖北路
Jessfield Road 極司非而路	Wanhangdu Road 萬航渡路
Avenue Joffre 霞飛路	Huaihai Road Middle 淮海中路
Kinnear Road 開納路	Wuding Road 武定路
Rue Massenet 馬斯南路	Sinan Road 思南路

Nanjing Road 南京路
Seymour Road 西摩路
Thibet Road 西藏路
Third Road 三馬路
Yuyuan Road 愚園路

Nanjing Road East 南京東路
Shaanxi Road North 陝西北路
Xizang Road 西藏路
Hankou Road 漢口路
Yuyuan Road 愚園路

FOOD

babaofan 八寶飯 "eight precious rice," sweet dessert of steamed red or glutinous rice with dates, nuts and mashed red beans

congyoubing 蔥油餅 deep-fried green onion cakes

dazhaxie 大閘蟹 Shanghai hairy crabs or "mitten crabs," a seasonal delicacy

dim sum (pinyin: *dianxin*) 點心 "dot heart," light refreshments in Cantonese cuisine

guoba 鍋巴 scorched crispy rice from the bottom of a pan

jiaohuaji 叫花雞 "beggar's chicken," a whole chicken roasted in clay

mantou 饅頭 steamed white bun made of milled wheat flour

rousong 肉鬆 pork-floss condiment that has been stewed, baked and fried

shengjianbao 生煎包 pan-fried dumplings filled with minced pork

tangyuan 湯圓 glutinous rice balls filled with sesame or red bean paste in sweet soup

tofu (pinyin: *doufu*) 豆腐 "bean curd" of coagulated soy milk pressed into blocks or sheets

    baiyejie 百葉結 "hundred-leaf knot," sheet tofu cut and tied into knots

    bingdoufu 冰豆腐 "iced tofu," tofu blocks frozen to resemble a sponge

    doufugan 豆腐乾 "dried tofu"

    doufupi 豆腐皮 "tofu skin," tofu shaped into thin sheets

    gansi 乾絲 "dry shreds," dried tofu cut into fine threads resembling noodles

    mianjin 麵筋 "noodle tendon," tofu that is sinuous in appearance and chewy in texture

    nendoufu 嫩豆腐 "soft tofu," moist, custard-like tofu

    youdoufu 油豆腐 "oily tofu," fried tofu with a soft, spongy core

wonton (pinyin: *huntun*) 餛飩 dumpling of minced meat and vegetables in a wheat-flour wrapper

xiaolongbao 小籠包 "little basket dumpling," steamed dumplings filled with minced pork and gelatin

zongzitang 粽子糖 hard candy of brown sugar and nuts

zhou 粥 rice porridge, also known as congee

EVERYTHING ELSE

aiya 哎呀 interjection of shock or wonder

Aruke aruke aruke aruke, kitaminami tōzai, aruke aruke! 歩け歩け歩け歩け, 北南東西, 歩け歩け! Japanese marching song: "Walk walk walk walk, north south east west, walk walk!"

baichi baizhuang, yang ge erzi kai diandang 白吃白壯，養個兒子開典當 "eat plain, get fat, raise a son who'll open a pawnshop"

bangpiao 綁票 "tie money," to kidnap

baofu 包袱 large square of cloth with four corners fastened into a topknot

baxianzhuo 八仙桌 "eight fairies table," square dining table for eight people

beitoufeng 被頭瘋 "blanket madness," morning grumpiness

Bieke 別克 Buick car

biesan 癟三 "empty three," beggar; missing the three necessities of clothing, food and shelter

Central Air Transport Corporation (CATC) 中央航空運輸公司 1943–1949, air transport company funded by the United Nations and later contracted by the Kuomintang government

changshan 長衫 "long shirt," traditional floor-length long-sleeved Chinese men's robe; in Hong Kong, the Cantonese *cheongsam* refers to both the men's robe and the women's high-collared dress known elsewhere as *qipao*

Changtong Shipping Company 常通輪船公司 passenger and cargo river shipping firm established by Taiyeye, with twelve ships serving Shanghai, Suzhou, Wuxi, Changshu and Hangzhou

cheongsam (pinyin: *changshan*) see *changshan* and *qipao*

chiku 吃苦 "eat bitterness," bear hardships

China National Aviation Corporation (CNAC) 中國航空公司 1929–1949, airline jointly owned by Pan American Airways and the Kuomintang government from 1937

chou 醜 male clown role in Beijing opera

chuan dao qiaotou zi hui zhi 船到橋頭自會直 "when the boat reaches the bridge, it will naturally straighten," things will work out in the end

cimu yanfu 慈母嚴父 "loving mother, strict father"

Civil Air Transport Inc. (CAT) 民航空運公司 1946–1968, airline involved in airlifting Kuomintang supplies into China's interior

comprador Portuguese for "buyer," agent who facilitates commercial transactions between Chinese and foreigners

coolie (pinyin: *kuli*) 苦力 "bitter work," loanword for an unskilled laborer

Cultural Revolution 文化大革命 1966–1976, Mao Zedong's call to arms for millions of young Red Guards to advance Communist ideology by purging society of "old customs, old culture, old habits and old ideas" and targeting nine categories of enemies

daigaomao 戴高帽 "wear a tall hat," to be branded or stigmatized by wearing a dunce cap

dan 旦 in Beijing opera, the portrayal of female characters by male artists

ding 丁 academic grade equivalent to a D

dingdongdan 叮咚担 "dingdong stand," peddler's trinket cart

Dingtai Qianzhuang 鼎泰錢莊 bank opened by Taiyeye in the 1880s

fen 分 monetary unit equivalent to one-hundredth of a yuan or of a renminbi

fengshui 風水 "wind water," Chinese metaphysical system incorporating astrology and the five elements

Forty-Eight Me's 四十八我 series of forty-eight casual photos

fu buguo sandai 富不過三代 "wealth does not surpass three generations"

gongshi 供石 "scholar's rocks" or "spirit stones," naturally formed rocks collected by Chinese literati

Great Leap Forward 大躍進 1958–1961, Mao Zedong's failed movement aimed at collectivizing farms and industrializing the economy

gua 褂 women's formal brocade gown

hahajing 哈哈鏡 "haha mirrors," distorting or fun-house mirrors

Hakebeili Fei-en Lixian Ji 哈克貝利費恩歷險記 *Adventures of Huckleberry Finn*, the Mark Twain classic about life on the Mississippi River

Hongkong and Shanghai Bank 香港上海滙豐銀行 bank founded in 1865 to finance trade between Asia and the West, today known as HSBC

Huadong Commercial Bank 華東商議銀行 bank established by Diedie in 1931

huqin 胡琴 two-stringed musical instrument resembling a fiddle

Jia-li-ke 茄立克 The Garrick brand cigarettes

jiao 角 monetary unit equivalent to one-tenth of a yuan or of a renminbi

jiawu 甲午 year of the horse and *yang* wood, portending conflict, instability and disaster

Jiefang Ribao 解放日報 *Liberation Daily*, Communist newspaper distributed in Shanghai

Jinfa Nülang 金髮女郎 "gold-haired maiden," *Blondie*, the American comic strip featuring Blondie and Dagwood Bumstead

jing 淨 painted-face male role in Beijing opera

juezi juesun 絕子絕孫 "cut short sons and grandsons," having no heirs

kang 炕 traditional bed of heatable bricks

keqi 客氣 polite, courteous

kowtow (pinyin: *koutou*) 叩頭 or *ketou* 磕頭 act of deep respect shown by kneeling and touching one's head to the ground

Kuomintang (pinyin: *Guomindang*) 國民黨 the Chinese Nationalist Party, established in 1912 by Sun Yat-sen and later led by Chiang Kai-shek; defeat by the Communists resulted in its members fleeing to Taiwan in 1949

Legend of the White Snake (Bai She Chuan) 白蛇傳 a *shuoshu* folk story

lihun 離婚 "to leave marriage," divorce

Little Red Book nickname for *Quotations from Chairman Mao Zedong* 毛主席
　語錄, a book of 267 Maoist quotations that was widely distributed during the
　Cultural Revolution

magua 馬褂 traditional men's jacket worn over a floor-length *changshan*

mahjong (pinyin: *majiang*) 麻將 game for four players using 144 tiles; suits are *wan*
　萬 ("10,000"), *tong* 筒 ("circles") and *suo* 索 ("bamboo"); examples of runs are
　yitiaolong 一條龍 ("dragon") and *sanjiemei* 三姐妹 ("three sisters")

manyue 滿月 "full moon," celebration held when an infant reaches one month of
　age

mayizhai 麻衣債 "hemp clothes debt," borrowing money in anticipation of an
　inheritance

meizhen 美珍 beautiful treasure

Menjiao Guniang 門角姑娘 "the girl in the corner of the door," occult game simi-
　lar to the Ouija board

Ming 明朝 Chinese dynasty, 1368–1644

Misi Fotuo 蜜絲佛陀 Max Factor cosmetics

mu huo tu jin shui 木火土金水 the five elements: wood, fire, earth, metal and water

Namo Emituofo 南無阿彌陀佛 the name of Amitabha Buddha

nianfo 念佛 "chant Buddha," Pure Land school of Buddhism prayer and meditation
　centered on chanting the name of Amitabha Buddha

nihao 你好 hello; how are you?

oolong cha (pinyin: *wulong cha*) 烏龍茶 "black dragon tea," traditional Chinese tea

paigow (pinyin: *paijiu*) 牌九 game played using thirty-two Chinese domino tiles

pedicab or *sanlunche* 三輪車 "three-wheeled cart" propelled by a pedaling driver

pinyin 拼音 "spelled sound," China's national phonetic system for romanizing the
　Mandarin dialect since 1958

pipa 琵琶 four-stringed musical instrument resembling a lute

pipa 枇杷 loquat fruit

Qing dynasty 清朝 China's last imperial dynasty, 1644–1911

qipao 旗袍 "banner gown," traditional Manchurian men's robe that evolved into the
　high-collared, hourglass-shaped women's dress; called *cheongsam* in Cantonese

ren 仁 benevolence, one of Confucius's Five Virtues

renminbi or RMB 人民幣 "people's note," monetary unit of the People's Republic
　of China

rickshaw from the Japanese *jinrikisha* 人力車, in Chinese known as *huangbaoche*
　黃包車 ("yellow package cart"), two- or three-wheeled passenger cart pulled by
　one man

sampan (pinyin: *shanban*) 舢舨 small boat propelled by oars or a pole, from
　Cantonese 三板 ("three boards")

sangui jiukoushou 三跪九叩首 "three kneelings and nine head knockings," gesture of deep respect shown by kowtowing three times, each time touching one's head to the floor three times

sangshi 喪事 funeral

sangshu 桑樹 white mulberry tree native to northern China and cultivated to feed silkworms

Sanmi 三咪 Muma's Persian cat

sheng 生 the main male role in Beijing opera

Shenbao 申報 *Shanghai News*, a widely circulated Chinese newspaper

shikumen 石庫門 "stone-framed gate," architectural style combining elements of a British row house with a traditional Chinese courtyard

shuda zhaofeng 樹大招風 "when a tree gets big, it invites the wind," a rich or famous person attracts criticism

shuoshu 說書 "speak book," traditional folk storytelling

tael or *liang* 兩 from the Malay *tahil*, "weight," unit of currency equivalent to 1.3 ounces of gold or silver (before China's national currency was standardized to yuan in 1933, bank reserves were held mostly in fifty-tael *yuanbao* silver ingots and Spanish or Mexican dollars)

taipan (pinyin: *daban*) 大班 big boss, foreign businessman; in Shanghai and Hong Kong, heads of the Western trading companies

Taiping Rebellion 太平天國 1850–1864, civil war fought by the Taiping Heavenly Kingdom against the Qing rulers

Tao 道 "the way," the path of morality in Taoism

Three Antis and Five Antis 三反五反 Maoist campaigns in 1951 and 1952 to eliminate political opponents

tingzijian 亭子間 "pavilion room," Isabel and Virginia's bedroom

tongfuyimu 同父異母 "same father, different mother," half-sibling with the same father but a different mother

tulaotou 土老頭 "old country bumpkin"

Two Girls flower dew water (Shuangmei hualushui) 雙妹花露水 brand of eau de cologne from Hong Kong

walla-walla 嘩啦嘩啦 small motorboat named for its noisy engine

Wujia Po 武家坡 *Wu Family Slope*, a Beijing opera similar to Homer's *Odyssey*

xianglan 香蘭 fragrant orchid

Xiansheng 先生 Mister; also teacher

xiexie 謝謝 thank you

Xinhua 新華 official news agency of the government of the People's Republic of China

yamen 衙門 county government office

Ye Bali 夜巴黎 Soir de Paris or Evening in Paris, a French perfume

yeman 野蠻 savage

yinyang 陰陽 from Chinese philosophy, the complementary principle of male/
   female, dark/light, negative/positive

yizhixiang 一枝香 time it takes to burn "one stick of incense," about an hour

yuan 元 unit of Chinese currency since 1933

yuanbao 元寶 boat-shaped gold or silver ingot valued by its weight in taels

zhongjian 中間 "middle room," in Isabel's home the salon between the formal
   dining room and the study

zitan 紫檀 rare, deep-purple hardwood

ACKNOWLEDGMENTS

MOST OF ALL, I THANK my mother for gifting me with her precious memories.

I extend loving gratitude to my husband, *John Falzarano*, for his unwavering support and uncomplaining tolerance of my distracted state, unkempt hair and workdays ending at three or four in the morning. He not only is far more than I dreamed of in a spouse, but also has been a deeply caring "favorite (only) son-in-law" to both my father and mother.

A project of this nature requires long spells of solitude but rests on the shoulders of many. We treasure the invaluable help and moral support that we've received from friends far and near at every stage of this book's evolution. Thank you, one and all!

Special thanks to *Deborah and Tom Cooney*, and Deborah's parents, *Ming-fai Hui* and *Eden Siu-hung Yu*. Our mutual affection for Old Shanghai has led to their involvement in myriad ways, from Ming's exquisite illustrations to Eden's memories and the Cooneys' ideas and introductions. During our friendship, Tom and Deborah's peripatetic life across three diplomatic postings in Shanghai, Honolulu and Hong Kong closely paralleled and aided the development of our book. I eagerly await the day that we are again living in the same city.

We are forever grateful to *Maggie McBride* and *Pat Malone*, cherished friends and mentors from my first job as a fresh university graduate at Hill & Knowlton Hong Kong. Maggie and Pat sacrificed blissful retirement to plough through early versions of the manuscript and provide constructive suggestions on many aspects of creating and marketing the book.

This journey may have stalled had it not been for the inspiration and encouragement of *Debra Lee Baldwin*. I met Debra, a noted garden author and photojournalist, over pots of succulent plants during a Garden Club of Honolulu workshop in 2013. Though she barely knew me, she offered to read the manuscript, and in ensuing years lent her expertise on many facets of writing and publishing. We cannot thank Debra enough for being our friend and mentor.

Tess Johnston, the writer and authority on Old Shanghai architecture, was born in the same year as my mother, and likewise worked for the US government for more than thirty years. We salute Tess for her resourcefulness in gleaning our only English-language reference to Diedie, in a 1939 *Shanghai Directory*.

We met *Vince Ungvary* in cyberspace during the book's late design stages. A dealer and collector of vintage maps and memorabilia, Vince could not have been more generous in sharing his treasures with us. To our knowledge, his rare and glorious illustrations of Nanjing Road and the Bund in the 1930s have never been published. We sincerely thank Vince for his kindness.

Sherman Tang graciously gifted us the biography of his mother, Nancy Chan, *A Movie Queen Chen Yunshang*, and gave us permission to publish excerpts and photos from it.

Nicholas von Sternberg kindly permitted the use of excerpts from his father's memoir, *Fun in a Chinese Laundry: An Autobiography by Josef von Sternberg—*

exuberant descriptions of the Great World that would have been difficult to improve upon.

The director and producer *Stanley Kwan* regaled us with stories about his retro Shanghai movies, including the difficulties of replicating 1930s finger wave hairstyles that Mom accomplished by sleeping with wet cotton wool rolled in her hair.

Publisher and editor *Dania Shawwa* championed the book from its formative stages, providing thoughtful guidance and encouragement. We thank *Martin Alexander*, editor in chief of the *Asia Literary Review*, for educating us on the ins and outs of the publishing industry, and ruminating on the order of characters in the book's subtitle. We greatly appreciate the efforts of our scholarly friend *William Zanella, PhD*, for reviewing the glossary with a fine-tooth comb, as well as *Betty Peh-T'i Wei, PhD*, whose acute observation uncovered several discrepancies. *Susan Fox-Wolfgramm, PhD*, read an early manuscript and provided useful feedback.

Hugues Martin generously allowed us access to his collection of vintage Shanghai photographs. *Dean Harden* accompanied us and took photos on our first visit to Zhenning Road in 2008. *Krista and Pete Mui* photographed the embroideries on three vintage qipao, which had been collected by Muma and now grace the book's sidebars.

Winnie Chiu gave us an insider's view of China's marketing and social media. *Joe Spitzer* and *Lilian Tang* provided expert feedback on design and Chinese typography. *Charlyn Masini* advised on trailer production resources. *Kyoko Talisman* and *Debbie Funakawa* transcribed and translated the Japanese officer's marching song.

Ji-Li Chang, Youngsuk Chi, Doug Childers, Frank Chu, Heather Diamond, Daniel Kwok, Fred Lau and *Sally Nhomi* generously shared knowledge and resources.

Classmates *Beth Chute, Bernice Glenn* and *Laurel Slaughter* served as my chief networkers and cheerleaders in the Princeton community.

My party maven friends advised on and coordinated convivial book launches: in Honolulu, *Vivien Stackpole, Mary Rose Shen* and *Judy Murata*; and in Hong Kong, *Jeanne Thornhill, Susan Paolini* and *Larry Quek*.

Karen Thorne served as strategic planner and adviser.

We are grateful to *Armando, Daisy and Jade Manalac* in Hong Kong and *Lorna Apo* in Honolulu for their loyal support over two decades.

Many pals may not have made specific contributions to the book but gave us unconditional moral support: *Julie Au, Heidi Ho, Lisa and Alfredo Lobo, Linda Mui, Joanne Pating, Don Thompson, Laurie Tom, Valerie Van Buren* and my surrogate Mom, *Rebecca Soong*. Their friendship means the world to us.

I am deeply indebted to my Princeton dorm mate *Adam Inselbuch.* After years of gentle encouragement, at a crucial juncture Adam reconnected me with his university roommate, the political writer *Charles Robbins,* who graciously led me on the path to securing professional help.

Fortunately, this help came not in the form of a psychological intervention, but from the talented editor *Gali Kronenberg,* whose intellectual heavy lifting accelerated the pace and heightened the intrigue of our stories. Editor *Diana Rico,* a self-described book midwife, gave the manuscript its vital final polish, taking a bird's-eye view to firm up chronology and connect the dots. We credit Gali's and Diana's multilingual skills and multicultural sensitivities for meeting the challenges of an English-language narrative packed with Chinese history and characters (of both the human and written sort), interweaving two voices representing five generations and spanning more than 170 years.

Our team at Girl Friday Productions handled every stage of publication with consummate professionalism: executive director *Meghan Harvey* in a couple of hours brought clarity to every unanswered question I'd had about publishing over the previous ten years; art director *Paul Barrett* transformed our ideas into our exquisite cover and interior design; photo editor *Emily Friedenrich* managed the book's many images; and *Rachel Marek* created our gorgeous website. Our task-juggling senior special projects editor *Emilie Sandoz-Voyer* corralled hundreds of moving parts to lead us to the finish line. In the process, she coached me on the arcane and the practical, including Oxford commas (she's pro, I'm anti), colophons, fleurons, screenbacks, running heads and, yes, deadlines.

A family memoir is inherently a family endeavor. I thank my aunts *Virginia Sun* and *Sun Shuquan* for relating many stories and anecdotes that added depth and perspective to my mother's recollections. Reaching this point makes me admire all the more the accomplishments of my uncle *Sun Shufen,* who emerged from the deprivations of the Cultural Revolution to produce his first manuscript of 320,000 handwritten Chinese characters, while working as a full-time teacher and without the aid of a computer or the Internet.

I have no doubt that my ancestors have served as my guides and inspiration, and am delighted that the project created the impetus to forge closer connections to my cousins *Anicet Dubonnet, Warren Zheng* and *Ginger Cheng.*

Distance prevents us from seeing enough of immediate family: my oldest brother, *Leslie Chao,* his wife, *Ann,* and sons, *Alex* and *Garrett*; and John's daughter, *Johanna,* and her husband, *Chris Boyte.* But we count our blessings to reside on the same island as John's son, *William Falzarano,* his wife, *Dawn,* and John's only grandchild, *John,* who brings light and laughter to our lives.

As a filmmaker and media executive, my second brother, *Lloyd Chao,* on countless occasions lent his keen eye and design sense, efficiently and uncomplainingly retouching virtually every photographic image in the book. As we face forward, I gleefully anticipate collaborating with him and our old friend, producer *Corey Tong,* on "the next chapter."

– Claire Chao, Honolulu, August 2017

Isabel in the 1950s.

ABOUT THE ILLUSTRATORS

MING-FAI HUI許明輝

Born and raised in Hong Kong, Ming-fai Hui credits her parents for encouraging her artistic pursuits from an early age. Since receiving a doctoral degree in art and art education from Southern Illinois University, she has been active in teacher training and curriculum design in the US and Hong Kong. Ming's unique brush-painting style combines Eastern and Western influences and has garnered numerous awards in international juried shows.

We especially appreciate this talented artist's re-creation of Isabel's childhood home. The unusual assignment took place in the summer of 2012, with Ming seated, paintbrushes in hand, at Claire's Honolulu dining table, alongside Isabel and three friends at their mahjong table. Over several days, Ming pulled together her lovely illustration from partial old photos and Isabel's sketches and tweaks between mahjong games.

SUN QIAN孫倩

Sun Qian was born in 1990 in Qingdao, Shandong Province. By happy coincidence, she shares Isabel's surname.

After receiving a degree in environmental art design from Shanghai University in 2014, Sun joined an international cosmetics company as a display designer, and in 2016 was promoted to visual merchandising supervisor.

Her whimsical style captures the essence of Isabel's early childhood. Sun tells us she acquired a taste for Shanghainese food after illustrating mouth-watering delicacies for this book.

ABOUT THE AUTHORS

Isabel Sun Chao's childhood in Shanghai coincided with the last eighteen years before Mao came to power. She left for Hong Kong on what she thought was a holiday in 1950 and never saw her father again. She has since lived in Hong Kong, where she worked for more than thirty years as a cultural affairs specialist in the US Consulate General. Now in her eighties, Isabel is fully retired, and most days can be found exercising her skills and diplomacy at the mahjong table.

Claire Chao is Isabel's daughter, a writer with more than thirty years' management experience for companies including Tiffany & Co., Harry Winston and Hill & Knowlton. *Avenue* magazine designated her one of the "500 Most Influential Asian Americans," and *Hong Kong Tatler* named her to "The 500 List" of "Who's Who in Hong Kong." She graduated with highest honors from Princeton University. She lives in Honolulu with her husband.

CPSIA information can be obtained
at www.ICGtesting.com
Printed in the USA
FSHW01n1626071018
52801FS